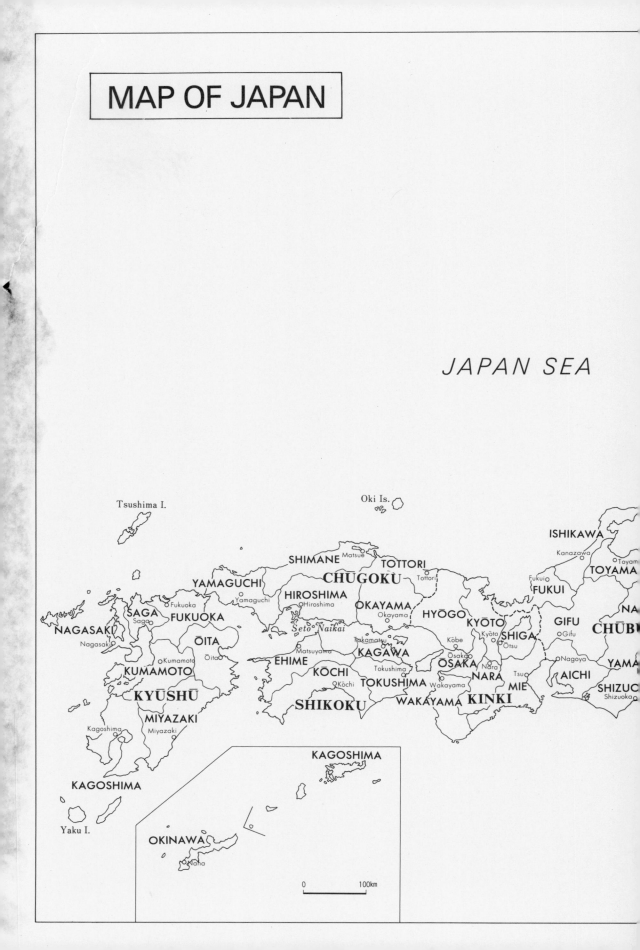

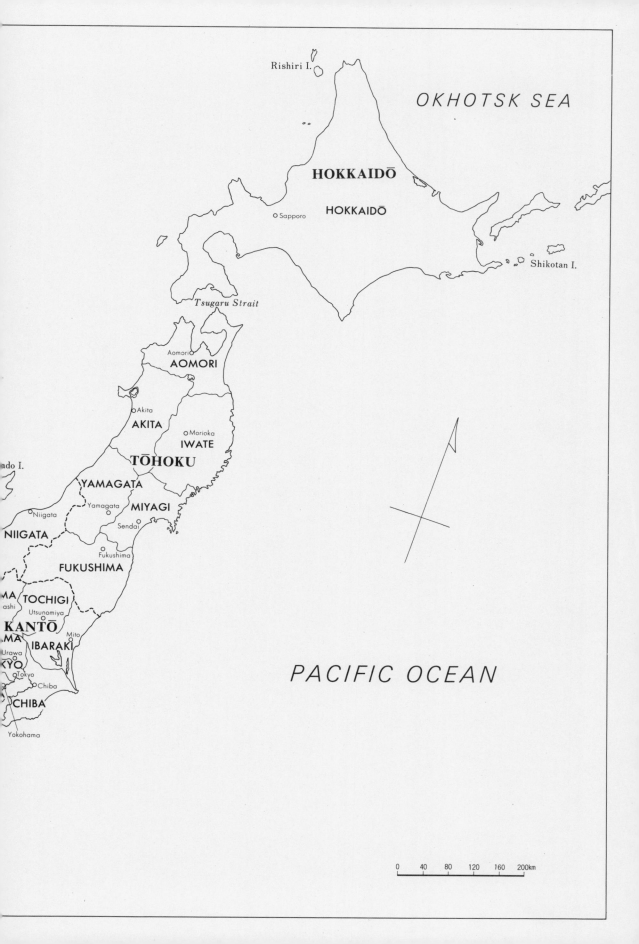

JAPANESE FOR BUSY PEOPLE

I

JAPANESE FOR BUSY PEOPLE

I

Association for Japanese-Language Teaching

40-1663

KODANSHA INTERNATIONAL
Tokyo and New York

Publication of this textbook has been assisted by a grant from the Japan Foundation.

A few, minor corrections have been made in the twelfth printing.

Distributed in the United States by Kodansha International/ USA Ltd., 114 Fifth Avenue, New York, New York 10011.

Published by Kodansha International Ltd., 17-14 Otowa 1-chome, Bunkyo-ku, Tokyo 112 and Kodansha International/ USA Ltd., 114 Fifth Avenue, New York, New York 10011. Copyright © 1984 by the Association for Japanese-Language Teaching. All rights reserved. Printed in Japan.
                              ISBN 4-7700-1099-0 (in Japan)
First edition, 1984
Twelfth printing, 1989

Library of Congress Cataloging in Publication Data
Main entry under title:
Japanese for busy people.
    Includes index.
    1. Japanese language—Textbooks for foreign speakers—English. II. Kokusai Nihongo Fukyū Kyōkai (Japan)
PL539.3.J28   1983   495.6'83421   83-80218
 ISBN 0-87011-599-5

CONTENTS

Introduction   7

Writing and Pronunciation   11

Characteristics of Japanese Grammar   14

Useful Daily Expressions   15

Signs in Daily Life   16

Lesson   1: Introductions   19

Lesson   2: Address and Telephone Number   25

Lesson   3: Day and Time   31

Lesson   4: How Much?   38

Lesson   5: Counting Objects   44

Lesson   6: Going and Coming   52

Lesson   7: Going by Taxi   60

Lesson   8: Existence of People and Things   65

Lesson   9: Place, Location   72

Lesson 10: Tickets Bought   78

Lesson 11: Reading Review   85

Lesson 12: Telephoning   87

Lesson 13: Delicious Cakes   94

Lesson 14: Yesterday's Enjoyable Kabuki   103

Lesson 15: Giving and Receiving   108

Lesson 16: Asking Preferences   113

Lesson 17: Invitation to a Party   119

Lesson 18: Ownership and Events   123

Lesson 19: Doing This and That   129

Lesson 20: Requests and Orders   136

Lesson 21: Having Things Done   141

Lesson 22: Public Transportation   144

Lesson 23: Asking Permission   149

Lesson 24: Refusal   154

Lesson 25: Now in Progress   158

Lesson 26: Reading Review   163

Lesson 27: Present Condition   167

Lesson 28: Expressing Preferences   173

Lesson 29: Dining Out   182

Lesson 30: Reading Review   187

Appendices

  A. Adjectives   191
  B. Common Japanese Names   191
  C. Counters   192
  D. Country, Nationality, Language   192
  E. Extent, Frequency, Quantity   193
  F. Parts of the Face and Body   194
  G. Time Expressions   194
  H. Verb Conjugation   196

Answers to Quizzes   199

Glossary   205

Index   213

INTRODUCTION

Japanese for Busy People is for people who want to learn essential Japanese as quickly and as effectively as possible.

Preparation of this textbook is based on more than ten years' experience of AJALT's specially trained staff in teaching beginning through advanced Japanese to students from approximately 40 countries. During the two years prior to publication, the material was reviewed and tested in the classroom with about 200 students, and revisions made as necessary.

This course might be described as "survival Japanese," for the language learned can be put to immediate use in conversational situations. The simplistic or childish ways of expression found in most beginning texts do not occur. While vocabulary and grammar patterns have been limited to about one third of those in the ordinary beginning text, the selection has been made after a careful study of the situations in which foreigners may have to speak Japanese. The objective is to enable the student to obtain the information he needs and to communicate what he or she wants to say in uncomplicated but *adult* language. The stress is not simply on grammatical accuracy. Careful consideration has been given to the actual linguistic patterns in Japanese communication.

To make the course effective, concise reference is made in the Notes to the linguistic customs underlying these communication patterns. The Grammar sections explain the structure and grammatical principles of Japanese whenever it is thought that such explanations would be helpful in understanding and applying the conversational patterns presented. Grammar and vocabulary are made available to the student as necessary, but he is not overburdened by having to learn excessive amounts of either for some undefined future contingency.

Although this is an introductory text, it does provide a solid foundation for the study of Japanese at a higher level. Every student should be able to obtain a good grasp of just *what kind of language* Japanese is while learning the basic conversational patterns. Because of this, it should be of value not only to people who are approaching Japanese for the first time but also a good review for people who already know a little Japanese but wish to confirm whether they are using the phrases they know in the right situations.

The amount of time needed to complete this course will naturally vary, depending on the individual. In AJALT classes, which meet two and a half hours a day, five days a week, the course takes four weeks, or a total of about fifty hours. In addition, two to three hours a day are needed for preparation and review.

Arrangement of the Book

Basic guides to writing, pronunciation and grammar are presented in the immediately following sections, after which come Useful Daily Expressions and Signs in Daily Life. The main text is divided into 30 lessons. At the end of the book are the appendices, Quiz Answers, Glossary and Index.

Nearly all of the lessons deal with conversational situations. These are supplemented by four reading and review lessons.

The two modes of communication, oral and written, are different. In a conversational situation, speaker and listener share a good deal of information. In a natural conversation, much of this information is omitted and the speakers are able to communicate in a rather elliptical fashion. In a story, a report or a letter, however, it is necessary to write an organized, well-structured composition in order to communicate all the information needed in a logical fashion. In our experience, the student can learn Japanese most effectively if he studies both conversation and written Japanese from the very beginning.

This is one reason for the short review lessons. From Lesson 3, there are Summary Sentences (marked by ■) in Japanese and English following the opening Dialogue or Text. These sentences also show the differences between the oral and written languages. In addition, besides a title for ready reference, most lessons have at the beginning a Topic Sentence in English to orient the student to the main situation in the lesson. These should be of special value when teaching students for whom English is a second language.

Lessons are generally based on a particular conversational situation, such as shopping, talking on the telephone and so on. Strategically placed throughout the book are ten Grammar sections to cover the most important grammar patterns. With the exception of the review lessons, each lesson has Notes, a Practice section consisting of Key Sentences, Exercises and Short Dialogue(s), and a Quiz. This arrangement will be especially helpful to people who want to study on their own.

To the Teacher

To understand the overall plan adopted in this book, it best to first read it from beginning to end.

Work on pronunciation is especially important at the introductory level. The sounds represented by double consonants in romanization, long vowels and the nasalized **n** sound are especially difficult for foreigners, but it is also important to help the student learn how to pronounce the five vowels correctly. Even though he has a Japanese teacher, the student should be encouraged to listen to the tapes both for basic pronunciation and for the flow of speech.

In teaching *kana*, you should consider using charts or a *kana* workbook. You should make it clear to the student that mastering *kana* will help him with pronunciation, and pronunciation should be emphasized whenever you are helping the student with *hiragana* or *katakana*. You may want to have the student learn *kana* before you begin the text. However, the text is designed so that it is quite possible to have the student work on both at the same time. He should be able to master *hiragana* by the time he reaches Lesson 10.

As much as possible, class time should be devoted to actually using Japanese. The student should study the Notes and Grammar sections before class.

The Dialogues are very short and, while the practice sections are designed to reinforce the patterns introduced, the Exercises give relatively few examples. You should select additional vocabulary—for example, from the appendices—that will be of interest to the student and have him practice each pattern using these new words in order to increase the amount of oral practice. But it is best not to try for too much at one time. It is better to proceed at a steady pace, increase vocabulary gradually, and work on improving weak points after several lessons, than to introduce a lot of new vocabulary and try for perfection in each lesson. Do not allow the class to get bogged down in one lesson.

Since each lesson is based on a particular conversational situation and emphasizes specific points of grammar, the time required for each lesson is not the same. One lesson may require only one hour while another requires three hours. Adjectives, for example, are introduced in Lessons 13 and 14, and these lessons will require more time simply because of the quantity of material to be covered.

The following suggestions concern the student's preparation. Before class, he should listen to the tape of the opening Dialogue to get a feeling for the flow of conversation between native speakers. Then he should listen to the vocabulary for each lesson while memorizing the English meanings. These two points should be the main emphasis of his preparation.

Encourage the student to review each lesson after each class meeting. At this time, it is important to insist that the student diligently memorize the Dialogues, Summary Sentences and Key Sentences.

The Quizzes may be done either in class or as homework. In either case, the teacher should check them carefully, not only to correct mistakes but also to identify individual problems and find ways to correct them.

Self-study

The main parts of each lesson are printed in both *hiragana* and *katakana* and romanized Japanese (*rōmaji*). Learning will be more effective if you try to master *hiragana* by the time you are halfway through the book.

We strongly recommend that you devote sufficient time to pronunciation, accent and intonation, either by taking advantage of the tapes or by having your Japanese friends help you.

It is essential that you read the Japanese portions of the text out loud. First, take a look at the Dialogue at the beginning of the lesson. Then carefully study the Notes and the Grammar, where applicable, until you understand them completely. The Practice section gives more examples of the important patterns in the Dialogue. You should spend plenty of time repeating these patterns in a clear voice. Frequent repetition is essential. Using the appendices, you can try substituting words in each pattern while imagining situations in which you might find yourself. Remember, these patterns will only be useful if you can use them in actual situations. When you feel that you have mastered the patterns in the lesson, do the Quiz at the end. Finally, after you have completed all these steps, go back to the beginning of the lesson and thoroughly memorize the opening Dialogue, Summary Sentences and Key Sentences.

ACKNOWLEDGMENTS

Compilation of this textbook has been a cooperative endeavor, and we deeply appreciate the collective efforts and individual contributions of Mss Sachiko Adachi, Nori Andō, Haruko Matsui, Shigeko Miyazaki, Sachiko Okaniwa, Terumi Sawada and Yuriko Yobuko. For English translations and editorial assistance, we wish to thank Ms. Dorothy Britton.

WRITING AND PRONUNCIATION

There are three kinds of Japanese writing:

1. *Kanji*: Chinese characters or ideographs, each conveying an idea, most of which have at least two readings.

2. *Hiragana*: A phonetic syllabary. The symbols are curvalinear in style.

3. *Katakana*: The second syllabary used primarily for foreign names and place names and words of foreign origin. The symbols are made up of straight lines.

Written Japanese normally makes use of all three, as in the following example:

"I am going to Canada."　私はカナダに行きます。

kanji	**Watashi** 私		**i-** 行	
hiragana	**wa** は	**ni** に	**kimasu** きます	
katakana	**Kanada** カナダ			

Besides these three forms of writing, Japanese is sometimes written in *rōmaji* (Roman letters), particularly for the convenience of foreigners. This is generally used in teaching conversational Japanese to foreigners when time is limited. There are various systems for transliterating Japanese in the Roman alphabet. In this book we use the modified Hepburn system.

HIRAGANA, KATAKANA AND RŌMAJI

The *kana* to the left are *hiragana*; *katakana* are in parentheses.

I Basic Syllables: Vowel, Consonant plus vowel and **n**

c \ v	a あ (ア)	i い (イ)	u う (ウ)	e え (エ)	o お (オ)
k	ka か (カ)	ki き (キ)	ku く (ク)	ke け (ケ)	ko こ (コ)
s	sa さ (サ)	shi し (シ)	su す (ス)	se せ (セ)	so そ (ソ)
t	ta た (タ)	chi ち (チ)	tsu つ (ツ)	te て (テ)	to と (ト)
n	na な (ナ)	ni に (ニ)	nu ぬ (ヌ)	ne ね (ネ)	no の (ノ)
h	ha は (ハ)	hi ひ (ヒ)	fu ふ (フ)	he へ (ヘ)	ho ほ (ホ)
m	ma ま (マ)	mi み (ミ)	mu む (ム)	me め (メ)	mo も (モ)
y	ya や (ヤ)	[i い (イ)]	yu ゆ (ユ)	[e え (エ)]	yo よ (ヨ)
r	ra ら (ラ)	ri り (リ)	ru る (ル)	re れ (レ)	ro ろ (ロ)
w	wa わ (ワ)	[i い (イ)]	[u う (ウ)]	[e え (エ)]	o を (ヲ)
n, m	— ん (ン)				

Note: The syllables **yi**, **ye**, **wi**, **wu** and **we** do not occur in modern Japanese.

II Modified Syllables: Consonant plus basic vowel

g	ga が（ガ）	gi ぎ（ギ）	gu ぐ（グ）	ge げ（ゲ）	go ご（ゴ）
z	za ざ（ザ）	ji じ（ジ）	zu ず（ズ）	ze ぜ（ゼ）	zo ぞ（ゾ）
d	da だ（ダ）	ji ぢ（ヂ）	zu づ（ヅ）	de で（デ）	do ど（ド）
b	ba ば（バ）	bi び（ビ）	bu ぶ（ブ）	be べ（ベ）	bo ぼ（ボ）
p	pa ぱ（パ）	pi ぴ（ピ）	pu ぷ（プ）	pe ぺ（ペ）	po ぽ（ポ）

III Modified Syllables: Consonant plus **ya, yu, yo**

kya きゃ（キャ）	kyu きゅ（キュ）	kyo きょ（キョ）
sha しゃ（シャ）	shu しゅ（シュ）	sho しょ（ショ）
cha ちゃ（チャ）	chu ちゅ（チュ）	cho ちょ（チョ）
nya にゃ（ニャ）	nyu にゅ（ニュ）	nyo にょ（ニョ）
hya ひゃ（ヒャ）	hyu ひゅ（ヒュ）	hyo ひょ（ヒョ）
mya みゃ（ミャ）	myu みゅ（ミュ）	myo みょ（ミョ）
rya りゃ（リャ）	ryu りゅ（リュ）	ryo りょ（リョ）
gya ぎゃ（ギャ）	gyu ぎゅ（ギュ）	gyo ぎょ（ギョ）
ja じゃ（ジャ）	ju じゅ（ジュ）	jo じょ（ジョ）
bya びゃ（ビャ）	byu びゅ（ビュ）	byo びょ（ビョ）
pya ぴゃ（ピャ）	pyu ぴゅ（ピュ）	pyo ぴょ（ピョ）

IV Double Consonants

kk, pp, ss, tt	っ（ッ）

(See Note 6.)

V Long Vowels

ā	ああ	（アー）
ii, ī	いい	（イー）
ū	うう	（ウー）
ē, ei	ええ, えい	（エー）
ō	おう, おお	（オー）

POINTS TO NOTE

1. The top line of the Japanese syllabary consists of the five vowels: **a, i, u, e, o**.
   They are short vowels, pronounced clearly and crisply. If you pronounce the
   vowels in the following English sentence, making them all short, you will have

their approximate sounds. The **u** is pronounced with no movement forward of the lips.

Ah, we soon get old.

a   i   u   e   o

2. Long vowels are written as shown in Chart V. **Ē** or **ei** is most often written えい but ええ is also sometimes encountered.
おう is the general rule for **ō** but in some words it is traditionally written おお. Long vowels are a doubling of the single vowel and care should be taken to pronounce them as a continuous sound, equal in value to two identical short vowels.

3. The rest of the syllabary from the second line down in Chart I are syllables formed by a consonant and a vowel.

4. Japanese consonants more or less resemble English. Listen to the cassette tape or a native speaker for the exact sounds. Especially note the following: *t* in the **ta** row, *f* in the syllable **fu** and *r* in the **ra** row. The *g* in the syllables **ga**, **gi**, **gu**, **ge** and **go** at the beginning of a word is hard (like the [g] in garden), but when it occurs in the middle or in the last syllable of a word, it often becomes nasal, as in **eiga** ("movie"). The particle **ga**, too, is usually pronounced in this way. However, many Japanese today use a *g* sound which is not nasal.
N is the only independent consonant not combined with a vowel. When it is at the end of a word it is pronounced somewhat nasally. Otherwise it is usually pronounced like the English [n]. But if it is followed by syllables beginning with *b*, *m* or *p*, it is pronounced more like [m] and accordingly spelled with an *m* in this textbook. Special care is necessary when syllabic **n** is followed by a vowel as in the word **kin'en**. (**ki-n-en**, "no smoking"). Note that this is different in syllable division from **kinen** (**ki-ne-n**, "anniversary").

5. As explained above, *hiragana* and *katakana* are phonetic symbols and each is one syllable in length. The syllables in Chart III which consist of two symbols—the second written smaller—are also only one syllable in length if the vowel is short, longer if the vowel is long.

6. What are written in Roman letters as the double consonants **kk**, **pp**, **ss** and **tt** in Chart IV are expressed in *kana* (*hiragana* and *katakana*) with a small **tsu** in place of the first consonant. I.e., けっこん **kekkon** ("marriage"), きっぷ **kippu** ("ticket"), まっすぐ **massugu** ("straight") and きって **kitte**, ("stamp"). This small っ is one syllable in length, and there is the slightest pause after it is pronounced (as in the English word *book'keeping*). In the case of the **chi** syllable, the **tsu** is represented by a *t* in Roman letters, i.e., マッチ **matchi** (" match").

7. In *hiragana*, the syllables **ji** and **zu** are written じ and ず as a general rule. In a few rare cases, they are traditionally written ぢ and づ

8. *Hiragana* follows a tradition in which the following three particles are written a special way:
    o when used as a particle is written を, not お.
    e when used as a particle is written へ, not え.
    wa when used as a particle is written は, not わ.

CHARACTERISTICS OF JAPANESE GRAMMAR

The grammar in this text is derived from a natural analysis of the Japanese language, rather than being an interpretation adapted to the syntax of Western languages. We have given as few technical terms as possible, choosing ones that will make for a smooth transition from the basic level to more advanced study.

The following points are basic and in most cases reflect differences between the grammar of Japanese and that of English, or other European languages. Specific explanations and examples are given in Grammar I through Grammar X, the notes and the appendices.

1. Japanese nouns have neither gender nor number. But plurals of certain words can be expressed by the use of a suffix.

2. The verb generally comes at the end of the sentence or clause.
   ex. **Watashi wa Nihon-jin desu**. I am a Japanese.
   Watashi wa Kyōtō ni ikimasu. I go to Kyoto.

3. Verb conjugation is not affected by the gender, number or person of the subject.

4. Verb conjugation shows only two tenses, the present form and the past form. Whether use of the present form refers to habitual action or the future, and whether the past form is equivalent to the English past tense, present perfect or past perfect can be determined from the context.

5. Japanese adjectives, unlike English ones, are inflected to show present and past, affirmative and negative.

6. The grammatical function of nouns is indicated by particles. Their role is similar to English prepositions, but since they always come after the word, they are sometimes referred to as postpositions.
   ex. **Tōkyō de**, at Tokyo
   15-nichi ni, on the 15 (of the month)

7. Many degrees of politeness are expressable in Japanese. In this book the style is one which anyone may use without being rude.

Note: The following abbreviations are used in this book:

aff.	affirmative
neg.	negative
A*a*:	Answer, affirmative
A*n*:	Answer, negative
ex.	example
-i adj.	**-i** adjective
-na adj.	**-na** adjective

USEFUL DAILY EXPRESSIONS

1. おはようございます。**Ohayōgozaimasu**. Good morning! Used until about 10 A.M.

2. こんにちは。**Konnichiwa**. Hello. A rather informal greeting used from about 10 A.M. until sundown.

3. こんばんは。**Kombanwa**. Good evening.

4. さようなら。**Sayōnara**. Good-bye. On more formal occasions one uses **Shitsurei shimasu**.

5. おやすみなさい。**Oyasumi nasai**. Good night. Said at night before going to bed. When parting at night outside the home, **Sayōnara** is more usual.

6. では　また。／じゃ　また。**Dewa mata./Ja mata**. Well then . . . Said informally when parting from relatives or friends.

7. いってらっしゃい。**Itte rasshai**. So long. (*lit.* "Go and come back.") Said to members of a household as they leave the house.

8. いってまいります。**Itte mairimasu**. So long. (*lit.* "[I'm] going and coming back.") This is the reply to **Itte rasshai**.

9. ただいま。**Tadaima**. I'm back. (*lit.* "[I have returned] Just now.") Said by a person on returning home.

10. おかえりなさい。**Okaeri nasai**. Welcome home. This is the reply to **Tadaima**.

11. おげんきですか。**O-genki desu ka.** How are you? (*lit.* "Are you well?")

12. ありがとうございます。　げんきです。**Arigatō gozaimasu. Genki desu**. Fine, thank you.

13. おめでとうございます。**Omedetō gozaimasu**. Congratulations!

14. おだいじに。**O-daijini**. Take care of yourself.

15. どうも　ありがとうございます。**Dōmo arigatō gozaimasu**. Thank you very much.

16. どういたしまして。**Dō itashimashite**. You're welcome.

17. ちょっと　まってください。**Chotto matte kudasai**. Wait just a moment, please.

18. もう　いちど　おねがいします。**Mō ichido onegaishimasu**. Once more, please.

19. おさきに。**Osakini**. Pardon my going first (before you). Said when going ahead of other people after being urged to do so.

20. どうぞ　おさきに。**Dōzo osakini**. Please, go ahead.

21. きをつけて。**Ki o tsukete**. Take care!/Be careful!

22. あぶない。**Abunai**. Look out! (*lit.* "It's dangerous.")

23. だめです。**Dame desu**. Out of the question./Impossible./No good.

24. がんばってください。**Gambatte kudasai**. Keep your chin up! Said to encourage someone.

15

annai
Information

eigyōchū
Open

takushī-noriba
Taxi Stand

eki
(railway) Station

jumbichū
Getting ready to open.
(May also indicate
"Closed for the day.")

chikatetsu
Subway, Underground

kippu-uriba
Ticket Office

kaisatsuguchi
Ticket Gate

seisanjo
(fare) Adjustment Office

kyūgyōchū
Closed

iriguchi
Entrance

deguchi
Exit

hijōguchi
Emergency Exit

osu
Push

hiku
Pull

uketsuke
Reception

erebētā
Elevator

esukarētā
Escalator

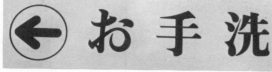

o-tearai
Toilet

otoko
Men, Gentlemen

keshō-shitsu
Powder Room

onna
Women, Ladies

usetsu kinshi
No right turn

sasetsu kinshi
No left turn

chūsha kinshi
No Parking

Te o furenaide kudasai.
Do not touch.

ippōtsūkōro
One Way Street

chūshajō
Parking lot

Gomi o sutenaide kudasai.
Please don't litter.

Shibafu no naka ni hairanaide kudasai.
Please keep off the grass.

kin'en
No Smoking

tachiiri kinshi
No Admittance

chūi
Caution!

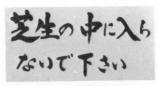

kōjichū
Under Construction

kiken
Danger!

LESSON 1 INTRODUCTIONS

Mr. Hayashi introduces Mr. Smith to Mr. Tanaka.

はやし：たなかさん、こちらは　スミスさんです。

スミス：はじめまして。〔わたしは〕スミスです。どうぞ　よろしく。

たなか：はじめまして。〔わたしは〕とうきょうでんきの　たなかです。
　　　　どうぞ　よろしく。

はやし：スミスさんは　ABCの　べんごしです。

Hayashi: **Tanaka-san, kochira wa Sumisu-san desu.**
Sumisu: **Hajimemashite. [Watashi wa] Sumisu desu. Dōzo yoroshiku.**
Tanaka: **Hajimemashite. [Watashi wa] Tōkyō Denki no Tanaka desu. Dōzo**
  yoroshiku.
Hayashi: **Sumisu-san wa ABC no bengoshi desu.**

Hayashi: Mr. Tanaka, this is Mr. Smith.
Smith: How do you do. My name's Smith. I'm very glad to meet you.
Tanaka: How do you do. I'm Tanaka from Tokyo Electric. I'm very glad to meet you.
Hayashi: Mr. Smith is ABC's lawyer.

Vocabulary

はやし	**Hayashi**	a surname
たなかさん	**Tanaka-san**	a surname with honorific
～さん	**-san**	Mr., Mrs., Ms., Miss (suffix)
こちら	**kochira**	this one (implies this person)
は	**wa**	as for (topic marker, particle)
スミス	**Sumisu**	Smith
です	**desu**	is
はじめまして	**hajimemashite**	How do you do.
わたし	**watashi**	I
どうぞよろしく	**dōzo yoroshiku**	*lit.* Please favor me.
とうきょうでんき	**Tōkyō Denki**	Tokyo Electric (company name)
の	**no**	= 's (possessive particle)
ABC	**ĒBĪSHĪ**	ABC (company name)
べんごし	**bengoshi**	lawyer

GRAMMAR I

Lessons 1–5 Identifying People and Things

1. noun 1 WA noun 2 DESU
2. noun 1 WA noun 2 DESU KA
   Hai, (noun 1 **wa**) noun 2 **desu**.
   Iie, (noun 1 **wa**) noun 2 **dewa/ja arimasen**.

Present Form		Past Form	
aff.	*neg.*	*aff.*	*neg.*
desu	**dewa arimasen**	**deshita**	**dewa arimasendeshita**
is	is not	was	was not

- Particle **wa**. Topic marker.
  Wa follows noun 1 indicating that it is the topic under discussion. Noun 2 is then identified and the phrase is concluded with **desu**. The topic is often the same as the subject, but not necessarily. It is also possible for the object to be the topic. (See Note 3, p. 183.) The . . . **wa** . . . **desu** structure is not affected by person or number.
  ex. **A-san wa bengoshi desu.** "Mr. A is a lawyer."
  A-san to B-san wa bengoshi desu. "Mr. A and Mrs. B are lawyers."

- Particle **ka**. Question marker.
  The formation of questions in Japanese is easy. Put **ka** at the end of a sentence and it becomes a question. No change in word order is required even when the question contains interrogative words such as who, what, when, etc. Intonation normally rises on the particle **ka** only, i.e., . . . **desu ka**. ⌏

- **Hai** and **Iie**
  Hai is virtually the same as "yes." **Iie** is virtually the same as "no." It is better, however, to think of **hai** as meaning, "That's right," and **iie** as meaning, "That's wrong." Otherwise negative questions can be a problem. I.e., to the question, **Ja, banana ga arimasen ka**, "So you have no bananas?" the reply is **Hai, arimasen**, "That's right, we have none." Or **Iie, arimasu**, "That's wrong, we have some."

- Omission of topic (noun 1)
  When it is obvious to the other person what the topic is, it is generally omitted.
  ex. **[Watashi wa] Sumisu desu**, "(As for me) I'm Smith."

- **Dewa arimasen./Ja arimasen**.
  Negative form of **desu. Ja** is more informal than **dewa**.

NOTES

1. Tanaka-san

San is a title of respect added to a name, so it cannot be used after one's own name. **San** may be used with both male and female names, and with either surname or given name. It may even be suffixed to the name of an occupation.
ex. **Bengoshi-san**, "Mr. Lawyer."

2. Kochira wa Sumisu-san desu.

Kochira, "this one," implies "this person here" and is a polite way of saying "this person."

3. Hajimemashite.

Salutation used on meeting a person for the first time. It is a form of the verb **hajimeru**, "to begin."

4. [Watashi wa] Sumisu desu.

"My name's Smith." (*lit.* "I'm Smith.")
Especially in conversational Japanese, **watashi**, "I," is hardly ever used. **Anata**, "you," is similarly avoided, especially when addressing superiors, in which case the person's surname, title or occupation is used when necessary.

5. Dōzo yoroshiku.

A phrase used when being introduced, it is usually combined with **hajimemashite**. It is also used when taking one's leave after having asked a favor. **Yoroshiku** means "good" and is a request for the other person's favorable consideration in the future. It can also be used as follows: **Tanaka-san ni yoroshiku**. "Please give my regards to Mr. Tanaka."

6. Tōkyō Denki no (Tanaka desu).

The possessive particle **no** indicates ownership or attribution and comes after the noun it modifies, like " 's" in English. Here it shows that Mr. Tanaka belongs to, in the sense that he works for, Tokyo Electric. Japanese customarily give their company and position when being introduced.

7. Dare/donata, "who?"

The basic word for "who" is **dare**, but **donata** is more polite.
ex. **Kochira wa dare desu ka**. "Who is this?"
Kochira wa donata desu ka. "Might I ask who this is?"

PRACTICE

KEY SENTENCES

1. **Watashi wa Sumisu desu.**
2. **Watashi wa Amerika Taishikan no Sumisu desu.**
3. **Kochira wa Tanaka-san desu.**
4. **Watashi wa bengoshi dewa arimasen.**

1. My name's Smith.

2. I'm Smith from the American Embassy.

3. This is Mr. Tanaka.

4. I'm not a lawyer.

Vocabulary

Amerika Taishikan	American Embassy
Amerika	America
taishikan	embassy

EXERCISES

I Practice the following pattern by changing the underlined part as in the example given.

 ex. **[Watashi wa] Sumisu desu.**

  1. **Amerika Taishikan no Sumisu**

  2. **Amerika-jin**

  3. **bengoshi**

II Make dialogues by changing the underlined parts as in the examples given.

 A. *ex.* **Q: [Anata wa] Sumisu-san desu ka.**

   A: Hai, Sumisu desu.

   1. **Tanaka**

 B. *ex.* **Q: [Anata wa] Nihon-jin desu ka.**

   A*a*: Hai, Nihon-jin desu.

   A*n*: Iie, Nihon-jin dewa arimasen.

   1. **bengoshi**

   2. **hisho**

 C. *ex.* **Q: [Anata wa] Nihon-jin desu ka, Chūgoku-jin desu ka.**

   A: Nihon-jin desu.

   1. **Amerika-jin, Doitsu-jin**

   2. **gakusei, kaishain**

   3. **bengoshi, hisho**

 D. *ex.* **Q: [Anata wa] Donata desu ka.**

   A: Sumisu desu.

   1. **Tanaka**

   2. **Amerika Taishikan no Tanaka**

   3. **Nihon Ginkō no Tanaka**

 E. *ex.* **Q: Kochira wa donata desu ka.**

   A: Sumisu-san desu.

   1. **Tanaka-san**

   2. **Nihon Ginkō no Tanaka-san**

Amerika-jin	an American	**Chūgoku-jin**	a Chinese
-jin	person (suffix)	**Doitsu-jin**	a German
anata	you	**gakusei**	student
ka	= ? (question marker, particle)	**kaishain**	company employee
		donata	who
hai	yes, certainly	**Nihon Ginkō**	Bank of Japan
Nihon-jin	a Japanese	**Nihon**	Japan
iie	no	**ginkō**	bank
hisho	secretary		

SHORT DIALOGUES

1. **Sumisu:** [Anata wa] Tanaka-san desu ka.
   Tanaka: Hai, Tanaka desu.
   Sumisu: Tanaka-san wa gakusei desu ka.
   Tanaka: Iie, gakusei dewa arimasen. Kaishain desu.

   Smith: Are you Mr. Tanaka?
   Tanaka: Yes, I am.
   Smith: Are you a student.
   Tanaka: No, I'm not a student. I'm a company employee.

2. Mr. Hayashi introduces Miss Yamada to Mr. Tanaka.
   Hayashi: Go-shōkai shimasu. Kochira wa Yamada-san desu. Sumisu-san no hisho desu. Kochira wa Tanaka-san desu.
   Yamada: Hajimemashite. Yamada desu. Dōzo yoroshiku.
   Tanaka: Hajimemashite. Tanaka desu. Dōzo yoroshiku.

   Hayashi: Let me introduce you. This is Miss Yamada. She is Mr. Smith's secretary. This is Mr. Tanaka.
   Yamada: How do you do. My name's Yamada. I'm very glad to meet you.
   Tanaka: How do you do. My name's Tanaka. I'm very glad to meet you.

Vocabulary

go-shōkai shimasu	Let me introduce you.
Yamada	a surname

QUIZ ▦

I Supposing you are Mr. Smith in the opening dialogue, answer the following questions.

  1. **[Anata wa] Donata desu ka.**

    A.

  2. **[Anata wa] Nihon-jin desu ka.**

    A.

  3. **[Anata wa] kaishain desu ka, bengoshi desu ka.**

    A.

II Complete the questions so that they fit the answers.

  1. **(   ) desu ka.**
    Hai, Sumisu desu.
  2. **Sumisu-san wa (   ) desu ka.**
    Iie, Doitsu-jin dewa arimasen.
  3. **Sumisu-san wa (   ) desu ka, kaishain desu ka.**
    Bengoshi desu.
  4. **Kochira wa (   ) desu ka.**
    Tanaka-san desu.

III Put the appropriate particles in the parentheses.

  1. **Kochira (   ) Yamada-san desu.**
  2. **[Anata wa] Bengoshi desu (   ), kaishain desu (   ).**
    Kaishain desu.
  3. **Sumisu-san wa ABC (   ) bengoshi desu.**
  4. **Anata (   ) donata desu ka.**
    Sumisu desu.

IV Translate into Japanese.

  1. I'm Smith.
  2. How do you do. I'm glad to meet you.
  3. Miss Yamada, this is Mr. Tanaka of Tokyo Electric.
  4. Is Mr. Smith American or German?

LESSON 2 ADDRESS AND TELEPHONE NUMBER

Mr. Tanaka gives Mr. Smith his business card. Mr. Smith cannot read *kanji*.

たなか： わたしの　めいしです。どうぞ。

スミス： どうも　ありがとうございます。これは　たなかさんの
　　　　　なまえですか。

たなか： ええ、わたしの　なまえです。たなかです。

スミス： これは？

たなか： かいしゃの　なまえです。とうきょうでんきです。

スミス： これは　かいしゃの　でんわばんごうですか。

たなか： はい、かいしゃのです。03-400-9031です。うちの　でんわ
　　　　　ばんごうは　045-326-8871です。

Tanaka: Watashi no meishi desu. Dōzo.
Sumisu: Dōmo arigatō gozaimasu. Kore wa Tanaka-san no namae desu ka.
Tanaka: Ee, watashi no namae desu. TA-NA-KA desu.
Sumisu: Kore wa?
Tanaka: Kaisha no namae desu. TŌ-KYŌ DEN-KI desu.
Sumisu: Kore wa kaisha no denwa-bangō desu ka.
Tanaka: Hai, kaisha no desu. Zero-san no yon-zero-zero no kyū-zero-san-ichi desu. Uchi no denwa-bangō wa zero-yon-go no san-ni-roku no hachi-hachi-nana-ichi desu.

Tanaka: This is my business card. Please . . .
Smith: Thank you very much. Is this (your) name?
Tanaka: Yes. That's my name. Tanaka.
Smith: And this?
Tanaka: (That's) the name of my company, Tokyo Electric.
Smith: Is this the company's telephone number?
Tanaka: Yes, it's the company's. (03) 400–9031. (My) home telephone number is (045) 326–8871.

わたしの	watashi no	my
めいし	meishi	business card (*lit.* "name card")
どうぞ	dōzo	please (accept)
どうも ありがとう ございます	dōmo arigatō gozaimasu	Thank you very much.
どうも	dōmo	very much
ありがとう ございます	arigatō gozaimasu	(I am) grateful
これ	kore	this
なまえ	namae	name
ええ	ee	yes
これは？	kore wa?	as for this?
かいしゃ	kaisha	company
でんわばんごう	denwa-bangō	telephone number
でんわ	denwa	telephone
ばんごう	bangō	number
かいしゃのです	kaisha no desu	It is the company's.
うち	uchi	home

NOTES

1. Meishi

Japanese, particularly those in business, carry business cards which they exchange during introductions. A few hand-written words on a business card can serve as a convenient introduction.

2. Kore wa Tanaka-san no namae desu ka.

Note that although addressing Mr. Tanaka, Mr. Smith uses his name rather than saying **anata no**, "your." (See Note 4, p. 21.)

3. Ee.

"Yes." Less formal than **hai**.

4. Kore wa?

A rising intonation on the particle **wa** makes this informal phrase a question without using the question marker **ka**.

5. Kaisha no desu.

Short for **kaisha no denwa-bangō desu**. This sort of abbreviated expression is often used in Japanese.

6. (03) 400–9031

Spoken as **zero-san no yon-zero-zero no kyū-zero-san-ichi**. The area code (Tokyo's is 03), the exchange and the number are joined by the particle **no**. In telephone numbers 0 is often pronounced **zero** in Japanese.

7. **Nani/nan**, "what"

"What" is **nani**, but it often becomes **nan**, as in **Kore wa nan desu ka**. "What is this?"

8. **Nan-ban**, "What number?"

   ex. **Tanaka-san no denwa-bangō wa nan-ban desu ka.** "What is Mr. Tanaka's telephone number?"

PRACTICE

KEY SENTENCES

1. **Kore wa meishi desu.**
2. **Kore wa meishi dewa arimasen.**
3. **Kore wa Tanaka-san no tokei desu. Kore wa Tanaka-san no desu.**
4. **Kaisha no denwa-bangō wa (03) 400–9031 desu.**

1. This is a business card. (These are business cards.)
2. This is not a business card.
3. This is Mr. Tanaka's watch. This is Mr. Tanaka's.
4. The company's telephone number is (03) 400–9031.

Vocabulary

tokei   clock, watch

EXERCISES

I Look at the pictures and practice the following pattern by changing the underlined part as in the example given.

   ex. **Kore wa meishi desu.**

ex.

1. hon
2. shimbun
3. tokei
4. kagi
5. denwa
6. kuruma

II Make dialogues by changing the underlined parts as in the examples given.

A. *ex.* Q: Kore wa meishi desu ka.

Aa: Hai, meishi desu.

An: Iie, meishi dewa arimasen. Hon desu.

1. hon, shimbun
2. jūsho, denwa-bangō

B. *ex.* Q: Kore wa nan desu ka.

A: Namae desu.

1. tokei
2. kagi
3. denwa

C. *ex.* Q: Kore wa Tanaka-san no kuruma desu ka.

Aa: Hai, Tanaka-san no kuruma desu. Tanaka-san no desu.

An: Iie, Tanaka-san no kuruma dewa arimasen. Tanaka-san no dewa arimasen.

1. Sumisu-san
2. kaisha

D. *ex.* Q: Kore wa dare no hon desu ka.

A: Tanaka-san no desu.

1. Sumisu-san
2. kaisha
3. watashi

III Numbers: Memorize the numbers from 0 to 20.

0, **zero/rei**	7, shichi/nana	14, jūshi/jūyon
1, ichi	8, hachi	15, jūgo
2, ni	9, kyū/ku	16, jūroku
3, san	10, jū	17, jūshichi/jūnana
4, shi/yon	11, jūichi	18, jūhachi
5, go	12, jūni	19, jūkyū/jūku
6, roku	13, jūsan	20, nijū

IV Telephone numbers: Practice saying the following telephone numbers.

(03) 742–8955. **Zero-san no nana-yon-ni no hachi-kyū-go-go.**

401–5634. **Yon-zero-ichi no go-roku-san-yon.**

V Make dialogues by changing the underlined parts as in the example given.

ex. Q: Kaisha no denwa-bangō wa nan-ban desu ka.

A: 742–8920 desu.

1. ginkō, 325–8871
2. gakkō, (03) 781–6493
3. Tanaka-san no uchi, 956–4158

hon	book	nan	what
shimbun	newspaper	dare no	whose
kagi	key	nan-ban	what number
kuruma	car	-ban	number
jūsho	address	gakkō	school

SHORT DIALOGUES

1. **Hayashi:** **Kore wa Sumisu-san no tokei desu ka.**
   Tanaka: **Hai, Sumisu-san no tokei desu.**

   Hayashi: Is this Mr. Smith's watch?
   Tanaka: Yes, it's Mr. Smith's watch.

2. **Hayashi:** **Kore wa Sumisu-san no tokei desu ka.**
   Sumisu: **Hai, watashi no tokei desu.**

   Hayashi: Is this your watch?
   Smith: Yes, it's my watch.

3. **Hayashi:** **Kore wa Tanaka-san no hon desu ka.**
   Sumisu: **Iie, Tanaka-san no dewa arimasen. Watashi no desu.**

   Hayashi: Is this Mr. Tanaka's book?
   Smith: No, it's not Mr. Tanaka's. It's mine.

4. **Sumisu:** **Taishikan no denwa-bangō wa nan-ban desu ka.**
   Hisho: **325–7634 desu.**
   Sumisu: **Ginkō no denwa-bangō wa?**
   Hisho: **423–6502 desu.**

   Smith: What is the telephone number of the embassy?
   Secretary: It's 325–7634.
   Smith: What about the telephone number of the bank?
   Secretary: It's 423–6502.

QUIZ ▓▒░░░░░

I Look at the illustrated business card and answer the questions.

1. **Kore wa nan desu ka.**
2. **Kore wa kaisha no namae desu ka.**
3. **Kore wa Tanaka-san no uchi no jūsho desu ka, kaisha no desu ka.**

4. **Kore wa Tanaka-san no uchi no denwa-bangō desu ka.**

5. **Tanaka-san no kaisha no denwa-bangō wa nan-ban desu ka.**

II Complete the questions so that they fit the answers.

1. **Kore wa (   ) no denwa-bangō desu ka.**
   Iie; kaisha no dewa arimasen. Uchi no desu.
2. **Kore wa (   ) no jūsho desu ka.**
   Tanaka-san no desu.
3. **Kore wa (   ) desu ka.**
   Tokei desu.
4. **Tanaka-san no uchi no denwa-bangō wa (   ) desu ka.**
   325–7634 desu.

III Put the appropriate particles in the parentheses.

1. **Kochira (   ) donata desu ka.**
2. **Kore (   ) nan desu (   ).**
   Kaisha (   ) denwa-bangō desu.
   Kore (   )?
   Kaisha (   ) jūsho desu.
3. **Kore (   ) watashi (   ) kuruma dewa arimasen. Kaisha (   )**
   desu.

IV Translate into Japanese.

1. This is Mr. Tanaka.
2. This is Mr. Tanaka's business card.
3. This is not Mr. Tanaka's home telephone number. It is that of his company.
4. What is your company's telephone number?

LESSON 3 DAY AND TIME

Mr. Smith goes to a department store. It is not open yet.

スミス： すみません。いま　なんじですか。
おんなの　ひと：9じ50ぷんです。
スミス： デパートは　なんじからですか。
おんなの　ひと：10じからです。
スミス： なんじまでですか。
おんなの　ひと：ごご　6じまでです。
スミス： どうも　ありがとう。
おんなの　ひと：どういたしまして。

■ デパートは　10じから　6じまでです。

Sumisu: Sumimasen. Ima nan-ji desu ka.
Onna no hito: Ku-ji gojuppun desu.
Sumisu: Depāto wa nan-ji kara desu ka.
Onna no hito: Jū-ji kara desu.
Sumisu: Nan-ji made desu ka.
Onna no hito: Gogo roku-ji made desu.
Sumisu: Dōmo arigatō.
Onna no hito: Dō itashimashite.

■ Depāto wa jū-ji kara roku-ji made desu.

Smith: Excuse me. What time is it now?
Woman: It's 9:50.
Smith: What time does the store open?
Woman: It opens at 10:00.
Smith: How late does it stay open?
Woman: It stays open until 6 P.M.
Smith: Thank you very much.
Woman: Don't mention it.

■ The department store's hours are from 10:00 to 6:00.

すみません	**sumimasen**	Excuse me./I'm sorry.
いま	**ima**	now
なんじ	**nan-ji**	what time
～じ	**-ji**	o'clock
おんなの ひと	**onna no hito**	woman
おんな	**onna**	woman, female
ひと	**hito**	person
9じ	**ku-ji**	9 o'clock
50ぷん	**gojuppun/gojippun**	50 minutes
～ふん、～ぷん	**-fun, -pun**	minute
デパート	**depāto**	department store
から	**kara**	from (particle)
10じ	**jū-ji**	10 o'clock
まで	**made**	until (particle)
ごご	**gogo**	P.M.
6じ	**roku-ji**	6 o'clock
どう いたしまして	**dō itashimashite**	Don't mention it./You're welcome. (*lit.* "What have (I) done?")

NOTES

1. **Sumimasen.**

   Sumimasen, "Excuse me," prefaces a request, such as asking a stranger for information. It can also mean "Thank you," "I'm sorry," or "Pardon me."

2. **Jū-ji kara desu. Gogo roku-ji made desu.**

   "From 10 o'clock." "Until 6 P.M."

   Particles follow words, rather than proceed them. (See Grammar II, p. 53.) Note that instead of **Jū-ji kara hirakimasu,** "It is open from 10 o'clock," the word "open" is omitted. When the verb is understood, only the key words, (here **jū-ji kara, roku-ji made**) followed by **desu** are often used.

3. When

   Hour. **Nan-ji,** "what time?"
   Day of the week. **Nan-yōbi,** "which day of the week?"
   Day of the month. **Nan-nichi,** "which day of the month?"
   Month. **Nan-gatsu,** "which month?"
   Time in general. **Itsu,** "when?"

PRACTICE

1. **Ima gozen 10-ji desu.**
2. **Hiru-yasumi wa 12-ji kara 1-ji han made desu.**
3. **Kyō wa 6-gatsu 18-nichi desu.**
4. **Ashita wa Hayashi-san no tanjōbi desu.**
5. **Kinō wa kin-yōbi deshita.**
6. **Kinō wa moku-yōbi dewa arimasendeshita.**

1. It's 10 A.M. now.
2. Lunch time is from 12:00 to 1:30.
3. Today is June 18.
4. Tomorrow is Mr. Hayashi's birthday.
5. Yesterday was Friday.
6. Yesterday was not Thursday.

Vocabulary

gozen	A.M.	**-nichi**	day (See Exercise VI, p. 35.)
hiru-yasumi	lunch time		
hiru	noon	**ashita**	tomorrow
yasumi	rest (period)	**tanjōbi**	birthday
1-ji han	half past 1 (*lit.* "1 o'clock half")	**kinō**	yesterday
		kin-yōbi	Friday
han	half	**-yōbi**	day of the week (See Exercise V, p. 35.)
kyō	today		
6-gatsu 18 nichi	June 18		
6-gatsu	June (*lit.* sixth month)		
-gatsu	month (See Exercise VII, p. 35.)	**deshita**	was
		moku-yōbi	Thursday
		arimasendeshita	was not
18-nichi	18 day		

EXERCISES

I Numbers: Memorize the numbers from 20 to 100.

20, **nijū**	50, **gojū**	80, **hachijū**
30, **sanjū**	60, **rokujū**	90, **kyūjū**
40, **yonjū**	70, **shichijū, nanajū**	100, **hyaku**

Intermediate numbers are made by adding to the above numbers, the numbers from 1 to 9.

  ex. 21, **nijū-ichi**

II Look at the pictures and practice the following pattern as in the example given.

  ex. **Ima gozen 1-ji desu.**

   1. **3-ji**

   2. **gogo 4-ji 10-pun**

   3. **gozen 6-ji 15-fun**

   4. **9-ji han**

III Time: Practice telling time.

  A. **Ima nan-ji desu ka?**

   1. A.M. 2. P.M. 3. A.M. 4. P.M. 5. A.M. 6. P.M.

  B. **Nan-ji kara nan-ji made desu ka?**

   1. 2. 3. 4.

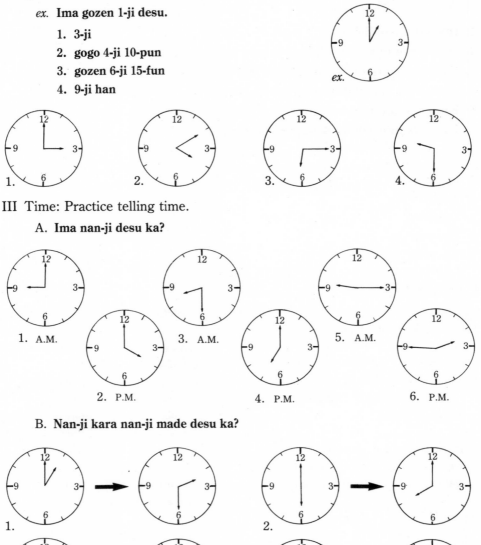

IV Make dialogues by changing the underlined parts as in the examples given.

  A. *ex.* **Q: Ima nan-ji desu ka.**

    A: 8-ji desu.

   1. 6:00

   2. 3:00 P.M.

   3. 9:30 A.M.

B. *ex.* Q: Pātī wa nan-ji kara desu ka.

    A: 7-ji kara desu.

    1. ginkō, 9:00

    2. eiga, 4:45

    3. kaigi, 9:30

C. *ex.* Q: Depāto wa nan-ji made desu ka.

    A: Gogo 6-ji made desu.

    1. hiru-yasumi, 1:30

    2. yūbinkyoku, gogo 5:00

    3. shigoto, 5:15

D. *ex.* Q: Hiru-yasumi wa nan-ji kara nan-ji made desu ka.

    A: 12-ji kara 1-ji made desu.

    1. eiga, 3:30, 4:45

    2. ginkō, 9:00, 3:00

V Days of the week: Memorize the names of the days of the week.

nichi-yōbi, Sunday	**sui-yōbi,** Wednesday	**do-yōbi,** Saturday
getsu-yōbi, Monday	**moku-yōbi,** Thursday	
ka-yōbi, Tuesday	**kin-yōbi,** Friday	

VI Days of the month: Memorize the days of the month.

1st, **tsuitachi**	11th, **jūichi-nichi**	21st, **nijūichi-nichi**
2nd, **futsuka**	12th, **jūni-nichi**	22nd, **nijūni-nichi**
3rd, **mikka**	13th, **jūsan-nichi**	23rd, **nijūsan-nichi**
4th, **yokka**	14th, **jūyokka**	24th, **nijūyokka**
5th, **itsuka**	15th, **jūgo-nichi**	25th, **nijūgo-nichi**
6th, **muika**	16th, **jūroku-nichi**	26th, **nijūroku-nichi**
7th, **nanoka**	17th, **jūshichi-nichi**	27th, **nijūshichi-nichi**
8th, **yōka**	18th, **jūhachi-nichi**	28th, **nijūhachi-nichi**
9th, **kokonoka**	19th, **jūku-nichi**	29th, **nijūku-nichi**
10th, **tōka**	20th, **hatsuka**	30th, **sanjū-nichi**
		31st, **sanjūichi-nichi**

VII Months. Memorize the names of the months.

ichi-gatsu, January	**go-gatsu,** May	**ku-gatsu,** September
ni-gatsu, February	**roku-gatsu,** June	**jū-gatsu,** October
san-gatsu, March	**shichi-gatsu,** July	**jūichi-gatsu,** November
shi-gatsu, April	**hachi-gatsu,** August	**jūni-gatsu,** December

VIII Make dialogues by changing the underlined parts as in the examples given.

    A. *ex.* Q: Kyō wa nan-nichi desu ka.

        A: 15-nichi desu.

1. 19-nichi
2. 23-nichi
3. 27-nichi

B. *ex.* Q: Ashita wa nan-yōbi desu ka.

A: <u>Ka-yōbi</u> desu.

1. sui-yōbi
2. moku-yōbi

C. *ex.* Q: Kinō wa nan-nichi deshita ka.

A: <u>11-nichi</u> deshita.

1. 12-nichi
2. 13-nichi

D. *ex.* Q: [Anata no] Tanjōbi wa itsu desu ka.

A: <u>3-gatsu</u> desu.

Q: <u>3-gatsu</u> nan-nichi desu ka.

A: <u>3-gatsu 26-nichi</u> desu.

1. 4-gatsu, 15-nichi
2. 9-gatsu, 21-nichi
3. 12-gatsu, 18-nichi

E. *ex.* Q: Kinō wa <u>moku-yōbi</u> deshita ka.

A: Iie, <u>moku-yōbi</u> dewa arimasendeshita. <u>Kin-yōbi</u> deshita.

1. getsu-yōbi, ka-yōbi
2. sui-yōbi, moku-yōbi
3. do-yōbi, nichi-yōbi

Vocabulary

pātī	party	**shigoto**	work
eiga	movie	**nan-nichi**	which day (of the month)
kaigi	conference, meeting	**nan-yōbi**	which day (of the week)
yūbinkyoku	post office	**itsu**	when

SHORT DIALOGUES

1. Sumisu: Ima nan-ji desu ka.
   Hisho: 9-ji han desu.
   Sumisu: Kaigi wa nan-ji kara desu ka.
   Hisho: 10-ji kara desu.

   Smith: What time is it now?
   Secretary: It's 9:30.
   Smith: What time does the meeting begin?
   Secretary: It's from 10:00.

2. **Tanaka:** Natsu-yasumi wa itsu kara desu ka.
   Sumisu: 7-gatsu 15-nichi kara desu.
   Tanaka: 7-gatsu 15-nichi wa nan-yōbi desu ka.
   Sumisu: Do-yōbi desu.

   Tanaka: When does summer vacation begin?
   Smith: It's from July 15.
   Tanaka: What day is July 15?
   Smith: It's a Saturday.

Vocabulary

natsu-yasumi   summer vacation
natsu   summer

QUIZ

I Read this lesson's opening dialogue and answer the following questions.

1. **Ima 10-ji desu ka.**
2. **Depāto wa nan-ji kara desu ka.**
3. **Depāto wa 7-ji made desu ka.**

II Complete the questions so that they fit the answers.

1. **Hiru-yasumi wa (   ) kara desu ka.**
   12-ji han kara desu.
2. **Kyō wa (   ) desu ka.**
   Ka-yōbi desu.
3. **Kinō wa (   ) deshita ka.**
   11-nichi deshita.

III Put the appropriate particles in the parentheses.

1. **Kinō (   ) kin-yōbi deshita.**
2. **Watashi (   ) kaisha no hiru-yasumi (   ) 12-ji kara desu.**
3. **Depāto (   ) nan-ji (   ) nan-ji (   ) desu ka.**

IV Translate into Japanese.

1. Thank you very much.
2. You're welcome.
3. Excuse me. Until what time does the post office stay open?
4. Today is the 15. Tomorrow is the 16.
5. Today is Thursday. Yesterday was Wednesday.

LESSON 4   HOW MUCH?

Mr. Smith goes shopping in the department store.

デパートの　てんいん：いらっしゃいませ。

スミス：　　　　　　　それを　みせてください。

デパートの　てんいん：はい、どうぞ。

スミス：　　　　　　　これは　いくらですか。

デパートの　てんいん：それは　3,000えんです。

スミス：　　　　　　　それは　いくらですか。

デパートの　てんいん：これも　3,000えんです。

スミス：　　　　　　　じゃ、それを　ください。

デパートの　てんいん：はい、ありがとうございます。

Depāto no ten'in: Irasshaimase.
Sumisu: Sore o misete kudasai.
Depāto no ten'in: Hai, dōzo.
Sumisu: Kore wa ikura desu ka.
Depāto no ten'in: Sore wa sanzen-en desu.
Sumisu: Sore wa ikura desu ka.
Depāto no ten'in: Kore mo sanzen-en desu.
Sumisu: Ja, sore o kudasai.
Depāto no ten'in: Hai, arigatō gozaimasu.

Store Clerk: May I help you, sir? (*lit.* "Welcome!")
Smith: Would you show me that, please?
Store Clerk: Certainly, sir. Here you are.
Smith: How much is this?
Store Clerk: That's 3,000 yen.
Smith: How much is that one?
Store Clerk: This one's 3,000 yen, too.
Smith: Well then, please give me that one.
Store Clerk: Very well, sir. Thank you.

Vocabulary		
てんいん	**ten'in**	store clerk
いらっしゃいませ	**irasshaimase**	Come in!/Welcome! (greeting to customers in stores/restaurants)
それ	**sore**	that, that one
を	**o**	(object marker, particle)
みせて　ください	**misete kudasai**	Please show me
みせます（みせる）	**misemasu (miseru)**	show
いくら	**ikura**	how much
3,000えん	**sanzen-en**	3,000 yen
～えん	**-en**	yen (¥)
も	**mo**	too (particle)
じゃ	**ja**	Well then . . .
ください	**kudasai**	Please give me . . .

NOTES

1. Kore, sore

Whereas English has only "this" and "that," Japanese has three separate indicators: **Kore**, **sore**, and **are**. (See Note 5, p. 46.)

Kore indicates something near the speaker.

Sore indicates something near the person spoken to.

Are indicates something not near either person.

ex. **Kore wa watashi no meishi desu.** "This is my business card."

2. Mo

The particle **mo** means "too, also, either." It is used in both affirmative and negative sentences.

ex. **Sore wa 3,000-en desu. Kore mo 3,000-en desu.** "That one is ¥3,000. This one is ¥3,000, too."

Kore wa watashi no kasa ja arimasen. Sore mo watashi no ja arimasen. "This is not my umbrella. That's not mine either."

3. Ja, sore o kudasai.

Dewa and **ja** correspond to "well" or "well then," an interjection expressing conclusion or resignation.

4. Sore o kudasai.

Kudasai, "please give me," follows the object (a noun referring to concrete things only) + object marker **o**.

ex. **Banana o kudasai.** "Please give me some bananas."

5. Ikura, "how much"

ex. **Kono fuirumu wa ikura desu ka.** "How much is this film?"

PRACTICE

KEY SENTENCES

1. **Kore wa tokei desu.**
2. **Sore mo tokei desu.**
3. **Are wa 3,000-en desu.**
4. **Kore o kudasai.**
5. **Are mo kudasai.**

1. This is a watch.
2. That is a watch, too.
3. That one (over there) is ¥3,000.
4. Give me this one, please.
5. Give me that one (over there), too, please.

Vocabulary

are   that (over there)

EXERCISES

I Look at the pictures and practice the following patterns.

    A. Imagine you are Mr. A and say the following.

        1. **Kore wa tokei desu.**
        2. **Sore wa kasa desu.**
        3. **Are wa terebi desu.**

    B. Now imagine you are Mr. B and say the following.

        1. **Kore wa kasa desu.**
        2. **Sore wa tokei desu.**
        3. **Are wa terebi desu.**

C. Imagine you are the clerk and state the prices of the objects illustrated.

    1. **Kore wa 3,000-en desu.**

    2. **Sore wa 3,500-en desu.**

    3. **Are mo 3,500-en desu.**

II Numbers: Memorize the numbers from 100 to 1,000,000,000,000 and note how decimals and fractions are read.

100. **hyaku**	1,000. **sen**	10,000. **ichiman**
200. **nihyaku**	2,000. **nisen**	100,000. **jūman**
300. **sambyaku**	3,000. **sanzen**	1,000,000. **hyakuman**
400. **yonhyaku**	4,000. **yonsen**	10,000,000. **senman**
500. **gohyaku**	5,000. **gosen**	100,000,000. **ichioku**
600. **roppyaku**	6,000. **rokusen**	1,000,000,000. **jūoku**
700. **nanahyaku**	7,000. **nanasen**	10,000,000,000. **hyakuoku**
800. **happyaku**	8,000. **hassen**	100,000,000,000. **sen'oku**
900. **kyūhyaku,**	9,000. **kyūsen**	1,000,000,000,000. **itchō**

Intermediate numbers are made by combining the numbers composing them.

ex. 135, **hyaku-sanjū-go**　　　　1,829, **sen-happyaku-nijū-kyū**

Decimals. (The word for "decimal point" is **ten**.)

      0, **rei, zero**

     0.7, **rei ten nana**

    0.29, **rei ten ni kyū**

   0.538, **rei ten go san hachi**

Fractions. (**Bun** means "part.")

    1/2, **nibun no ichi**　　　　1/4, **yombun no ichi**　　　　2/3, **sambun no ni**

III Make dialogues by changing the underlined parts as in the examples given.

  A. *ex.* **Q: Kore wa ikura desu ka.**

        A: [Sore wa] <u>2,000-en</u> desu.

    1. **1,800-en**

    2. **1,200-en**

    3. **7,500-en**

  B. *ex.* **Q: Sore wa <u>hon</u> desu ka.**

        A: Hai, kore wa <u>hon</u> desu.

        Q: Are mo <u>hon</u> desu ka.

        A: Hai, are mo <u>hon</u> desu.

    1. **tokei**

    2. **rajio**

  C. *ex.* **Q: Kore wa <u>ikura</u> desu ka.**

        A: Sore wa <u>3,500-en</u> desu.

        Q: Are mo <u>3,500-en</u> desu ka.

        A: Hai, are mo <u>3,500-en</u> desu.

1. ikura, 5,000-en
2. nan, rajio

D. *ex.* Q: Sore wa 3,000-en desu ka.

A: Hai, kore wa 3,000-en desu.

Q: Are mo 3,000-en desu ka.

A: Iie, are wa 3,000-en dewa arimasen. 3,500-en desu.

1. tēpurekōdā, rajio
2. Tanaka-san no hon, Sumisu-san no hon

IV Practice the following pattern by changing the underlined part as in the example given.

ex. **Kore** o kudasai.

1. sore
2. haizara
3. mizu
4. ringo
5. reshīto

Vocabulary

kasa	umbrella	haizara	ashtray
terebi	TV (set)	mizu	water
rajio	radio	ringo	apple
tēpurekōdā	tape recorder	reshīto	receipt

SHORT DIALOGUE

Sumisu: Sumimasen. Are wa rajio desu ka.
Ten'in: Iie, rajio dewa arimasen. Are wa tēpurekōdā desu.
Sumisu: Kore wa rajio desu ka.
Ten'in: Hai, rajio desu.
Sumisu: Ikura desu ka.
Ten'in: 28,000-en desu.
Sumisu: Dewa, kore o kudasai.

Smith: Excuse me. Is that a radio?
Clerk: No, it's not a radio. It's a tape recorder.
Smith: Is this a radio?
Clerk: Yes, it's a radio.
Smith: How much is it?
Clerk: It's ¥28,000.
Smith: Then, I'll take this.

Vocabulary

dewa   well then

QUIZ

I Imagine you are B in the illustration and answer A's questions.

1. **Kore wa tokei desu.**
   Sore mo tokei desu ka.
2. **Are wa nan desu ka.**
3. **Are wa ikura desu ka.**
4. **Kore mo 50,000-en desu ka.**
5. **Kore wa ikura desu ka.**
6. **Sore mo 5,000-en desu ka.**

II Complete the questions so that they fit the answers.

1. **Sore wa (   ) desu ka.**
   Kore wa tēpurekōdā desu.
2. **Kore wa (   ) desu ka.**
   Sore wa 13,000-en desu.
3. **Kochira wa (   ) desu ka.**
   Tanaka-san desu.
4. **(   ) wa ikura desu ka.**
   Are wa 3,500-en desu.

III Put the appropriate particles in the parentheses.

1. **Kore (   ) kudasai.**
2. **Kore (   ) ikura desu ka.**
   5,000-en desu.
   Sore (   ) 5,000-en desu ka.
   Hai, kore (   ) 5,000-en desu.
   Are (   ) 5,000-en desu ka.
   Iie, are (   ) 5,000-en dewa arimasen. Are (   ) 3,500-en desu.

IV Answer with the appropriate expressions in Japanese.

1. When you want a store clerk to show you an article that is near him, what do you say?
2. When you have decided to buy an article that is near you, what do you say to the clerk?
3. When you want to know the price of an article near you, what do you say?
4. What does a store clerk say when a customer enters the store?

LESSON 5   COUNTING OBJECTS

Mr. Smith buys a camera at a camera shop.

スミス：　すみません。その　カメラは　いくらですか。

カメラや：どれですか。

スミス：　その　ちいさい　カメラです。

カメラや：これですか。25,000えんです。どうぞ。

スミス：　これを　ください。それから　フイルムを　みっつ
　　　　　　ください。

■ちいさい　カメラは　25,000えんです。

Sumisu:	**Sumimasen. Sono kamera wa ikura desu ka.**
Kamera-ya:	**Dore desu ka.**
Sumisu:	**Sono chiisai kamera desu.**
Kamera-ya:	**Kore desu ka. 25,000-en desu. Dōzo.**
Sumisu:	**Kore o kudasai. Sorekara fuirumu o mittsu kudasai.**

■**Chiisai kamera wa 25,000-en desu.**

Smith:	Excuse me. How much is that camera?
Salesman:	Which one, sir?
Smith:	That small camera.
Salesman:	This one? It's ¥25,000. Here you are.
Smith:	I'll take this. And please let me have three (rolls of) film.

■The small camera is ¥25,000.

Vocabulary		

その	**sono**	that
カメラ	**kamera**	camera
カメラや	**kamera-ya**	camera store, camera seller
～や	**-ya**	store, seller
どれ	**dore**	which
ちいさい	**chiisai**	small (**-i** adj.)

それから	**sorekara**	and
フィルム	**fuirumu**	film
みっつ	**mittsu**	3

NOTES

1. Kamera-ya

Kamera-ya means not only "camera store" but also the store owner or store clerk. **Ya** is added to many things to mean the store or the person selling something.

ex. **Hana-ya**, "flower shop, florist"; **sakana-ya**, "fish shop, fish seller"; **hon-ya**, "book store, book seller."

2. Sorekara

Sorekara, "and, and also, and then, after that, in addition," is a connective placed at the beginning of a new sentence to connect it to the previous one.

3. Mittsu

In Japanese there are two numerical systems, the **hitotsu, futatsu, mittsu** system and the abstract **ichi, ni, san** system. Counting things can be done in two ways:

1. Using the **hitotsu, futatsu, mittsu** system independently. (See Exercise III, p. 48.)

ex. **Fuirumu o mittsu kudasai.** "Please give me three (rolls of) film."

2. Using the **ichi, ni, san** system combined with a counter. Two counters are **-mai**, for thin, flat objects such as paper, records, etc., and **-hon (-bon, -pon)**, for long, slender objects such as pencils, bottles, etc. Other counters appear in the appropriate place in the text, and they are given comprehensively in Appendix C.

-mai (how many . . . **nan-mai**)		**-hon** (how many . . . **nan-bon**)	
ichi-mai	shichi-mai, nana-mai	ippon	nana-hon
ni-mai	hachi-mai	ni-hon	happon
san-mai	kyū-mai	sam-bon	kyū-hon
yon-mai	jū-mai	yon-hon	juppon
go-mai	jūichi-mai	go-hon	jūippon
roku-mai	jūni-mai	roppon	jūni-hon

ex. **Hagaki o san-mai kudasai.** "Please give me three postcards." (*lit.* "three 'sheets of' ")

Note: The **hitotsu, futatsu, mittsu** system only goes as far as **tō** (10), after which the **ichi, ni, san** system is used.

4. **Fuirumu o mittsu kudasai.**

Note the word order: thing + **o** + numeral (or numeral and counter) + **kudasai.**

5. **Kono chiisai kamera**

Chiisai is an adjective. Adjectives will be given in detail in Lesson 13 and Lesson 14.

In Lesson 4 it was pointed out that there are three words for this and that: **kore**, **sore** and **are**. The demonstratives **kono**, **sono** and **ano** are used with nouns and have similar meanings from the viewpoint of the speaker. Study the following diagram and chart to understand the meaning of these words.

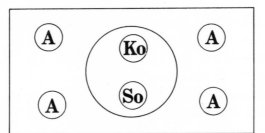

	ko words	**so** words	**a** words	**do** words
direction	**kochira** here, this way	**sochira** there, that way	**achira** over there	**dochira** where
people	**kochira** this person	**sochira** that person	**achira** that person over there	**donata, dare** who
thing	**kore** this	**sore** that	**are** that over there	**dore** which
place	**koko** here	**soko** there	**asoko** over there	**doko** where
demonstrative	**kono kamera** this camera	**sono kamera** that camera	**ano kamera** that camera over there	**dono kamera** which camera

6. **Ikutsu**, "How many?"
   ex. **Fuirumu o kudasai.** "Please give me some film."
   Hai, ikutsu desu ka. "Certainly sir, how many do you wish?"

PRACTICE

KEY SENTENCES

1. **Kono kamera wa 25,000-en desu.**
2. **Kono ringo wa hitotsu 200-en desu.**
3. **Kore wa Nihon no kamera desu.**
4. **Sono chiisai denchi o mittsu kudasai.**

1. This camera is ¥25,000.
2. One of these apples is ¥200.
3. This is a Japanese camera.
4. Please give me three of those small batteries.

Vocabulary

kono   this
hitotsu   1
denchi   battery

EXERCISES

I Look at the picture and practice how to use **kore/kono**, **sore/sono** and **are/ano**.

    1. **Kore wa 30,000-en desu.**

      Kono kamera wa 30,000-en desu.

    2. **Sore wa 20,000-en desu.**

      Sono tokei wa 20,000-en desu.

    3. **Are wa 10,000-en desu.**

      Ano têpurekōdā wa 10,000-en desu.

II Make dialogues by changing the underlined parts as in the examples given.

    A. *ex.* **Q: <u>Sono kamera</u> wa ikura desu ka.**

       A: <u>Kore</u> wa 30,000-en desu.

     1. **kono rajio, sore**

     2. **ano têpurekōdā, are**

B. *ex.* **Kore wa Nihon no kuruma desu ka.**

    A: Iie, Nihon no dewa arimasen. Doitsu no desu.

    1. **Amerika, Igirisu**

    2. **Itaria, Furansu**

C. *ex.* **Q: Kore wa doko no kamera desu ka.**

    A: Nihon no kamera desu.

    1. **Doitsu**

    2. **Amerika**

D. *ex.* **Q: Ano akai kasa wa ikura desu ka.**

    A: Are wa 5,000-en desu.

    1. **chiisai kamera, 20,000-en**

    2. **Doitsu no tokei, 10,000-en**

E. *ex.* **Q: Hayashi-san no kasa wa kore desu ka.**

    A: Hai, sore desu.

    1. **sore, kore**

    2. **are, are**

F. *ex.* **Hayashi-san no kasa wa dore desu ka.**

    A: Kore desu.

    1. **Nihon-go no têpu**

    2. **Sumisu-san no kuruma**

III Practice how to count things.

1, **hitotsu**	4, **yottsu**	7, **nanatsu**	10, **tō**
2, **futatsu**	5, **itsutsu**	8, **yattsu**	11, **jūichi**
3, **mittsu**	6, **muttsu**	9, **kokonotsu**	12, **jūni**

IV Look at the pictures and practice the following pattern by changing the underlined parts as in the example given.

    ex. **Kono fuirumu o futatsu kudasai.**

    1. **kono denchi, hitotsu**

    2. **sono ōkii ringo, itsutsu**

    3. **kono mikan, 2-kiro**

    4. **100-en no kitte, 10-mai**

    5. **biru, 12-hon**

ano	that, that one (over there)	ōkii	big (**-i** adj.)
Igirisu	United Kingdom	itsutsu	5
Itaria	Italy	mikan	tangerine
Furansu	France	2-kiro	2 kilograms
doko	where, belonging to or coming from what place?	-kiro	kilogram
		kitte	postage stamp
akai	red (**-i** adj.)	10-mai	*lit.* 10 (sheets)
Nihon-go	Japanese language	-mai	(counter)
-go	language	bīru	beer
tēpu	tape	12-hon	12 bottles
futatsu	2	-hon, -bon, -pon	(counter)

SHORT DIALOGUES

1. Sumisu: **Sumimasen. Rajio o misete kudasai.**
   Ten'in: **Dono rajio desu ka.**
   Sumisu: **Ano chiisai rajio desu.**
   Ten'in: **Hai, dōzo.**

   Smith: Excuse me. Would you show me that radio?
   Clerk: Which radio?
   Smith: That small radio (over there).
   Clerk: Certainly, sir. Here you are.

2. Sumisu: **Ano kasa wa ikura desu ka.**
   Ten'in: **Dore desu ka.**
   Sumisu: **Ano aoi kasa desu.**
   Ten'in: **Are wa 5,000-en desu.**
   Sumisu: **Ano kuroi kasa mo 5,000-en desu ka.**
   Ten'in: **Iie, are wa 7,000-en desu.**
   Sumisu: **Ja, ano aoi kasa o kudasai.**

   Smith: How much is that umbrella (over there)?
   Clerk: Which one?
   Smith: That blue one.
   Clerk: That's ¥5,000.
   Smith: Is that black umbrella ¥5,000, too?
   Clerk: No, it's ¥7,000.
   Smith: Well then, I'll take that blue one.

Vocabulary	

dono   which
aoi   blue (**-i** adj.)
kuroi   black (**-i** adj.)

QUIZ ▪▪▪▪▨▨▨

I Supposing you are the store clerk in the illustration. Answer the customer's
questions.

1. **Kono Doitsu no kamera wa ikura desu ka.**
2. **Sono kamera mo Doitsu no desu ka.**
3. **Sono kamera wa ikura desu ka.**
4. **Ano chiisai rajio wa doko no desu ka.**

II Complete the questions so that they fit the answers.

1. **Kono denchi wa (   ) desu ka.**
   100-en desu.
2. **(   ) wa ikura desu ka.**
   Are wa 30,000-en desu.
3. **Are wa (   ) no kitte desu ka.**
   Iie, Igirisu no dewa arimasen.
   (   ) no desu ka.
   Amerika no desu.

III Put the appropriate particles in the parentheses. (If a particle is not required,
put an X in the parentheses.)

1. **Kore (   ) Nihon (   ) tēpurekōdā desu. Sono tēpurekōdā (   )**
   Nihon (   ) desu.

2. **Kamera (   ) misete kudasai.**
3. **Bīru (   ) 15-hon (   ) kudasai.**
4. **Kore (   ) 150-en desu.**
5. **Kono (   ) ringo (   ) hitotsu (   ) 200-en desu.**

IV Translate into Japanese.

1. How much is this?
2. How much is this radio?
3. My watch is not Japanese. It is American.
4. Please show me that small tape recorder.
5. Please give me 3 (rolls of) film.
   Which film?
   That film.

LESSON 6 GOING AND COMING

Mr. Tanaka meets Mr. Hayashi at Tokyo Station. Mr. Hayashi looks as if he is going on a trip.

たなか：どこに　いきますか。

はやし：きょうとの　ししゃに　いきます。

たなか：ひとりで　いきますか。

はやし：いいえ、かいしゃの　ひとと　いきます。

たなか：おおさかにも　いきますか。

はやし：いいえ、おおさかには　いきません。

たなか：いつ　とうきょうに　かえりますか。

はやし：あさって　かえります。

■ はやしさんは　かいしゃの　ひとと　きょうとの　ししゃに　
　いきます。そして　あさって　とうきょうに　かえります。

Tanaka:	Doko ni ikimasu ka.
Hayashi:	Kyōto no shisha ni ikimasu.
Tanaka:	Hitori de ikimasu ka.
Hayashi:	Iie, kaisha no hito to ikimasu.
Tanaka:	Ōsaka ni mo ikimasu ka.
Hayashi:	Iie, Ōsaka ni wa ikimasen.
Tanaka:	Itsu Tōkyō ni kaerimasu ka.
Hayashi:	Asatte kaerimasu.

■ Hayashi-san wa kaisha no hito to Kyōto no shisha ni ikimasu. Soshite asatte Tōkyō ni kaerimasu.

Tanaka:	Where are you going?
Hayashi:	I'm going to our branch office in Kyoto.
Tanaka:	Are you going alone?
Hayashi:	No, I'm going with a person from the company.
Tanaka:	Are you going to Osaka, too?
Hayashi:	No, we're not going to Osaka.

Tanaka: When are you coming back to Tokyo?
Hayashi: We're returning the day after tomorrow.

■ Mr. Hayashi is going to the company's branch office in Kyoto with a colleague. They will return to Tokyo the day after tomorrow.

Vocabulary

に	**ni**	to (particle)
いきます（いく）	**ikimasu (iku)**	go, is going
きょうと	**Kyōto**	Kyoto (city and prefecture)
ししゃ	**shisha**	branch office
ひとりで	**hitori de**	alone
と	**to**	with (particle)
おおさか	**Ōsaka**	Osaka (city and prefecture)
とうきょう	**Tōkyō**	Tokyo (city and prefecture)
かえります（かえる）	**kaerimasu (kaeru)**	return, come back
あさって	**asatte**	the day after tomorrow
そして	**soshite**	and then

GRAMMAR II

Lessons 6–7   NI/E verb

1. noun **wa** place NI/E IKIMASU
2. noun **wa** place NI/E IKIMASU KA

    Hai, (noun **wa** place **ni**) ikimasu.

    Iie, (noun **wa** place **ni**) ikimasen.

• Particles **ni/e**

Particles are an important part of Japanese sentence structure. They resemble English prepositions in the way they connect words, but unlike English *pre*positions, which come before nouns, Japanese particles are *post*positions, always coming after nouns. Particles show the grammatical role of nouns in Japanese. The role of the preposition "to" in English is played by the particles **ni** and **e** in Japanese, placed after the noun—something like the English suffix "-ward," as in "northward."

ex. **Tōkyō ni/e ikimasu.** "I am going to Tokyo." (*lit.* " 'Tokyo-ward' I am going.")

Theoretically the use of **ni** and **e** are divided as given below, but in actual practice they are interchangeable. In this book, in situations where either might occur, we use **ni**.

   e: expresses direction
         ex. **Higashi e ikimasu.** "(I) am going towards the east."
   ni: expresses arrival at a destination

ex. **Kyonen no 12-gatsu ni Nihon ni kimashita.** "(I) came to Japan last December."

Note that some particles, like **ka**, may come at the end of phrases, clauses or sentences. See Lesson 1, **ka**; Lesson 9, **kara**, **yo**, **ne**; Lesson 10, **ne**; Lesson 12, **ga**; and Lesson 16, **ni**.

- Verbs

Japanese sentences end with the verb. (**Desu** in Grammar I is not strictly speaking a verb, but its use in sentences is similar to that of a verb and so it comes at the end.) The endings of verbs show the tense and whether they are positive or negative.

Tenses of Japanese verbs can be divided roughly into two large categories:

1. Present Form

   Habitual action: *ex.* **Tanaka-san wa mainichi kaisha ni ikimasu.** "Mr. Tanaka goes to the office (*lit.* company) every day."

   Future: *ex.* **[Watashi wa] Ashita kaerimasu.** "I return/am returning/ will return tomorrow."

2. Past Form

   Past: *ex.* **[Watashi wa] Senshū Kyōto ni ikimashita.** "Last week (I) went to Kyoto."

   Present perfect: *ex.* **Ima kimashita.** "(He) has just come."

In simple sentences like the above, tenses of Japanese verbs closely resemble those in English. However, verbs that occur within a sentence in addition to the main verb at the end (i.e., Before I *left* home, I turned off the TV), do not necessarily take the same form they would in English. But that kind of sentence is outside the scope of this book and must be studied at a higher level.

Note: The **-u** form of the verb given in the vocabulary lists (**-u**, **-ku**, **-su**, **-ru**, etc.) is the so-called plain (uninflected) form found in dictionaries. Used at the end of a sentence, it is less formal than the **-masu** form. This book uses only the more polite **-masu** form.

NOTES

1. A. **Hitori de ikimasu.**

   Number of people takes the particle **de**.

   ex. **Hitori de**, "alone, by oneself"

   San-nin de, "three of us/them"

   B. **Kaisha no hito to ikimasu.**

   Individual or individuals take the particle **to**, "with."

   ex. **Tanaka-san to**, "with Mr. Tanaka"

2. **Ōsaka ni mo ikimasu ka.**

   Iie, Ōsaka ni wa ikimasen.

   Mr. Hayashi says he is going to Kyoto, which is close to the important industrial city of Osaka, so Mr. Tanaka asks him if he is going to Osaka too. **Ōsaka ni mo . . .?** Note the position after the noun of the particles **ni**, "to, towards," and **mo**, "too, also."

In his reply, Mr. Hayashi uses the topic marker particle **wa** to show that motion towards Osaka is the topic, "As for Osaka, I am not going there." Note that while two particles may normally follow one another, as do **ni mo** and **ni wa** above, **wa** and **mo** never follow the particles **ga** and **o**, but simply take their place. Similarly, **wa** and **mo** are never used together. One or the other is used.

ex. **Sumisu-san wa bengoshi desu.** "Mr. Smith is a lawyer." **Buraun-san mo bengoshi desu.** "Mr. Brown, too, is a lawyer."

Mo can follow any of the other particles such as **ni**, **kara**, **de**, etc.

3. **Asatte kaerimasu.**

"Yesterday," "next week," "this month," "last year," and certain other time expressions do not take particles.

4. **Soshite, asatte Tōkyō ni kaerimasu.**

In Japanese many sentences begin with connectives, like **soshite**, meaning "and then," which link them to the previous sentence.

5. **A. Doko**, "where"
   ex. **Doko ni ikimasu ka.** "Where are you going?"
   B. Itsu, "when." Time in general.
   ex. **Itsu kimasu ka.** "When are you coming?"
   C. Dare/donata (ga), "who"
   ex. **Dare ga Ōsaka ni ikimasu ka.** "Who is going to Osaka?" When the subject is unknown, the particle **ga** should be used after **dare/donata** instead of the topic marker **wa**. (See Grammer III, p. 66.)

PRACTICE

KEY SENTENCES

1. **Watashi wa ashita ginkō ni ikimasu.**
2. **Kono densha wa Tōkyō Eki ni ikimasen.**
3. **Watashi wa kinō yūbinkyoku ni ikimashita.**
4. **Watashi wa senshū gakkō ni ikimasendeshita.**
5. **Sumisu-san wa kyonen Amerika kara Nihon ni kimashita.**
6. **Sumisu-san wa rainen Amerika ni kaerimasu.**

1. I'm going to the bank tomorrow.
2. This train doesn't go to Tokyo Station.
3. I went to the post office yesterday.
4. I didn't go to school last week.
5. Mr. Smith came to Japan from America last year.
6. Mr. Smith will go back to America next year.

densha	(electric) train	**kara**	from (particle)
Tōkyō Eki	Tokyo Station	**kimashita**	came
eki	station	**kimasu (kuru)**	come
senshū	last week	**rainen**	next year
kyonen	last year		

EXERCISES

I Verbs: Memorize the following verbs in their present and past forms.

	Present Form		Past Form	
	aff.	*neg.*	*aff.*	*neg.*
go	**ikimasu**	**ikimasen**	**ikimashita**	**ikimasendeshita**
come	**kimasu**	**kimasen**	**kimashita**	**kimasendeshita**
return	**kaerimasu**	**kaerimasen**	**kaerimashita**	**kaerimasendeshita**

II Practice the following by changing the underlined part as in the example given.

> *ex.* **A. [Watashi wa] Ginkō ni ikimasu.**
>
> 1. **kaisha**
> 2. **Amerika**

III Make dialogues by changing the underlined part as in the examples given.

> A. *ex.* **Q: [Anata wa] Ashita kaisha ni ikimasu ka.**
>
> **A*a*: Hai, ikimasu.**
>
> **A*n*: Iie, ikimasen.**
>
> 1. **tomodachi no uchi**
> 2. **depāto**
> 3. **taishikan**

> B. *ex.* **Q: Kono densha wa Tōkyō Eki ni ikimasu ka.**
>
> **A*a*: Hai, ikimasu.**
>
> **A*n*: Iie, ikimasen.**
>
> 1. **basu**
> 2. **chikatetsu**

> C. *ex.* **Q: Sumisu-san wa kinō Amerika ni kaerimashita ka.**
>
> **A*a*: Hai, kaerimashita.**
>
> **A*n*: Iie, kaerimasendeshita.**
>
> 1. **senshū**

2. sengetsu

3. kyonen

D. *ex.* **Q: Dare ga kyō taishikan ni ikimasu ka.**

    A: <u>Tanaka-san</u> ga ikimasu.

    1. **tomodachi**

    2. **Tanaka-san no hisho**

E. *ex.* **Q: [Anata wa] Itsu Nihon ni kimashita ka.**

    A: <u>Sengetsu</u> kimashita.

    1. **senshū**

    2. **kyonen**

F. *ex.* **Q: Tanaka-san wa kinō doko ni ikimashita ka.**

    A: <u>Depāto</u> ni ikimashita.

    1. **yūbinkyoku**

    2. **tomodachi no uchi**

    3. **ginkō**

G. *ex.* **Q: Sumisu-san wa dare to Narita Kūkō ni ikimashita ka.**

    A: <u>Tanaka-san</u> to ikimashita.

    1. **tomodachi to**

    2. **kaisha no hito to**

    3. **hitori de**

Vocabulary

tomodachi	friend	**sengetsu**	last month
basu	bus	**ga**	(subject marker, particle)
chikatetsu	subway, *lit.* under-ground railway	**Narita Kūkō**	Narita Airport
		kūkō	airport

SHORT DIALOGUES

1. **Tanaka:**   **Kyō ginkō ni ikimasu ka.**
   Hisho: **Hai, ikimasu.**
   Tanaka: **Yūbinkyoku ni mo ikimasu ka.**
   Hisho: **Iie, yūbinkyoku ni wa ikimasen.**

   Tanaka: Are you going to the bank today?
   Secretary: Yes, I am.
   Tanaka: Will you go to the post office, too?
   Secretary: No, I'm not going to the post office.

2. **Sumisu:**   **Kono densha wa Tōkyō Eki ni ikimasu ka.**
   Otoko no hito: **Iie, ikimasen.**
   Sumisu: **Dono densha ga ikimasu ka.**
   Otoko no hito: **Ano aoi densha ga ikimasu.**

Smith: Does this train go to Tokyo Station?
Man: No, it doesn't.
Smith: Which train goes there?
Man: That blue train over there does.

Vocabulary

otoko no hito	man
otoko	man, male

QUIZ ▰▰▰▰▰▰

I Read this lesson's opening dialogue and answer the following questions.

1. **Hayashi-san wa Ōsaka no shisha ni ikimasu ka, Kyōto no shisha ni ikimasu ka.**
2. **Hayashi-san wa dare to Kyōto no shisha ni ikimasu ka.**
3. **Hayashi-san wa itsu Tōkyō ni kaerimasu ka.**

II Complete the questions so that they fit the answers.

1. **(   ) ni ikimasu ka.**
   Hai, ginkō ni ikimasu.
   (   ) ni mo ikimasu ka.
   Iie, yūbinkyoku ni wa ikimasen.
2. **(   ) Nihon ni kimashita ka.**
   Kyonen kimashita.
3. **(   ) ni ikimashita ka.**
   Kūkō ni ikimashita.
   (   ) to ikimashita ka.
   Hitori de ikimashita.

III Put the appropriate particles in the parentheses. (If a particle is not required, put an X in the parentheses.)

1. **Tanaka-san wa ashita (   ) Ōsaka (   ) ikimasu.**
2. **Yamada-san wa kaisha no hito (   ) kūkō (   ) ikimashita.**
3. **Tanaka-san (   ) itsu (   ) Ōsaka kara kaerimasu ka.**
4. **Tomodachi wa senshū hitori (   ) Amerika ni kaerimashita.**
5. **Ashita Kyōto (   ) ikimasu.**
   Ōsaka ni (   ) ikimasu ka.
   Iie, Ōsaka ni (   ) ikimasen.

6. **Dare (   ) kimashita ka.**
   Yamada-san ga kimashita.

IV Translate into Japanese.

   1. Excuse me, does this bus go to Tokyo Station?
   2. Mr. Tanaka went to Osaka yesterday with a person from his company. And
      he will return to Tokyo the day after tomorrow.
   3. Mr. Smith came to Japan alone last year.
   4. Who went to the airport?
      Mr. Tanaka's secretary went.

LESSON 7 GOING BY TAXI

Mr. Smith visits Mr. Tanaka on Sunday.

たなか：スミスさん、よく　いらっしゃいました。

スミス：こんにちは。

たなか：どうぞ　おはいりください。

スミス：しつれいします。

たなか：どうぞ　こちらに。バスで　きましたか。

スミス：いいえ、タクシーで　きました。

たなか：どうぞ　おかけください。

スミス：ありがとうございます。

■スミスさんは　にちようびに　タクシーで　たなかさんの　うちに
　いきました。

Tănaka:	**Sumisu-san, yoku irasshaimashita.**
Sumisu:	**Konnichiwa.**
Tanaka:	**Dōzo ohairi kudasai.**
Sumisu:	**Shitsurei shimasu.**
Tanaka:	**Dōzo kochira ni. Basu de kimashita ka.**
Sumisu:	**Iie, takushī de kimashita.**
Tanaka:	**Dōzo okake kudasai.**
Sumisu:	**Arigatō gozaimasu.**

■**Sumisu-san wa nichiyōbi ni takushī de Tanaka-san no uchi ni ikimashita.**

Tanaka:	Mr. Smith, how nice of you to come.
Smith:	Hello.
Tanaka:	Do come in.
Smith:	May I?
Tanaka:	This way, please. Did you come by bus?
Smith:	No. I came by taxi.
Tanaka	Do sit down.
Smith:	Thank you.

■Mr. Smith went to Mr. Tanaka's house by taxi on Sunday.

よく　いらっしゃいました	**yoku irasshaimashita**	How nice of you to come. (*lit.* "Welcome!")
よく	**yoku**	well
いらっしゃいました	**irasshaimashita**	came
いらっしゃいます（いらっしゃる）	**irasshaimasu (irassharu)**	come (polite word for **kuru**)
おはいり　ください	**ohairi kudasai**	Do come in.
はいります（はいる）	**hairimasu (hairu)**	enter
しつれいします	**shitsurei shimasu**	May I? (I'm afraid I'll be disturbing you.)
こちらに	**kochira ni**	this way
こちら	**kochira**	this direction
で	**de**	by (particle)
タクシー	**takushi**	taxi
おかけ　ください	**okake kudasai**	Please have a seat. (*lit.* "Please sit down.")
かけます（かける）	**kakemasu (kakeru)**	sit
に	**ni**	on (particle)

NOTES

1. **Shitsurei shimasu.**

   "May I." (*lit.* "I'll be so bold as to do so.")

   Shitsurei essentially means "rudeness" and is used when entering a house or room, passing in front of someone, leaving in the middle of a gathering and so on, in other words, when creating some sort of disturbance and interrupting the status quo. Some people use it as a form of "good-bye," instead of **sayōnara**, when leaving a house or room.

2. **Basu de kimashita ka.**

   The particle **de** follows nouns to express means.

   ex. **basu de**, (travel) "by bus"

   pen de, (write) "with pen"

   Nihon-go de, (speak) "in Japanese"

   iyahōn de, (listen) "with earphones"

   funabin de, (send) "by sea mail"

3. **Nichi-yōbi ni ikimashita.**

   The particle **ni** is used here and in cases such as the following:

   5-ji ni, "at 5 o'clock"

   do-yōbi ni, "on Saturday"

   12-nichi ni, "on the 12"

   1960-nen ni, "in 1960"

4. **Nani/nan de**, "how"

    ex. **Nan de ikimasu ka.** "How will you go?"

    Basu de ikimasu. "I'll go by bus."

An exception to this pattern is **aruite ikimasu**, "I'll walk."

PRACTICE

KEY SENTENCES

1. **Kurāku-san wa 5-gatsu 18-nichi ni Kanada kara Nihon ni kimashita.**
2. **Kurāku-san wa rainen no 3-gatsu ni Kanada ni kaerimasu.**
3. **Watashi wa chikatetsu de kaisha ni ikimasu.**

1. Mr. Clark came to Japan on May 18 from Canada.
2. Mr. Clark will go back to Canada in March of next year.
3. I go to the office by subway.

Vocabulary	
Kurāku	Clark
Kanada	Canada

EXERCISES

I Practice the following pattern by changing the underlined part as in the example given.

    ex. **Howaito-san wa <u>5-gatsu 18-nichi ni</u> Nihon ni kimashita.**

        1. **15-nichi ni**

        2. **1980 nen ni**

        3. **senshū no moku-yōbi ni**

        4. **sengetsu**

        5. **ototoi**

        6. **senshū**

II Make dialogues by changing the underlined part as in the examples given.

    A. *ex.* **Q: Howaito-san wa itsu Nihon ni kimasu ka.**

        A: <u>5-gatsu 18-nichi ni</u> kimasu.

        1. **getsu-yōbi**

        2. **raishū no do-yōbi**

        3. **raigetsu no 15-nichi**

        4. **rainen no 10-gatsu**

    B. *ex.* **Q: Tanaka-san wa nan de uchi ni kaerimashita ka.**

        A: <u>Kuruma</u> de kaerimashita.

        1. **takushī**

2. **basu**

3. **densha**

C. *ex.* Q: **Hayashi-san wa nan-nen ni Igirisu ni ikimashita ka.**

   A: <u>1981-nen</u> ni ikimashita.

   1. **1975-nen**

   2. **1982-nen**

D. *ex.* Q: **Dare ga kyō Kyōto no shisha ni ikimasu ka.**

   A: <u>Hayashi-san</u> ga ikimasu.

   Q: <u>Hayashi-san</u> wa itsu Tōkyō ni kaerimasu ka.

   A: **Asatte kaerimasu.**

   1. **Tanaka-san**

   2. **Sumisu-san**

Vocabulary

Howaito	White	**raishū**	next week
1980-nen	(the year) 1980	**raigetsu**	next month
-nen	year (See Appendix G.)	**nan de**	how, by what means
ototoi	the day before yesterday	**nan-nen**	what year?

SHORT DIALOGUE

Tanaka: **Kurāku-san wa itsu Nihon ni kimashita ka.**

Kurāku: **Kyonen no 5-gatsu 18-nichi ni kimashita.**

Tanaka: **Kyōto ni ikimashita ka.**

Kurāku: **Ee, senshū Shinkansen de ikimashita. Kin-yōbi ni Tōkyō ni kaerimashita.**

Tanaka: When did you come to Japan?

Clark: I came on May 18 last year.

Tanaka: Did you go to Kyoto?

Clark: Yes, I went (there) by Shinkansen last week. I returned to Tokyo on Friday.

Vocabulary

Shinkansen   Shinkansen, New Trunk Line

QUIZ ■▨▨▨▨░

I Read this lesson's opening dialogue and answer the following questions.

1. **Dare ga Tanaka-san no uchi ni ikimashita ka.**

2. **Sumisu-san wa itsu Tanaka-san no uchi ni ikimashita ka.**

3. **Sumisu-san wa Tanaka-san no uchi ni densha de ikimashita ka.**

4. **Sumisu-san wa Tanaka-san no uchi ni nan de ikimashita ka.**

II Complete the questions so that they fit the answers.

1. **Nichi-yōbi ni (   ) ni ikimashita ka.**
   Tomodachi no uchi ni ikimashita.
2. **Tanaka-san wa (   ) Kyōto kara kaerimashita ka.**
   Senshū no do-yōbi ni kaerimashita.
3. **Kurāku-san wa (   ) ni Osaka ni ikimasu ka.**
   18-nichi ni ikimasu.
   (   ) de ikimasu ka.
   Shinkansen de ikimasu.
   (   ) to ikimasu ka.
   Hitori de ikimasu.

III Put the appropriate particles in the parentheses. (If a particle is not required, put an X in the parentheses.)

1. **Watashi wa basu (   ) kaisha (   ) kimasu. Anata (   ) basu de kimasu ka.**
2. **Itsu (   ) Nihon ni kimashita ka.**
   5-gatsu 18-nichi (   ) kimashita.

IV Answer with the appropriate expressions in Japanese.

1. How does one greet a person one meets in the daytime?
2. What does one say to a guest who has just arrived?
3. How does one offer a chair to a guest?

V Translate into Japanese.

1. Please come this way.
2. Do come in.
3. Mr. Tanaka went home yesterday by taxi.
4. Miss White is going to the Osaka branch office on Friday.

LESSON 8 EXISTENCE OF PEOPLE AND THINGS

Let's have a look at Mr. Tanaka's house.

いまに　いすや　テーブルや　テレビが　あります。テーブルの
うえに　しんぶんと　はなが　あります。いまに　たなかさんの
おくさんが　います。にわに　たなかさんと　おとこの　こが　います。
だいどころに　だれも　いません。

Ima ni isu ya tēburu ya terebi ga arimasu. Tēburu no ue ni shimbun to hana ga arimasu. Ima ni Tanaka-san no okusan ga imasu. Niwa ni Tanaka-san to otoko no ko ga imasu. Daidokoro ni dare mo imasen.

There is a chair, a table, a TV set (etc.) in the living room. There are some flowers and a newspaper on (top of) the table. Mrs. Tanaka is in the living room. Mr. Tanaka and a boy are in the garden. There isn't anybody in the kitchen.

Vocabulary

いま	**ima**	living room
に	**ni**	in (particle)
いす	**isu**	chair
や	**ya**	and (etc.) (particle)
テーブル	**tēburu**	table
あります（ある）	**arimasu (aru)**	are (for inanimate things)
うえ	**ue**	top
と	**to**	and (particle)
はな	**hana**	flower
おくさん	**okusan**	(his) wife (See Note 2, p. 168.)
います（いる）	**imasu (iru)**	is (for living things)
にわ	**niwa**	garden
おとこのこ	**otoko no ko**	boy (*lit.* "male child")
こ	**ko**	child
だいどころ	**daidokoro**	kitchen
だれも～ません	**dare mo . . . -masen**	nobody . . . is

GRAMMAR III

Lessons 8–9　Existence of People and Things

1. place **NI** noun **GA ARIMASU/IMASU**
2. noun **WA** place **NI ARIMASU/IMASU**
3. noun **WA** place **DESU**

- **Arimasu/Imasu**
  Both verbs express "being." **Arimasu** is used for inanimate things (books, buildings, tree, etc.) and **imasu** for animate things (people, animals, insects, etc.)

- Particle **ni**
  Existence in a place is indicated by the particle **ni**, not **e**.
  ex. **Niwa ni Tanaka-san ga imasu.** "Mr. Tanaka is in the garden."

- Particle **ga**. Subject marker.
  When a subject is introduced for the first time, or when the speaker believes the information to be new to the listener, the subject marker **ga** is used after the noun instead of the topic marker **wa**. Noun + **ga** + verb is the pattern used.
  ex. **Basu ga kimasu.** "The bus is coming."
  　　Yamada-san ga kinō kimashita. "Mr. Yamada came yesterday."
  Ga is also used when the subject is unknown, i.e., with question words like "who" and "what." (See Note 4, below.)
  ex. **Dare ga kimashita ka.** "Who came?"

Ga is used similarly in the reply.

ex. **Hayashi-san ga kimashita.** "Mr. Hayashi came."

• **Ga——→wa**

As soon as the existence of someone or something is understood by both parties, it can become the topic.

ex. **Tana no ue ni hon ga arimasu.** "There is a book on the shelf."
Ano hon wa Tanaka-san no hon desu. "That book is Mr. Tanaka's book."

• **Verb——→desu**

When the verb is understood, **desu** sometimes takes its place at the end of the sentence.

ex. **Terebi wa doko ni arimasu ka.** "Where is the TV set?"
Tēburu no ue desu. (for **Tēburu no ue ni arimasu.**) "It's on the table."

If it is not certain whether there is a TV or not, **desu** cannot be substituted and **arimasu** must be repeated to make the meaning clear.

ex. **Tēburu no ue ni terebi ga arimasu ka.** "Is there a TV set on the table?"
Hai, arimasu./Hai, terebi ga arimasu. "Yes, there is./Yes, there is a TV set."

In this case, one may not say: **Hai, terebi desu./Hai, tēburu no ue desu.**

NOTES

1. **Ima ni isu ya tēburu ya terebi ga arimasu.**

   The particle **ya** is used for "and" when listing two or more things or people and implying the existence of others as well.

2. **Tēburu no ue ni shimbun to hana ga arimasu.**

   The particle **to** is used for "and" when the existence of nothing or nobody else is implied. From the Japanese sentence it is clear that there is nothing on the table besides the newspaper and the flowers. Note that unlike "and," both **to** and **ya** are used only to connect nouns. They cannot be used to connect verbs or clauses.

3. **Dare mo imasen.**

   Dare, "who," combines with the particle **mo** to mean "nobody" when followed by a verb with the negative ending **-masen**. Similarly, **nani mo**, "nothing," and **doko ni mo**, "nowhere," take the negative verb ending **-masen**.

   ex. **Dare mo kimasen deshita.** "Nobody came."
   Tanaka-san wa ashita doko ni mo ikimasen. "Mr. Tanaka is not going anywhere tomorrow."

4. **Nani ga**

   Like **dare**, "who," **nani**, "what," is never followed by the topic marker **wa**. It always takes the subject marker **ga**.

   ex. **Isu no ue ni nani ga arimasu ka.** "What is there on the chair?"
   Hon ga arimasu. "There is a book."

PRACTICE

KEY SENTENCES

1. Ikkai ni ima ga arimasu.
2. Hako no naka ni kitte to hagaki ga arimasu.
3. Tana no ue ni shashin ya hon ga arimasu.
4. Mado no chikaku ni onna no ko ga imasu.
5. Genkan ni dare mo imasen.
6. Todana no mae ni nani mo arimasen.

1. There is a living room on the first floor.
2. There are stamps and postcards in the box.
3. There are pictures, books (etc.) on the shelf.
4. There is a girl near the window.
5. There isn't anybody in the entrance hall.
6. There isn't anything in front of the cabinet.

Vocabulary

ikkai	first floor, ground floor	mado	window
-kai	floor (See Appendix C.)	chikaku	near, close to
hako	box	onna no ko	girl (*lit.* "female child")
naka	inside	genkan	entrance hall
hagaki	postcard	todana	cabinet
tana	shelf	mae	in front of, before
shashin	photograph		

EXERCISES

I Verbs: Memorize the following verbs and their present and past forms.

	Present Form		Past Form	
	aff.	*neg.*	*aff.*	*neg.*
be	arimasu	arimasen	arimashita	arimasendeshita
be	imasu	imasen	imashita	imasendeshita

II Practice the following pattern by changing the underlined part as in the example given.

    ex. Ikkai ni <u>ima</u> ga arimasu.

        1. daidokoro
        2. shokudō
        3. o-tearai

III Make dialogues by changing the underlined parts as in the examples given.

A. *ex.* Q: Ima ni <u>terebi</u> ga arimasu ka.

A*a*: Hai, arimasu.

A*n*: Iie, arimasen.

1. todana
2. isu
3. denwa

B. *ex.* Q: Ima ni <u>kodomo</u> ga imasu ka.

A*a*: Hai, imasu.

A*n*: Iie, imasen.

1. otoko no ko
2. onna no ko

C. *ex.* Q: <u>Hako no naka</u> ni nani ga arimasu ka.

A: <u>Hagaki to kitte</u> ga arimasu.

1. tēburu no ue, hana to shimbun
2. tana no ue, shashin ya hon

D. *ex.* Q: <u>Niwa</u> ni dare ga imasu ka.

A: <u>Otoko no ko</u> ga imasu.

1. otoko no ko to onna no ko
2. Tanaka-san

E. *ex.* Q: <u>Daidokoro</u> ni dare ga imasu ka.

A: Dare mo imasen.

1. genkan
2. shokudō

F. *ex.* Q: <u>Todana no mae</u> ni nani ga arimasu ka.

A: Nani mo arimasen.

1. isu no ue
2. isu no shita

Vocabulary

shokudō	dining room	**kodomo**	child
o-tearai	lavatory	**nani mo . . . -masen**	nothing is
o-	(Traditionally added to certain words to give them elegance.) (prefix)	**shita**	under

SHORT DIALOGUE

Otoko no hito: Kono biru ni denwa ga arimasu ka.

Onna no hito: Hai, arimasu. Asoko ni uketsuke ga arimasu ne. Ano uketsuke no mae ni arimasu.

Otoko no hito: Dōmo arigatō.

Man: Is there a telephone in this building?

Woman: Yes, there is. There's a reception desk over there, you see? It's in front of the reception desk.

Man: Thank you.

Vocabulary

biru	building
asoko	over there, that place (over there)
uketsuke	reception (desk)
ne	You see . . . (*lit.* . . . "isn't there?")

QUIZ ▮▮▮▓▒░

I Read this lesson's opening text and answer the following questions.

    1. **Ima ni nani ga arimasu ka.**

    2. **Tēburu no ue ni nani ga arimasu ka.**

    3. **Ima ni dare ga imasu ka.**

    4. **Daidokoro ni dare ga imasu ka.**

II Complete the questions so that they fit the answers.

    1. **Niwa ni (   ) ga imasu ka.**
       Tanaka-san ga imasu.

    2. **Ima ni (   ) ga arimasu ka.**
       Isu ya tēburu ga arimasu.

    3. **Daidokoro ni (   ) ga imasu ka.**
       Dare mo imasen.

    4. **Isu no ue ni (   ) ga arimasu ka.**
       Nani mo arimasen.

III Circle the correct verb of the two in parentheses.

    1. **Tana no ue ni shashin ya hon ga (arimasu, imasu).**

    2. **Niwa ni Tanaka-san ga (arimasu, imasu) ka.**

    3. **Daidokoro ni dare mo (imasu, imasen).**

    4. **Terebi no ue ni nani mo (arimasu, arimasen).**

IV Put the appropriate particles in the parentheses. (If a particle is not required, put an X in the parentheses.)

    1. **Hako (   ) naka (   ) kitte (   ) arimasu.**

2. **Tēburu (   ) ue ni hana (   ) shimbun (   ) arimasu.** (There is nothing else there besides the flowers and the newspapers.)
3. **Hako no naka ni hagaki (   ) kitte (   ) arimasu.** (There are other things besides postcards and stamps.)
4. **Genkan ni dare (   ) imasu ka.**
   Dare (   ) imasen.

V Translate into Japanese.

1. There are chairs, tables (etc.) in the living room.
2. Mr. Tanaka and a boy are in the garden.
3. Who is in the kitchen?
   There isn't anybody (there).
4. There isn't anything on the chair.

LESSON 9 PLACE, LOCATION

Mr. Smith wants to send a parcel home. He is in front of the apartment building asking the superintendent how to go about it.

スミス： この ちかくに ゆうびんきょくが ありますか。

かんりにん：ええ、ありますよ。

スミス： どこですか。

かんりにん：あそこに スーパーが ありますね。ゆうびんきょくは
あの スーパーの となりです。きょうは どようびです
から、ゆうびんきょくは 12じまでです。

スミス： どうも ありがとう。

■ゆうびんきょくは スーパーの となりです。

Sumisu: Kono chikaku ni yūbinkyoku ga arimasu ka.
Kanrinin: Ee, arimasu yo.
Sumisu: Doko desu ka.
Kanrinin: Asoko ni sūpā ga arimasu ne. Yūbinkyoku wa ano sūpā no tonari
desu. Kyō wa do-yōbi desu kara, yūbinkyoku wa 12-ji made desu.
Sumisu: Dōmo arigatō.

■ Yūbinkyoku wa sūpā no tonari desu.

Smith: Is there a post office near here?
Superintendent: Yes, there is.
Smith: Where is it?
Superintendent: See that supermarket over there? The post office is next to that super-
market. Today is Saturday, so the post office closes at 12:00.
Smith: Thank you.

■ The post office is next to the supermarket.

| Vocabulary |

かんりにん	**kanrinin**	superintendent
よ	**yo**	I tell you (particle)
スーパー	**sūpā**	supermarket
となり	**tonari**	next to
から	**kara**	so, because (particle)

NOTES

1. Ee, arimasu yo.

The particle **yo** is added to the end of a sentence to call attention to information the speaker thinks the other person does not know.

2. Doko desu ka.

The same as **doko ni arimasu ka. Desu** is used in place of **ni arimasu.** (See Grammar III, p. 66.)

3. Asoko ni sūpā ga arimasu ne.

"See that supermarket over there?" (*lit.* "There's a supermarket over there, isn't there?")

The particle **ne** comes at the end of a sentence or phrase and, like "you see?" or "isn't there/it?" in English, seeks the confirmation and agreement of the other person. The particle **yo** *tells*, while the particle **ne** *asks*.

4. Kyō wa do-yōbi desu kara.

The particle **kara** means "because, so, therefore" and comes after the phrase or clause. The Japanese meaning can be expressed in English in two ways: "Because today is Saturday," or "Today is Saturday, so . . ."

5. Dōshite, "why"

ex. **Dōshite yūbinkyoku wa 12-ji made desu ka.** "Why is the post office only (open) until 12 o'clock?
Kyō wa do-yōbi desu kara. "Because today is Saturday."

PRACTICE

KEY SENTENCES

1. Eki no chikaku ni tatemono ga takusan arimasu.
2. Hon-ya no mae ni kodomo ga 5-nin imasu.
3. Takushi-noriba wa eki no mae desu.
4. Kyō wa do-yōbi desu kara, yūbinkyoku wa 12-ji made desu.

1. There are many buildings near the station.
2. There are 5 children in front of the book store.
3. The taxi stand is in front of the station.
4. Today is Saturday, so the post office is only (open) until 12:00.

Vocabulary

tatemono	building	**-nin**	(counter for people)
takusan	many, lots of		(See Appendix C.)
hon-ya	book store	**takushi-noriba**	taxi stand
5-nin	5 people	**noriba**	*lit.* "boarding place"

EXERCISES

I Practice the following patterns by changing the underlined parts as in the examples given.

A. *ex.* **Tēburu no ue ni ringo ga itsutsu arimasu.**

    1. **hagaki, 3-mai**

    2. **biru, 2-hon**

    3. **hana, takusan**

B. *ex.* **Niwa ni otoko no ko ga futari imasu.**

    1. **onna no ko, 3-nin**

    2. **otoko no hito, hitori**

II Make dialogues by changing the underlined parts as in the examples given.

A. *ex.* **Q: Tēburu no ue ni ringo ga ikutsu arimasu ka.**

    A: Mittsu arimasu.

    1. **hagaki, nan-mai, 3-mai**

    2. **biru, nan-bon, 2-hon**

    3. **hana, nan-bon, takusan**

B. *ex.* **Q: Niwa ni otoko no hito ga nan-nin imasu ka.**

    A: Hitori imasu.

    1. **onna no ko, 3-nin**

    2. **otoko no ko, futari**

C. *ex.* **Q: Kono chikaku ni takushi-noriba ga arimasu ka.**

    A: Hai, arimasu. Takushī-noriba wa eki no mae ni arimasu.

    1. **kippu-uriba, eki no naka**

    2. **chikatetsu no iriguchi, depāto no mae**

    3. **byōin, asoko**

    4. **kusuri-ya, soko**

D. *ex.* **Q: Kuruma no kagi wa doko ni arimasu ka.**

    A: Koko ni arimasu.

1. watashi no megane
2. kono heya no kagi

E. *ex.* Q: Tanaka-san wa doko ni imasu ka.

A: 2-kai ni imasu.

1. niwa
2. tonari no heya

F. *ex.* Q: Basu-noriba wa doko desu ka.

A: Eki no mae desu.

1. hon-ya, depāto no tonari
2. kaisatsuguchi, eki no naka
3. kusuri-ya, kōban no tonari
4. byōin, eki no chikaku

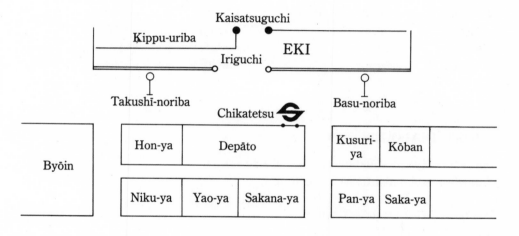

III A. Connect the following sentences using **kara**, "because," as in the example given.

ex. Kyō wa yasumi desu. Watashi wa gakkō ni ikimasen.

Kyō wa yasumi desu kara, watashi wa gakkō ni ikimasen.

1. Kyō wa nichi-yōbi desu. Watashi wa kaisha ni ikimasen.

B. Read the short dialogues and make the appropriate statements (S) using **kara**.

ex. Q: Dōshite kyō yūbinkyoku wa 12-ji made desu ka.

A: Kyō wa do-yōbi desu kara.

S: Kyō wa do-yōbi desu kara, yūbinkyoku wa 12-ji made desu.

1. Q: Dōshite anata wa kyō gakkō ni ikimasen ka.

A: Kyō wa nichi-yōbi desu kara.

S:

2. Q: Dōshite Sumisu-san wa kūkō ni ikimasu ka.

A: Okusan ga hikōki de kimasu kara.

S:

Vocabulary

futari	2 people (See Appendix C.)	**yaoya**	vegetable store
hitori	1 person	**sakana-ya**	fish store
ikutsu	how many	**sakana**	fish
nan-mai	how many sheets	**pan-ya**	bread store, bakery
nan-bon	how many bottles	**pan**	bread
nan-nin	how many people	**saka-ya**	liquor store
kippu-uriba	ticket office	**soko**	there, that place
kippu	ticket	**koko**	here, this place
-uriba	*lit.* "selling place"	**megane**	(eye) glasses
iriguchi	entrance	**heya**	room
byōin	hospital	**basu-noriba**	bus terminal
kusuri-ya	pharmacy, drug store	**kaisatsuguchi**	ticket gate
kusuri	medicine	**kōban**	police box
niku-ya	meat store	**yasumi**	holiday
niku	meat	**dōshite**	why
		hikōki	airplane

SHORT DIALOGUE

Smith: **Kyō no shimbun wa doko ni arimasu ka.**
Yamada: **Koko ni arimasu. Hai, dōzo.**

Smith: Where is today's paper?
Yamada: It's here. Here you are.

QUIZ

I Read this lesson's opening dialogue and answer the following questions.

1. **Yūbinkyoku wa sūpā no mae desu ka.**
2. **Yūbinkyoku wa kyō nan-ji made desu ka.**
3. **Dōshite yūbinkyoku wa 12-ji made desu ka.**

II Complete the questions so that they fit the answers.

1. **Takushi-noriba wa (   ) desu ka.**
   Asoko desu.
2. **Eki no chikaku ni (   ) ga arimasu ka.**
   Basu-noriba ya yūbinkyoku ya depāto ga arimasu.
3. **Hon-ya wa (   ) ni arimasu ka.**
   Sūpā no tonari ni arimasu.

4. (   ) yūbinkyoku wa kyō 12-ji made desu ka.
   Do-yōbi desu kara.

5. Tēburu no ue ni ringo ga (   ) arimasu ka.
   Mittsu arimasu.

6. Eki no mae ni otoko no hito ga (   ) imasu ka.
   Futari imasu.

III Put the appropriate particles in the parentheses. (If a particle is not required, put an X in the parentheses.)

1. Basu-noriba (   ) doko (   ) desu ka.
   Depāto (   ) mae (   ) arimasu.

2. Tēburu no ue (   ) bīru ga nan-bon (   ) arimasu ka.
   2-hon (   ) arimasu.

3. Dōshite kyō kaisha (   ) ikimasen ka.
   Do-yōbi desu (   ).

4. O-tearai (   ) doko (   ) arimasu ka.
   Asoko desu.

IV Translate into Japanese.

1. The liquor store is next to the vegetable store.
2. Excuse me, where is the lavatory?
   It's over there.
3. Miss White went to Osaka, so she isn't in the office today.
4. Why is the post office (open) until 12:00 today?
   Because it's Saturday.
5. There are five children in front of the book store.

LESSON  TICKETS BOUGHT

Mr. Smith and Mr. Tanaka are talking about their plans for the weekend.

たなか：しゅうまつに　なにを　しますか。

スミス：にちようびに　ともだちと　かぶきを　みます。

たなか：いいですね。もう　きっぷを　かいましたか。

スミス：ええ、せんしゅう　ぎんざの　プレイガイドで　かいました。

■ スミスさんは　せんしゅう　ぎんざの　プレイガイドで　かぶきの
きっぷを　かいました。にちようびに　ともだちと　かぶきを
みます。

Tanaka:　Shūmatsu ni nani o shimasu ka.
Sumisu:　Nichi-yōbi ni tomodachi to kabuki o mimasu.
Tanaka:　Ii desu ne. Mō kippu o kaimashita ka.
Sumisu:　Ee, senshū Ginza no pureigaido de kaimashita.

■ Sumisu-san wa senshū Ginza no pureigaido de kabuki no kippu o kaimashita. Nichi-yōbi ni tomodachi to kabuki o mimasu.

Tanaka:　What are you doing this weekend?
Smith:　I'm going to see the Kabuki with friends on Sunday.
Tanaka:　How nice. Have you bought your tickets yet?
Smith:　Yes, I bought them last week at a theater booking agency in the Ginza.

■ Mr. Smith bought tickets for the Kabuki at a theater booking agency in the Ginza last
week. He is going to see the Kabuki with friends on Sunday.

Vocabulary		
しゅうまつ	**shūmatsu**	weekend
します（する）	**shimasu (suru)**	do
かぶき	**kabuki**	Kabuki (Japanese theater)
みます（みる）	**mimasu (miru)**	see

78

いいですね	**ii desu ne**	*lit.* It's nice (good, all right).
いい	**ii**	good (**-i** adj.)
もう	**mō**	already
かいました	**kaimashita**	bought
かいます（かう）	**kaimasu (kau)**	buy
ぎんざ	**Ginza**	Ginza (place name)
プレイガイド	**pureigaido**	theater booking agency
で	**de**	at (particle)

GRAMMAR IV

Lessons 10–12   . . . O verb/ . . . NI . . . O verb

1. person **WA** noun **O** verb
2. person **WA** person **NI** noun **O** verb

• Verbs

	Present Form		Past Form	
	aff.	*neg.*	*aff.*	*neg.*
see	**mi-masu**	**mi-masen**	**mi-mashita**	**mi-masendeshita**
buy	**kai-masu**	**kai-masen**	**kai-mashita**	**kai-masendeshita**
read	**yomi-masu**	**yomi-masen**	**yomi-mashita**	**yomi-masendeshita**
show	**mise-masu**	**mise-masen**	**mise-mashita**	**mise-masendeshita**
tele-phone	**denwa o shi-masu**	**denwa o shi-masen**	**denwa o shi-mashita**	**denwa o shi-masen deshita**

• Particle **o**. Object marker.
  Placed after a noun, **o** indicates that the noun is the object. **O** is used with verbs such as "see," "read," "drink," "buy" and many others.
  ex. **Terebi o mimasu**, "(I) watch TV."

• Particle **ni**. Indirect object marker.
  In Japanese, the indirect object, or recipient, in the case of verbs such as "give," "teach," "telephone" and so on is indicated by the particle **ni**.
  ex. **Hayashi-san wa Sumisu-san ni denwa o shimashita.** "Mr. Hayashi telephoned Mr. Smith."

NOTES

1. Ii desu ne.
Here the particle **ne** does not seek confirmation or agreement. It is a sharing of the other persons's pleasure. Nuances can be conveyed by the amount of stress given any syllable. Compare this **ne** with the **ne** in Lesson 9.

2. Ginza no pureigaido de kaimashita.
Nouns and place names concerned with actions such as where things are bought, seen, eaten and so on take the particle **de**.

3. Doko, "where"
ex. **Doko de terebi o mimasu ka.** "Where do you watch television?"
Ima de mimasu. "I watch it in the living room."

4. Nani, "what"
ex. **Nani o kaimashita ka.** "What did you buy?"
Kippu o kaimashita. "I bought a/some ticket/tickets."

PRACTICE

KEY SENTENCES

1. [Watashi wa] Ashita eiga o mimasu.
2. Tanaka-san wa mainichi uchi de benkyō o shimasu.
3. [Watashi wa] Kinō resutoran de hiru-gohan o tabemashita.
4. [Watashi wa] Kinō depāto de nani mo kaimasendeshita.

1. I am going to see a movie tomorrow.
2. Mr. Tanaka studies at home every day.
3. I had lunch at a restaurant yesterday.
4. I didn't buy anything yesterday at the department store.

Vocabulary

mainichi	every day	**resutoran**	restaurant
mai-	every (See Appendix G.)	**hiru-gohan**	lunch
		gohan	meal
benkyō o shimasu	study	**tabemashita**	ate
(benkyō o suru)		**tabemasu (taberu)**	eat

EXERCISES

I Verbs: Memorize the following verbs and their present and past forms.

	Present Form		Past Form	
	aff.	*neg.*	*aff.*	*neg.*
see	mimasu	mimasen	mimashita	mimasendeshita
listen	kikimasu	kikimasen	kikimashita	kikimasendeshita
eat	tabemasu	tabemasen	tabemashita	tabemasendeshita
drink	nomimasu	nomimasen	nomimashita	nomimasendeshita
buy	kaimasu	kaimasen	kaimashita	kaimasendeshita
read	yomimasu	yomimasen	yomimashita	yomimasendeshita
study	benkyō o shimasu	shimasen	shimashita	shimasendeshita
shop	kaimono o shimasu	shimasen	shimashita	shimasendeshita
give a party	pātī o shimasu	shimasen	shimashita	shimasendeshita
work	shigoto o shimasu	shimasen	shimashita	shimasendeshita
play tennis	tenisu o shimasu	shimasen	shimashita	shimasendeshita

II Practice the following patterns by changing the underlined part as in the examples given.

A. *ex.* [Watashi wa] Eiga o mimasu.

1. terebi
2. kabuki
3. e

B. *ex.* [Watashi wa] Rajio o kikimasu.

1. nyūsu
2. ongaku no tēpu
3. rekōdo

C. *ex.* [Watashi wa] Hiru-gohan o tabemasu.

1. asa-gohan
2. ban-gohan
3. sandoitchi to sarada

D. *ex.* [Watashi wa] O-cha o nomimasu.

1. o-sake
2. sūpu
3. kusuri

E. *ex.* [Watashi wa] <u>Hana</u> o kaimasu.

    1. zasshi

    2. kitte

    3. Nihon no chizu

F. *ex.* [Watashi wa] <u>Hon</u> o yomimasu.

    1. tegami

    2. Nihon-go no shimbun

G. *ex.* [Watashi wa] <u>Benkyō</u> o shimasu.

    1. kaimono

    2. **pātī**

    3. shigoto

    4. tenisu

III Make dialogues by changing the underlined parts as in the examples given. Convert verbs to their appropriate form as necessary.

A. *ex.* Q: [Anata wa] Komban <u>eiga</u> o <u>mimasu</u> ka.

    A*a*: Hai, <u>mimasu</u>.

    A*n*: Iie, <u>mimasen</u>.

    1. hon, yomimasu

    2. Nihon-go no benkyō, shimasu

B. *ex.* Q: [Anata wa] Kinō <u>hon-ya</u> de <u>hon</u> o <u>kaimashita</u> ka.

    A*a*: Hai, <u>kaimashita</u>.

    A*n*: Iie, <u>kaimasendeshita</u>.

    1. kaisha, shigoto, shimasu

    2. kissaten, kōhi, nomimasu

C. *ex.* Q: [Anata wa] Maiasa nani o nomimasu ka.

    A: <u>Kōhī</u> o nomimasu.

    1. kōcha

    2. miruku

    3. jūsu to kōhī

D. *ex.* Q: [Anata wa] Kinō nani o shimashita ka.

    A: <u>Uchi de hon o yomimashita</u>.

    1. depāto de kutsu o kaimasu

    2. uchi de Nihon-go no benkyō o shimasu

    3. byōin ni ikimasu

E. *ex.* Q: [Anata wa] Kyō doko de hiru-gohan o tabemasu ka.

    A: <u>Uchi</u> de tabemasu.

    1. eki no chikaku no resutoran

    2. tomodachi no uchi

F. *ex.* Q: [Anata wa] Itsu Nihon-go no benkyō o shimasu ka.

    A: <u>Mainichi</u> shimasu.

1. maiban
2. getsu-yōbi to ka-yōbi ni
3. maishū ka-yōbi ni

G. *ex.* Q: [Anata wa] Shūmatsu ni dare to tenisu o shimasu ka.
    A: <u>Tanaka-san</u> to shimasu.
1. tomodachi
2. kazoku

H. *ex.* Q: [Anata wa] Depāto de nani o <u>kaimashita</u> ka.
    A: Nani mo <u>kaimasendeshita</u>.
1. tabemasu
2. nomimasu

Vocabulary

e	picture	**zasshi**	magazine
kikimasu (kiku)	listen	**chizu**	map
nyūsu	news	**yomimasu (yomu)**	read
ongaku	music	**tegami**	letter
rekōdo	record	**kaimono**	shopping
asa-gohan	breakfast (*lit.*	**tenisu**	tennis
	"morning meal")	**komban**	this evening
asa	morning	**kissaten**	coffee shop
ban-gohan	dinner (*lit.*	**kōhī**	coffee
	"evening meal")	**nomimasu (nomu)**	drink
ban	evening	**maiasa**	every morning
sandoitchi	sandwich	**kōcha**	black tea
sarada	salad	**miruku**	milk
o-cha	tea	**jūsu**	juice
cha	tea	**kutsu**	shoes
o-sake	Japanese rice wine	**maiban**	every evening
sake	Japanese rice wine	**maishū**	every week
sūpu	soup	**kazoku**	(my) family

SHORT DIALOGUE

Hayashi:	Kinō Nihon-go no benkyō o shimashita ka.
Howaito:	Iie, shimasendeshita.
Hayashi:	Dōshite benkyō o shimasendeshita ka.
Howaito:	Tomodachi ga uchi ni kimashita kara.

Hayashi:	Did you study Japanese yesterday?
White:	No, I didn't.
Hayashi:	Why didn't you study?
White:	Because some friends came to my house.

QUIZ

I Read this lesson's opening dialogue and answer the following questions.

1. Sumisu-san wa nichi-yōbi ni eiga o mimasu ka, kabuki o mimasu ka.
2. Sumisu-san wa hitori de kabuki o mimasu ka.
3. Sumisu-san wa itsu kabuki no kippu o kaimashita ka.
4. Sumisu-san wa doko de kabuki no kippu o kaimashita ka.

II Complete the questions so that they fit the answers.

1. (   ) ni eiga o mimashita ka.
   Nichi-yōbi ni mimashita.
2. Kyō (   ) de hiru-gohan o tabemasu ka.
   Eki no chikaku no resutoran de tabemasu.
3. Do-yōbi ni (   ) o shimasu ka.
   Tomodachi no uchi ni ikimasu. Soshite tomodachi no uchi de ban-gohan o tabemasu.
4. Depāto de (   ) o kaimashita ka.
   Nani mo kaimasen deshita.

III Put the appropriate particles in the parentheses. (If a particle is not required, put an X in the parentheses.)

1. Sumisu-san wa shokudō (   ) imasu.
2. Howaito-san wa chikatetsu (   ) kaisha (   ) ikimasu.
3. Tanaka-san wa kaisha no chikaku no resutoran (   ) hiru-gohan (   ) tabemashita.
4. Watashi wa kinō depāto (   ) nani (   ) kaimasen deshita.
5. Shūmatsu ni nani (   ) shimasu ka.
6. Watashi wa maiasa (   ) uchi (   ) shimbun (   ) yomimasu.

IV Translate into Japanese.

1. I bought a camera at the department store on Sunday. It was ¥45,000.
2. What did you do yesterday?
   I listened to a tape of Japanese at home in the morning. I went to the Ginza in the afternoon and bought a camera (there).
3. Miss White doesn't eat anything in the morning.

　ブラウンさんは　ABCの　べんごしです。そして　スミスさんの
ともだちです。ブラウンさんは　ことしの　6がつに　ひとりで　にほん
に　きました。おくさんは　らいしゅう　にほんに　きます。

　ブラウンさんの　かいしゃは　とうきょうえきの　ちかくに　あります。
しごとは　げつようびから　きんようびまでです。

　ブラウンさんは　まいあさ　コーヒーを　のみますが、なにも　たべ
ません。そして　しんぶんを　よみます。ちかてつで　かいしゃに
いきます。ときどき　ちかてつで　ほんや　ざっしを　よみます。

　かいしゃは　9じから　5じはんまでです。レストランや　かいしゃの
しょくどうで　ひるごはんを　たべます。ひるやすみは　12じはんから
2じまでですから、ときどき　かいしゃの　ひとと　デパートや
きっさてんに　いきます。

　うちに　7じごろ　かえります。きのうは　かいしゃから　スミスさ
んの　うちに　いきましたから、11じごろ　うちに　かえりました。

　ブラウンさんは　あした　しんかんせんで　きょうとに　いきます。
きょうとの　ししゃで　かいぎを　します。そして　きんようびに
とうきょうに　かえります。

Buraun-san wa ABC no bengoshi desu. Soshite Sumisu-san no tomodachi
desu. Buraun-san wa kotoshi no 6-gatsu ni hitori de Nihon ni kimashita.
Okusan wa raishū Nihon ni kimasu.

　Buraun-san no kaisha wa Tōkyō Eki no chikaku ni arimasu. Shigoto wa
getsu-yōbi kara kin-yōbi made desu.

　Buraun-san wa maiasa kōhī o nomimasu ga, nani mo tabemasen. Soshite
shimbun o yomimasu. Chikatetsu de kaisha ni ikimasu. Tokidoki chikatetsu
de hon ya zasshi o yomimasu.

　Kaisha wa 9-ji kara 5-ji han made desu. Resutoran ya kaisha no shokudō de
hiru-gohan o tabemasu. Hiru-yasumi wa 12-ji han kara 2-ji made desu kara,
tokidoki kaisha no hito to depāto ya kissaten ni ikimasu.

Uchi ni 7-ji goro kaerimasu. Kinō wa kaisha kara Sumisu-san no uchi ni ikimashita kara, 11-ji goro uchi ni kaerimashita.

Buraun-san wa ashita Shinkansen de Kyōto ni ikimasu. Kyōto no shisha de kaigi o shimasu. Soshite kin-yōbi ni Tōkyō ni kaerimasu.

Mr. Brown is a lawyer with ABC. And he is a friend of Mr. Smith's. Mr. Brown came to Japan alone this June. His wife will come to Japan next week.

Mr. Brown's company is near Tokyo Station. He works from Monday to Friday.

Mr. Brown drinks coffee every morning, but he doesn't eat anything. And he reads the paper. He goes to his office by subway. Sometimes he reads a book or a magazine on the subway.

His office hours are from 9:00 to 5:30. He has lunch at a restaurant or in the company cafeteria. Lunch time is from 12:30 to 2:00, so sometimes he goes to a department store or a cafe with people from the office.

He gets home about 7:00. Last night he got home about 11:00 because he went from the office to the Smiths' house.

Mr. Brown is going to Kyoto tomorrow on the Shinkansen. He is holding a meeting at the branch office in Kyoto. He will return to Tokyo on Friday.

Vocabulary		
ブラウン	**Buraun**	Brown
ことし	**kotoshi**	this year
が	**ga**	but (particle)
ときどき	**tokidoki**	sometimes (See Appendix E.)
しょくどう	**shokudō**	cafeteria
７じごろ	**7-ji goro**	about 7:00
～ごろ	**goro**	about
かいぎを します	**kaigi o shimasu**	hold a meeting/conference
（かいぎを する）	**(kaigi o suru)**	

LESSON 12 TELEPHONING

Mr. Katō telephones Mr. Smith.

かとう：もしもし、スミスさんの　おたくですか。

スミス：はい、そうです。

かとう：かとうですが、ごしゅじんは　いらっしゃいますか。

スミス：いま　いません。9じごろ　かえります。

かとう：そうですか。では　また　あとで　でんわを　します。

スミス：はい、おねがいします。

かとう：しつれいします。

スミス：さようなら。

■ かとうさんは　スミスさんの　うちに　でんわを　しましたが、スミ
　スさんの　ごしゅじんは　いませんでした。

Katō:　　Moshi moshi, Sumisu-san no o-taku desu ka.
Sumisu:　Hai, sō desu.
Katō:　　Katō desu ga, go-shujin wa irasshaimasu ka.
Sumisu:　Ima imasen. 9-ji goro kaerimasu.
Katō:　　Sō desu ka. Dewa mata ato de denwa o shimasu.
Sumisu:　Hai, onegaishimasu.
Katō:　　Shitsurei shimasu.
Sumisu:　Sayōnara.

■ Katō-san wa Sumisu-san no uchi ni denwa o shimashita ga, Sumisu-san no
　go-shujin wa imasendeshita.

Katō:　　Hello. Is that Mr. Smith's residence?
Smith:　 Yes, it is.
Katō:　　This is Katō. Is your husband there?
Smith:　 He's not here now. He'll be back about 9:00.
Katō:　　I see. Then I'll call again later.
Smith:　 Yes. Please do.
Katō:　　Good-bye.
Smith:　 Good-bye.

■ Mr. Katō telephoned the Smiths' house but Mr. Smith was not there.

かとう	**Katō**	a surname
もしもし	**moshi moshi**	hello
おたく	**o-taku**	(his) residence
そうです	**sō desu**	That's right.
そう	**sō**	so
が	**ga**	(particle) (See Note 4 below.)
ごしゅじん	**go-shujin**	(your) husband
ご～	**go-**	(honorific, referring to some-one else's . . .)
いらっしゃいます (いらっしゃる)	**irasshaimasu (irassharu)**	is (polite word for **imasu**)
そう ですか	**sō desu ka**	I see.
また	**mata**	again
あとで	**ato de**	afterwards
おねがいします	**onegaishimasu**	Please (do).
しつれいします	**shitsurei shimasu**	good-bye (*lit.* "I'll be rude.")
に	**ni**	to (particle)

NOTES

1. **Moshi moshi.**

   This is the conventional beginning of a telephone conversation and may be repeated during the call to confirm whether the other party is still on the line. It is sometimes also like "I say!" used to attract the attention of someone one does not know. (See Lesson 24.) It is best to confine its use to the telephone.

2. **Sumisu-san no o-taku**

   The honorific **o** (or **go** as in **go-shujin**) is often prefixed to nouns to mean "your," i.e., **o-namae**, "your name." Similarly, **o-taku** means "your house," or, as here, "Mr. Smith's residence." It is very polite.

   The word **taku** alone is seldom used. **Uchi**, "house," is more common. I.e., **Are wa dare no uchi desu ka.** "Whose house is that?" **Uchi** is also used to mean "my/our house" or simply "our," as in **uchi no kuruma**, "our car."

3. **Hai, sō desu.**

   When replying in the affirmative to questions that end in **desu ka**, one may generally use this phrase.

4. A. **Katō desu ga, go-shujin wa irasshaimasu ka.**
   B. **Katō-san wa Sumisu-san ni denwa o shimashita ga, Sumisu-san wa imasendeshita.**

This **ga** is a connective, joining two clauses. It can usually be translated as "but," as in B, but sometimes it cannot, as in A. In A, it has no particular meaning. It is just a kind of courteous hesitation and indicates that the phrase before it is merely a preliminary to the principal matter.

5. 9-ji goro

The suffix **goro**, "about," is used to indicate approximate time.

ex. **3-ji goro**, "about 3 o'clock"

9-gatsu goro, "about September"

6. Onegaishimasu

A very convenient phrase, used when making a request. Literally, it means "I beg you," and the verb may be simply implied, as here, where it means "I beg you (to do that)."

ex. **Taipu o onegaishimasu.** "Could you type this, please?"

Ginza made onegaishimasu. "Please take me to the Ginza." (Said to a taxi driver.)

The reply to **onegaishimasu** is often **Hai, wakarimashita**. "Certainly./I see."

PRACTICE

KEY SENTENCES

1. [Watashi wa] Ashita bengoshi ni aimasu.
2. [Watashi wa] Hayashi-san ni denwa o shimasu.
3. [Watashi wa] Yoku tomodachi ni tegami o kakimasu.
4. [Watashi wa] Amari eiga o mimasen.
5. [Watashi wa] Sumisu-san no kaisha ni denwa o shimashita ga, Sumisu-san wa imasendeshita.

1. I am going to see the lawyer tomorrow.
2. I will telephone Mr. Hayashi.
3. I often write to (my) friends.
4. I don't see movies very often.
5. I telephoned Mr. Smith's office, but he wasn't there.

Vocabulary	
aimasu (au)	meet
denwa o shimasu (denwa o suru)	make a phone call
yoku	often (See Appendix E.)
kakimasu (kaku)	write
amari . . . -masen	does not . . . often (See Appendix E.)

EXERCISES

I Verbs: Memorize the following verbs and their present and past forms.

	Present Form		Past Form	
	aff.	*neg.*	*aff.*	*neg.*
telephone	denwa o shimasu	shimasen	shimashita	shimasendeshita
write	kakimasu	kakimasen	kakimashita	kakimasendeshita
ask	kikimasu	kikimasen	kikimashita	kikimasendeshita
tell	oshiemasu	oshiemasen	oshiemashita	oshiemasendeshita
meet	aimasu	aimasen	aimashita	aimasendeshita

II Practice the following pattern by changing the underlined part as in the example given.

    ex. [Watashi wa] Hayashi-san ni denwa o shimasu.

      1. Sumisu-san

      2. gakkō

      3. kaisha

III Make dialogues by changing the underlined parts as in the examples given.

    A. *ex.* Q: [Anata wa] Mainen tomodachi ni kurisumasu kādo o kakimasu ka.

        A*a*: Hai, kakimasu.

        A*n*: Iie, kakimasen.

        1. nengajō

    B. *ex.* Q: [Anata wa] Dare ni denwa o shimasu ka.

        A: Tanaka-san ni shimasu.

        1. tomodachi

        2. haha

    C. *ex.* Q: [Anata wa] Doko ni denwa o shimasu ka.

        A: Kaisha ni shimasu.

        1. gakkō

        2. hoteru

    D. *ex.* Q: Tanaka-san wa Sumisu-san ni nani o oshiemashita ka.

        A: Tanaka-san no uchi no denwa-bangō o oshiemashita.

        1. mise no namae

        2. naisen-bangō

    E. *ex.* Q: Tanaka-san wa dare ni Hayashi-san no jūsho o kikimashita ka.

        A: Hisho ni kikimashita.

1. Sumisu-san

2. kaisha no hito

F. *ex.* **Q:** [Anata wa] Ashita dare ni aimasu ka.

   A: <u>Tomodachi</u> ni aimasu.

   1. gakkō no sensei

   2. Hayashi-san no otōsan to okāsan

G. *ex.* **Q:** [Anata wa] Yoku tomodachi ni tegami o kakimasu ka.

   A*a***:** <u>Hai, yoku</u> kakimasu.

   A*n***:** <u>Iie, amari</u> kakimasen.

   1. hai, tokidoki. iie, zenzen

IV Connect the following sentences using **ga,** "but," as in the example given.

   ex. **Ashita wa nichi-yōbi desu. [Watashi wa] Kaisha de shigoto o shimasu.**

   Ashita wa nichi-yōbi desu ga, [watashi wa] kaisha de shigoto o shimasu.

   1. Watashi wa kinō Tanaka-san no uchi ni ikimashita. Tanaka-san wa ima-sendeshita.

   2. Watashi wa kinō depāto ni ikimashita. Depāto wa yasumi deshita.

| Vocabulary |

mainen	every year	**naisen-bangō**	extension number
kurisumasu kādo	Christmas card		
nengajō	New Year's card	**kikimasu (kiku)**	ask
haha	(my) mother	**sensei**	teacher
hoteru	hotel	**otōsan**	(your) father
oshiemasu (oshieru)	tell	**okāsan**	(your) mother
mise	store, shop	**zenzen . . . -masen**	never (do) (See Appendix E.)

SHORT DIALOGUES

1. On the telephone.

   Otoko no hito: Moshi moshi, Tanaka-san no o-taku desu ka.

   Onna no hito: Iie, chigaimasu.

   Otoko no hito: Dōmo sumimasen.

   Onna no hito: Iie. Dō itashimashite.

   Man: Hello. Is this Mr. Tanaka's residence?
   Woman: No, you have the wrong number.
   Man: Sorry to have troubled you.
   Woman: That's quite all right.

2. On the telephone.

   Kōkanshu: Tōkyō Denki de gozaimasu.

Hayashi:	Tanaka-san o onegaishimasu.
Kōkanshu:	Hai, shōshō omachi kudasai.

Operator:	This is Tokyo Electric.
Hayashi:	May I speak to Mr. Tanaka, please?
Operator:	Just a moment, please.

3. **Sumisu:** **[Watashi wa] Maiasa jogingu o shimasu ga, Hayashi-san mo jogingu o shimasu ka.**

Hayashi: **Hai, watashi mo yoku shimasu.**

Smith:	I jog every morning. Do you jog, too?
Hayashi:	Yes, I often do.

Vocabulary

chigaimasu (chigau)	That's wrong.
kōkanshu	switchboard operator
Tōkyō Denki de gozaimasu	This is Tokyo Electric.
de gozaimasu	(polite word for **desu**)
shōshō	a moment
omachi kudasai	Please wait.
machimasu (matsu)	wait
jogingu o shimasu	jog
(jogingu o suru)	

QUIZ ▰▰▰▰▰

I Read this lesson's opening dialogue and answer the following questions.

1. **Dare ga Sumisu-san no uchi ni denwa o shimashita ka.**
2. **Sumisu-san no go-shujin wa uchi ni imashita ka, imasendeshita ka.**
3. **Sumisu-san no go-shujin wa nan-ji goro uchi ni kaerimasu ka.**
4. **Katō-san wa mata ato de Sumisu-san ni denwa o shimasu ka.**

II Complete the questions so that they fit the answers.

1. **Kinō (   ) o shimashita ka.**
   Tegami o kakimashita.
   (   ) ni kakimashita ka.
   Haha ni kakimashita.
2. **Hayashi-san wa (   ) ni Kurāku-san no jūsho o kikimashita ka.**
   Howaito-san ni kikimashita.

3. (   ) ga Kyōto no shisha ni denwa o shimashita ka.
   Sumisu-san ga shimashita.

III Circle the correct word of the two in parentheses.

1. **Yoku kono resutoran ni kimasu ka.**
   (Hai, Iie), amari (kimasu, kimasen).
2. **Yoku terebi o (mimasu, mimasen) ka.**
   (Hai, Iie), zenzen (mimasu, mimasen).
3. **Yamada-san wa (yoku, amari) tomodachi ni denwa o shimasu.**
4. **Sumisu-san wa yoku densha de shimbun o (yomimasu, yomimasen)**
   ga, Kurāku-san wa zenzen (yomimasu, yomimasen).

IV Put the appropriate particles in the parentheses. (If a particle is not required,
   put an X in the parentheses.)

1. **Sumisu-san wa Hayashi-san (   ) denwa o shimashita.**
2. **Doko (   ) denwa o shimasu ka.**
   Gakkō ni shimasu.
3. **Yoku (   ) dare (   ) tenisu o shimasu ka.**
   Kazoku to shimasu.
4. **Tanaka-san wa Howaito-san (   ) Yamada-san no uchi no denwa-**
   bangō (   ) oshiemashita.
5. **Moshi moshi, Sumisu desu (   ), Hayashi-san (   ) irasshaimasu**
   ka.

V Translate into Japanese.

1. Hello. Is this the Tanaka residence?
2. This is Tanaka of Tokyo Electric. Is Mr. Hayashi there?
3. I'll call again later.
4. I asked Mr. Clark for his office telephone number.
5. Mr. Clark doesn't write letters to his friends very often but Miss White
   does (write often).

LESSON 13 DELICIOUS CAKES

Mr. Tanaka is offering Mr. Smith a cup of tea.

たなか：おちゃを　どうぞ。

スミス：ありがとうございます。

たなか：おかしは　いかがですか。

スミス：はい、いただきます。きれいな　おかしですね。にほんの
　　　　おかしですか。

たなか：ええ、そうです。どうぞ　めしあがってください。

スミス：とても　おいしいです。

たなか：おちゃを　もう　いっぱい　いかがですか。

スミス：いいえ、もう　けっこうです。

■スミスさんは　たなかさんの　うちで　きれいな　にほんの　おかし
　を　たべました。　おちゃを　いっぱい　のみました。

Tanaka:　O-cha o dōzo.
Sumisu:　Arigatō gozaimasu.
Tanaka:　O-kashi wa ikaga desu ka.
Sumisu:　Hai, itadakimasu. Kireina o-kashi desu ne. Nihon no o-kashi desu
　　　　ka.
Tanaka:　Ee, sō desu. Dōzo meshiagatte kudasai.
Sumisu:　Totemo oishii desu.
Tanaka:　O-cha o mō ippai ikaga desu ka.
Sumisu:　Iie, mō kekkō desu.

■Sumisu-san wa Tanaka-san no uchi de kireina Nihon no o-kashi o tabemashita. O-cha o ippai nomimashita.

Tanaka:　Do have some tea.
Smith:　Thank you.
Tanaka:　Will you have a cake?
Smith:　Yes, I'd love one. What pretty cakes! Are they Japanese cakes?
Tanaka:　Yes, they are. Please, help yourself.
Smith:　They are delicious.

94

Tanaka: Will you have another cup of tea?
Smith: No (thank you). That was enough.

■ Mr. Smith ate (some) pretty Japanese cakes at Mr. Tanaka's house. He drank a cup of tea.

Vocabulary

おかし	**o-kashi**	cake
いかがですか	**ikaga desu ka**	How about . . . ?
いかが	**ikaga**	how
いただきます（いただく）	**itadakimasu (itadaku)**	eat (polite word for **tabemasu**)
きれい（な）	**kireina**	pretty, clean (**-na** adj.)
めしあがって　ください	**meshiagatte kudasai**	Please eat/have (some)
とても	**totemo**	very (See Appendix E.)
おいしい	**oishii**	good, tasty (**-i** adj.)
もう	**mō**	more (another)
1ぱい	**ippai**	1 cupful
～はい、ばい、ぱい	**-hai, -bai, -pai**	(counter. See Appendix C.)
いいえ、もう　けっこうです	**iie, mō kekkō desu**	No (thank you). That was enough.

GRAMMAR V

Lessons 13–14   Adjectives

1. **ADJECTIVE** + noun
2. noun **wa ADJECTIVE desu**

1. Modifying Nouns: Adjective + Noun		
-i adj.	**ōkii kōen**	big park
-na adj.	**yūmeina kōen**	famous park

2. Adjective as Predicate: Adjective + **Desu**				
	Present Form		Past Form	
	aff.	*neg.*	*aff.*	*neg.*
-i adj.	**ōkii desu**	**ōkikunai desu**	**ōkikatta desu**	**ōkikunakatta desu**
-na adj.	**yūmei desu**	**yūmei dewa arimasen**	**yūmei deshita**	**yūmei dewa arimasendeshita**

- Japanese adjectives can either modify nouns by immediately preceding them or act as predicates. In this they resemble English.

There are two kinds of adjectives: **-i** adjectives and **-na** adjectives. Unlike English adjectives, Japanese adjectives are inflected as shown above. Either **-i** or **-na** adjectives can take the place of noun 2 in the noun 2 + **desu** construction given in Grammar I.

NOTES

1. Dōzo.

Dōzo, "please (accept/do)," is used when making an offer to someone or when begging their kindness and consideration.

2. Ikaga desu ka.

A politer way of saying **Dō desu ka**, *lit.* "How is it?" This phrase is often used when offering things like food and drink, meaning "Would you like one?" or "How about some?" It can be used in a variety of situations, such as when enquiring about a person's preferences or circumstances, when asking whether the person is free to do something (Lesson 17), or his state of health (Lesson 22).

3. Itadakimasu.

A polite equivalent of **tabemasu**, "I eat," and **moraimasu**, "I receive." Said when taking something that is offered, implying both acceptance and gratitude. Japanese mealtime conventions:

Before eating: **Itadakimasu.** "I gratefully partake."

After eating: **Gochisōsama.** "Thank you for a lovely meal." (*lit.* "It was indeed a feast!")

4. Iie, mō kekkō desu.

The polite way of refusing something offered. **Kekkō** means "good, fine, splendid." **Mō** in this case means "already." The expression **kekkō desu** implies, "I am all right as I am," or "What I've had was fine. It was enough."

5. Donna, "what kind of"

When one wants to know more about things, people or places, one uses **donna** + noun. Answers can be given in various ways.

ex. Q: **Donna okashi o tabemashita ka.** "What kind of cakes did (you) eat?"

A1: **Oishii okashi o tabemashita.** "(I) had (some) delicious cakes."

A2: **Kireina okashi o tabemashita.** "(I) ate (some) pretty cakes."

A3: **Nihon no okashi o tabemashita.** "(I) ate Japanese cakes."

A4: **Kukkī o tabemashita.** "(I) ate cookies."

PRACTICE

KEY SENTENCES

1. **Kono ringo wa totemo oishii desu.**
2. **Ano ringo wa amari oishikunai desu.**
3. **[Watashi wa] Oishii ringo o tabemashita.**
4. **Kono heya wa shizuka desu.**
5. **Ano heya wa shizuka dewa arimasen.**
6. **[Watashi wa] Shizukana heya de benkyō o shimasu.**

1. This apple is very good.
2. That apple doesn't taste very good.
3. I ate some delicious apples.
4. This room is quiet.
5. That room is not quiet.
6. I study in a quiet room.

Vocabulary

amari . . . -nai/-masen not very . . . (See Appendix E.)
shizukana quiet (**-na** adj.)

EXERCISES

I **-i** adjective: Memorize the following **-i** adjectives.

	As Predicate: Present Form		Modifying Noun
	aff.	*neg.*	
big	ōkii (desu)	ōkikunai (desu)	ōkii
expensive	takai	takakunai	takai
good	ii	yokunai*	ii
new, fresh	atarashii	atarashikunai	atarashii
small	chiisai	chiisakunai	chiisai
cheap	yasui	yasukunai	yasui
bad	warui	warukunai	warui
old	furui**	furukunai	furui
interesting	omoshiroi	omoshirokunai	omoshiroi
difficult	muzukashii	muzukashikunai	muzukashii
far	tōi	tōkunai	tōi
good, tasty	oishii	oishikunai	oishii
busy	isogashii	isogashikunai	isogashii

boring	tsumaranai	tsumaranakunai	tsumaranai
easy	yasashii	yasashikunai	yasashii
near	chikai	chikakunai	chikai

*All inflected forms of **ii** come from the **i**-adjective **yoi**, which also means "good."
**Not used for people.

II Practice the following patterns by changing the underlined parts in the examples given.

    A. *ex.* **Kono kamera wa ōkii desu.**

        Ano kamera wa chiisai desu.

        1. **kono kuruma, ano kuruma**

        2. **kono tamago, ano tamago**

    B. *ex.* **Kono rajio wa takai desu.**

        Ano rajio wa yasui desu.

        1. **kono tokei, ano tokei**

        2. **gyūniku, toriniku**

    C. *ex.* **Kore wa atarashii uchi desu.**

        Are wa furui uchi desu.

        1. **terebi**

        2. **sakana**

        3. **yasai**

III Make dialogues by changing the underlined part as in the examples given.

    A. *ex.* **Q: Nihon-go wa yasashii desu ka.**

        A*a***: Hai, yasashii desu.**

        A*n***: Iie, yasashikunai desu.**

        1. **muzukashii**

        2. **omoshiroi**

    B. *ex.* **Q: Kono hon wa omoshiroi desu ka.**

        A*a***: Hai, omoshiroi desu.**

        A*n***: Iie, amari omoshirokunai desu.**

        1. **takai**

        2. **ii**

    C. *ex.* **Q: Kore wa ii hon desu ka.**

        A*a***: Hai, totemo ii hon desu.**

        A*n***: Iie, amari ii hon dewa arimasen.**

        1. **omoshiroi**

        2. **muzukashii**

    D. *ex.* **Q: Kōen wa koko kara tōi desu ka.**

        A: Iie, tōkunai desu. Chikai desu.

        1. **basu-noriba**

2. **gakkō**

3. **chikatetsu no eki**

IV **-na** adjective: Memorize the following **-na** adjectives.

	As Predicate: Present Form		Modifying Noun
	aff.	*neg.*	
pretty, clean	**kirei desu**	**kirei dewa arimasen**	**kireina**
quiet	**shizuka desu**	**shizuka dewa arimasen**	**shizukana**
famous	**yūmei desu**	**yūmei dewa arimasen**	**yūmeina**
kind, helpful	**shinsetsu desu**	**shinsetsu dewa arimasen**	**shinsetsuna**
free	**hima desu**	**hima dewa arimasen**	**himana**
lively	**nigiyaka desu**	**nigiyaka dewa arimasen**	**nigiyakana**
convenient	**benri desu**	**benri dewa arimasen**	**benrina**
well, healthy	**genki desu**	**genki dewa arimasen**	**genkina**

V Practice the following patterns by changing the underlined parts as in the examples given.

A. *ex.* <u>**Kono hana**</u> **wa kirei desu.**

1. **Howaito-san**

2. **ano kissaten**

B. *ex.* <u>**Kono daidokoro**</u> **wa benri desu.**

1. **kono kamera**

2. **Tokyo no chikatetsu**

C. *ex.* **Watashi-tachi wa** <u>**kireina**</u> **resutoran de shokuji o shimashita.**

1. **shizukana**

2. **yūmeina**

VI Make dialogues by changing the underlined part as in the examples given.

A. *ex.* **Q: Tanaka-san wa** <u>**genki**</u> **desu ka.**

A*a*: Hai, <u>**genki**</u> **desu.**

A*n*: Iie, <u>**genki**</u> **dewa arimasen.**

1. **shinsetsu**

B. *ex.* **Q: Are wa** <u>**yūmeina**</u> **resutoran desu ka.**

A*a*: Hai, totemo <u>**yūmeina**</u> **resutoran desu.**

A*n*: Iie, amari <u>**yūmeina**</u> **resutoran dewa arimasen.**

1. **kireina**

2. **shizukana**

C. *ex.* **Q: [Anata wa]** <u>**Ashita**</u> **hima desu ka.**

A: Iie, hima dewa arimasen. Isogashii desu.

1. ashita no gogo

2. raishū no kin-yōbi

D. *ex.* Q: Tōkyō Hoteru wa donna hoteru desu ka.

    A: <u>Atarashii</u> hoteru desu.

1. ōkii

2. shizukana

3. totemo ii

E. *ex.* Q: Hayashi-san wa donna hito desu ka.

    A: <u>Shinsetsuna</u> hito desu.

1. omoshiroi

2. genkina

Vocabulary

tamago	egg	watashi-tachi	we
takai	expensive (-i adj.)	-tachi	(plural suffix for peo-
yasui	cheap (-i adj.)		ple)
gyū-niku	beef	shokuji o shimasu	have a meal
tori-niku	chicken meat	(shokuji o suru)	
atarashii	new, fresh (-i adj.)	shokuji	meal
furui	old, not fresh (-i adj.)	yūmeina	famous (-na adj.)
yasai	vegetable	genkina	well, healthy (-na adj.)
yasashii	easy (-i adj.)	shinsetsuna	kind, helpful (-na adj.)
muzukashii	difficult (-i adj.)	himana	free (-na adj.)
omoshiroi	interesting (-i adj.)	isogashii	busy (-i adj.)
kōen	park	Tōkyō Hoteru	Tokyo Hotel
benrina	convenient (-na adj.)	donna	what kind of

SHORT DIALOGUES

1. **Tanaka:** Sumisu-san, o-genki desu ka.

   Sumisu: Ee, arigatō gozaimasu. Genki desu.

   Tanaka: How are you, Mr. Smith?

   Smith: Fine, thank you.

2. **Tanaka:** Kyō wa ii tenki desu ne.

   Sumisu: Ee, hontō ni ii tenki desu ne.

   Tanaka: Kyō wa isogashii desu ka.

   Sumisu: Iie, amari isogashikunai desu.

   Tanaka: It's a fine day today, isn't it?

   Smith: Yes, it really is lovely weather.

   Tanaka: (Are you) busy today?

   Smith: No, (I'm) not so busy.

3. **Tanaka:** Sumisu-san no uchi wa kaisha kara tōi desu ka.
   Sumisu: Iie, tōkunai desu. Chikai desu. Chikatetsu de 20-pun gurai desu.
   Tanaka: Sō desu ka. Benri desu ne.

   Tanaka: Is your house far from your office?
   Smith: No, it isn't. It's near by. It's about 20 minutes by subway.
   Tanaka: I see. How convenient.

4. **Howaito:** Koko wa shizukana kōen desu ne.
   Yamada: Ee, ōkii ki ya kireina hana ga takusan arimasu ne. Howaito-san wa yoku
   kōen ni ikimasu ka.
   Howaito: Ee, nichi-yōbi no asa tokidoki uchi no chikaku no kōen ni ikimasu.

   White: This is a quiet park, isn't it?
   Yamada: Yes. There are lots of big trees and beautiful flowers (etc.), aren't there? Do
   you go to parks often?
   White: Yes. I sometimes go to the park near my house on Sunday morning.

| Vocabulary |

tenki	weather
hontō ni	really, truly
20-pun gurai	about 20 minutes (for about 20 minutes)
gurai	about, approximately
ki	tree

QUIZ ▦▩▩▩

I Read this lesson's opening dialogue and answer the following questions.

1. **Sumisu-san wa o-kashi o tabemashita ka.**
2. **Sumisu-san wa doko no o-kashi o tabemashita ka.**
3. **Sumisu-san wa nani o nomimashita ka.**

II Complete the questions so that they fit the answers.

1. **Tanaka-san wa (   ) desu ka.**
   Hai, genki desu.
2. **Sono hon wa (   ) desu ka.**
   Iie, amari omoshirokunai desu.
3. **Ano hito wa (   ) desu ka.**
   Tanaka-san desu.
4. **Ano hito wa (   ) hito desu ka.**
   Shinsetsuna hito desu.

III Circle the correct adjective in the parentheses.

1. **Ano kissaten no kōhī wa amari (oishii desu, oishikunai desu).**
2. **Uchi no chikaku ni (kirei, kireina) kōen ga arimasu.**
3. **Kono hon wa (omoshirokunai desu, omoshiroi dewa arimasen).**
4. **Watashi no rajio wa (ikunai desu, yokunai desu, ii dewa arimasen).**
5. **Are wa (yūmei, yūmeina) resutoran desu.**
6. **Yamada-san no uchi wa koko kara totemo (chikai desu, chikakunai desu).**

IV Translate into Japanese.

1. Would you like some coffee?
   Thank you, I'll have some.
2. Would you like another cup of coffee?
   No, thank you. That was enough.
3. We had dinner at a famous restaurant.
4. That cafe is clean, but it isn't quiet.
5. I am busy today.

LESSON 14   YESTERDAY'S ENJOYABLE KABUKI

Mr. Tanaka is asking Mr. Smith about the Kabuki he saw.

たなか：かぶきは　どうでしたか。

スミス：とても　きれいでした。

たなか：にほんごが　わかりましたか。

スミス：いいえ、ぜんぜん　わかりませんでしたから、イヤホーンで
　　　　えいごの　せつめいを　ききました。とても　おもしろかった
　　　　です。

■スミスさんは　かぶきを　みました。イヤホーンで　えいごの　せつ
　めいを　ききました。かぶきは　とても　おもしろかったです。

Tanaka:　Kabuki wa dō deshita ka.
Sumisu:　Totemo kirei deshita.
Tanaka:　Nihon-go ga wakarimashita ka.
Sumisu:　Iie, zenzen wakarimasendeshita kara, iyahōn de Ei-go no setsumei
　　　　o kikimashita. Totemo omoshirokatta desu.

■Sumisu-san wa kabuki o mimashita. Iyahōn de Ei-go no setsumei o kikimashita. Kabuki wa totemo omoshirokatta desu.

Tanaka:　How was the Kabuki?
Smith:　It was very beautiful.
Tanaka:　Did you understand the Japanese?
Smith:　No, I didn't understand it at all, so I listened to the English explanation with ear-
　　　　phones. It was fascinating.

■Mr. Smith saw a Kabuki play. He listened to the English explanation with earphones. He
enjoyed the Kabuki very much.

Vocabulary		
どう　でしたか	**dō deshita ka**	How was it?
どう	**dō**	how

わかりました	wakarimashita	understood
わかります（わかる）	wakarimasu (wakaru)	understand
ぜんぜん〜ません	zenzen . . . -masen	(not) at all (See Appendix E.)
イヤホーン	iyahōn	earphones
えいご	Ei-go	English language
せつめい	setsumei	explanation

NOTES

1. Dō deshita ka.

Used when asking a person his impression of something.

ex. **Eiga wa dō deshita ka.** "How was the movie?"
Omoshirokatta desu. "It was delightful."

2. Nihon-go ga wakarimashita ka.

Note that with the verb **wakarimasu**, the noun usually takes the particle **ga** rather than **o**. (See Grammar X, p. 174.)

PRACTICE

KEY SENTENCES

1. **Kinō wa samukatta desu.**
2. **Kinō wa atsukunakatta desu.**
3. **Kinō no pātī wa nigiyaka deshita.**
4. **[Watashi wa] Senshū hima dewa arimasendeshita.**

1. It was cold yesterday.
2. It wasn't hot yesterday.
3. Yesterday's party was lively.
4. I had no free time last week.

Vocabulary	
samukatta	was cold
samui	cold (**-i** adj.)
atsukunakatta	was not hot
atsui	hot (**-i** adj.)
nigiyakana	lively (**-na** adj.)

EXERCISES

I A. **-i** adjectives: Memorize the following **-i** adjectives and their present and past forms.

	Present Form		Past Form	
	aff.	*neg.*	*aff.*	*neg.*
cold	**samui (desu)**	**samukunai (desu)**	**samukatta (desu)**	**samukunakatta (desu)**
hot	**atsui**	**atsukunai**	**atsukatta**	**atsukunakatta**
enjoyable	**tanoshii**	**tanoshiku-nai**	**tanoshikatta**	**tanoshikuna-katta**
good	**ii**	**yokunai**	**yokatta**	**yokunakatta**
interesting	**omoshiroi**	**omoshiro-kunai**	**omoshiro-katta**	**omoshiroku-nakatta**
tasty	**oishii**	**oishikunai**	**oishikatta**	**oishikunakatta**
expensive	**takai**	**takakunai**	**takakatta**	**takakunakatta**

B. **-na** adjectives: Study the following **-na** adjectives.

	Present		Past	
	aff.	*neg.*	*aff.*	*neg.*
quiet	**shizuka desu**	**shizuka dewa arimasen**	**shizuka deshita**	**shizuka dewa arimasendeshita**
well, healthy	**genki desu**	**genki dewa arimasen**	**genki deshita**	**genki dewa arimasendeshita**

II Practice the following patterns by changing the underlined part as in the examples given.

    A. *ex.* **Kinō no eiga wa <u>omoshirokatta</u> desu.**

        1. **ii**

        2. **tanoshii**

    B. *ex.* **Kinō machi wa <u>shizuka</u> deshita.**

        1. **nigiyaka**

III Make dialogues by changing the underlined parts as in the examples given.

    A. *ex.* **Q: <u>Kinō no pātī</u> wa tanoshikatta desu ka.**

        A*a*: Hai, tanoshikatta desu.

        A*n*: Iie, tanoshikunakatta desu.

        1. **ryokō**

        2. **gorufu**

B. *ex.* **Q:** <u>Tanaka-san</u> wa genki deshita ka.

    A*a*: Hai, totemo genki deshita.

    A*n*: Iie, amari genki dewa arimasendeshita.

    1. sensei

    2. Tanaka-san no hisho

C. *ex.* **Q:** Kono hon wa <u>yokatta</u> desu ka.

    A*a*: Hai, <u>yokatta</u> desu.

    A*n*: Iie, <u>yokunakatta</u> desu.

    1. omoshiroi

    2. muzukashii

D. *ex.* **Q:** Kinō no pātī wa dō deshita ka.

    A*a*: Totemo <u>tanoshikatta</u> desu.

    A*n*: Amari <u>tanoshikunakatta</u> desu.

    1. omoshiroi

    2. nigiyaka

E. *ex.* **Q:** <u>Ryokō</u> wa dō deshita ka.

    A: Totemo <u>tanoshikatta</u> desu.

    1. eiga, omoshiroi

    2. ryōri, oishii

Vocabulary

tanoshii	enjoyable (**-i** adj)
machi	town, street
ryokō	trip
gorufu	golf
ryōri	food, cooking

SHORT DIALOGUE

Tanaka: Kinō eki no chikaku no resutoran ni ikimashita.

Sumisu: Donna resutoran deshita ka.

Tanaka: Shizukana resutoran deshita.

Sumisu: Ryōri wa dō deshita ka.

Tanaka: Totemo oishikatta desu.

Sumisu: Yokatta desu ne.

Tanaka: Yesterday I went to the restaurant near the station.

Smith: What was the restaurant like?

Tanaka: It was a quiet restaurant.

Smith: How was the food?

Tanaka: It was very good.

Smith: It turned out well (then), didn't it?

QUIZ ▇▇▇▇▇

I Read this lesson's opening dialogue and answer the following questions.

1. **Sumisu-san wa nani o mimashita ka.**
2. **Kabuki wa omoshirokatta desu ka, omoshirokunakatta desu ka.**
3. **Sumisu-san wa nan de Ei-go no setsumei o kikimashita ka.**

II Give the antonyms of the following.

1. **muzukashii**	4. **chiisai**	7. **samui**	10. **ii**
2. **tōi**	5. **yasui**	8. **nigiyakana**	
3. **omoshiroi**	6. **himana**	9. **atarashii**	

III Complete the questions so that they fit the answers.

1. **Shūmatsu ni (   ) o shimashita ka.**
   Kyōto ni ikimashita.
   Kyōto wa (   ) deshita ka.
   Totemo kirei deshita.
   Tenki wa (   ) deshita ka.
   Ee, totemo yokatta desu.
2. **(   ) hiru-gohan o tabemasen ka.**
   Isogashii desu kara.
3. **Ano hito wa (   ) hito desu ka.**
   Omoshiroi hito desu.

IV Circle the correct words in the parentheses.

1. **Kinō no tenki wa totemo (yokatta desu, ii deshita, ikatta desu).**
2. **Ryokō wa (nan, dō) deshita ka.**
   Tanoshikatta desu.
3. **Do-yōbi no pātī wa (nigiyakatta desu, nigiyaka deshita).**
4. **Ano resutoran wa amari (kirekunai desu, kirei desu, kirei dewa arimasen).**
5. **Kinō eiga o mimashita ga, zenzen (omoshirokatta desu, omoshiro-kunai deshita, omoshirokunakatta desu).**
6. **Tanaka-san wa senshū (genkikatta desu, genki deshita).**

V Translate into Japanese.

1. How was yesterday's meeting?
2. Yesterday's weather was good.
3. That restaurant's food was not very good.

LESSON 15 GIVING AND RECEIVING

Mr. Tanaka and Mr. Smith are talking about a vase Mr. Tanaka received from Mr. Clark.

スミス：きれいな　かびんですね。

たなか：ええ、たんじょうびに　ともだちの　クラークさんに
　　　　もらいました。

スミス：いい　いろですね。

たなか：ええ、わたしの　すきな　いろです。

■たなかさんは　クラークさんに　かびんを　もらいました。クラー
クさんは　たなかさんに　かびんを　あげました。

Sumisu:　Kireina kabin desu ne.
Tanaka:　Ee, tanjōbi ni tomodachi no Kurāku-san ni moraimashita.
Sumisu:　Ii iro desu ne.
Tǎnaka:　Ee, watashi no sukina iro desu.

■ Tanaka-san wa Kurāku-san ni kabin o moraimashita. Kurāku-san wa Tanaka-san ni kabin o agemashita.

Smith:　　What a lovely vase!
Tanaka:　Yes. My friend Mr. Clark gave it to me on my birthday.
Smith:　　It's a nice color, isn't it?
Tanaka:　Yes, it's a favorite color of mine.

■ Mr. Tanaka received a vase from Mr. Clark. Mr. Clark gave Mr. Tanaka a vase.

Vocabulary

かびん	kabin	vase
に	ni	from (particle)
もらいました	moraimashita	received
もらいます（もらう）	moraimasu (morau)	receive
いろ	iro	color

108

すき（な）	sukina	likable, favorite (**-na** adj.)
に	ni	to (particle)
あげました	agemashita	gave
あげます（あげる）	agemasu (ageru)	give

GRAMMAR VI

Lesson 15   Giving and Receiving

...NI ... O verb

1. person **WA** person **NI** noun **O AGEMASU**
2. person **WA** person **NI** noun **O MORAIMASU**

• **Agemasu/Kuremasu**, "give"
Moraimasu, "receive"
There are two words in Japanese meaning "give," and great care must be taken in their correct use. **Agemasu,** *lit.* "to raise up," implies "to humbly present," and can never be used when speaking of something that someone gives *you*. **Kuremasu**, on the other hand, literally means "to hand down" and must *only* be used in connection with things given to you.

ex. **Watashi wa Tanaka-san ni kabin o agemashita.** "I gave Mr. Tanaka a vase."
Kurāku-san wa watashi ni kabin o kuremashita. "Mr. Clark gave me a vase."
Watashi wa Kurāku-san ni kabin o moraimashita. "I received a vase from Mr. Clark."

Note: **Kuremasu** is not used in this book since **moraimasu**, "receive," is more frequently used. Also, **kara** is often used with **moraimasu** instead of **ni**.
Agemasu may also be freely used when the speaker is not involved in the giving.

ex. **Kurāku-san wa Tanaka-san ni kabin o agemashita.** "Mr. Clark gave Mr. Tanaka a vase."

NOTE

1. **Tomodachi no Kurāku-san**
   This is not the possessive **no**. It is the appositive, "my friend, Mr. Clark."

PRACTICE

KEY SENTENCES

1. **Hayashi-san wa Sumisu-san ni hon o agemashita.**
2. **Sumisu-san wa Hayashi-san ni hon o moraimashita.**

1. Mr. Hayashi gave Mr. Smith a book.
2. Mr. Smith received a book from Mr. Hayashi.

I Verbs: Memorize the following verbs and their present and past forms.

	Present Form		Past Form	
	aff.	*neg.*	*aff.*	*neg.*
give	**agemasu**	**agemasen**	**agemashita**	**agemasendeshita**
receive	**moraimasu**	**moraimasen**	**moraimashita**	**moraimasendeshita**

II Practice the following pattern by changing the underlined parts as in the example given.

  ex. **Hayashi-san wa Sumisu-san ni hon o agemasu. Sumisu-san wa Hayashi-san ni hon o moraimasu.**

  1. **Sumisu-san, Sumisu-san no hisho**
  2. **Nihon-go no sensei, Kurāku-san**

III Make dialogues by changing the underlined part as in the examples given.

  A. *ex.* **Q: [Anata wa] Kurāku-san ni hon o agemashita ka.**

  A*a***: Hai, agemashita.**

  A*n***: Iie, agemasendeshita.**

  1. **kireina kitte**
  2. **atarashii jisho**
  3. **ryokō no shashin**

  B. *ex.* **Q: Dare ga Kurāku-san ni atarashii jisho o agemasu ka.**

  A: Tanaka-san ga agemasu.

  1. **Haruko-san**
  2. **kaisha no hito**

  C. *ex.* **Q: [Anata wa] Dare ni eiga no kippu o moraimashita ka.**

  A: Tomodachi ni moraimashita.

  1. **chichi**
  2. **ane**

  D. *ex.* **Q: [Anata wa] Otōsan no tanjōbi ni otōsan ni nani o agemasu ka.**

  A: Nekutai o agemasu.

  1. **tokei**
  2. **rekishi no hon**

Vocabulary

jisho	dictionary	**ane**	(my) elder sister
Haruko	a given name (female)	**nekutai**	necktie
chichi	(my) father	**rekishi**	history

SHORT DIALOGUES

1. **Hayashi:** **Ii nekutai desu ne.**
   Kurāku: **Dōmo arigatō. Kinō kanai ni moraimashita. Kinō wa watashi no tanjōbi deshita.**

   Hayashi: What a nice necktie.
   Clark: Thank you. I received it from my wife yesterday. Yesterday was my birthday.

2. **Sumisu:** **Watashi wa Amerika de Nihon-go no benkyō o shimashita.**
   Tanaka: **Hiragana ya kanji no benkyō mo shimashita ka.**
   Sumisu: **Hai, shimashita. Kanji wa totemo omoshiroi desu. Watashi wa yoku Nihon-go no hon o yomimasu. Nihon-go no sensei ni kono hon o moraimashita. Totemo omoshiroi hon desu.**

   Smith: I studied Japanese in America.
   Tanaka: Did you study *hiragana, kanji* (and so on), too?
   Smith: Yes, I did. Kanji is fascinating. I often read books in Japanese. I was given this book by my Japanese teacher. It's a very entertaining book.

Vocabulary	
kanai	(my) wife
hiragana	*hiragana* (Japanese script)
kanji	*kanji* (Chinese characters)

QUIZ

I Read this lesson's opening dialogue and answer the following questions.

1. **Tanaka-san wa itsu kireina kabin o moraimashita ka.**
2. **Tanaka-san wa dare ni kireina kabin o moraimashita ka.**
3. **Dare ga Tanaka-san ni kireina kabin o agemashita ka.**
4. **Kurāku-san wa dare ni kireina kabin o agemashita ka.**

II Complete the questions so that they fit the answers.

1. **Tanaka-san wa (   ) ni ryokō no shashin o agemashita ka.**
   Kurāku-san ni agemashita.
2. **Hayashi-san wa (   ) ni eiga no kippu o moraimashita ka.**
   Sumisu-san ni moraimashita.
3. **Tomodachi ni (   ) o agemashita ka.**
   Nihon-go no jisho o agemashita.

III Put the appropriate particles in the parentheses. (If a particle is not required, put an X in the parentheses.)

1. **Watashi wa kono kabin o kaimasen deshita. Tomodachi (   ) morai-mashita.**
2. **Dare (   ) Hayashi-san ni eiga no kippu (   ) agemashita ka.**
3. **Sumisu-san wa tomodachi (   ) Amerika no kireina kitte (   ) agemashita.**
4. **Tanjōbi (   ) nani (   ) moraimashita ka.**
   Nani (   ) moraimasen deshita.

IV Translate into Japanese.

1. Mr. Tanaka received a pretty vase from Mr. Clark.
2. Mr. Hayashi gave Mr. Smith a map of Kyoto.
3. Did you give that person a business card?
   Yes, I did (give him one).

LESSON 16 ASKING PREFERENCES

Mr. Hayashi invites Mr. Smith to go skiing.

はやし：どようびに　にっこうに　スキーに　いきます。スミスさん、
　　　　いっしょに　いきませんか。

スミス：いいですね。いきましょう。なんで　いきますか。

はやし：でんしゃで　いきます。とうきょうえきで　あいませんか。

スミス：はい。なんじに　あいましょうか。

はやし：あさの　7じに　とうきょうえきの　かいさつぐちで
　　　　あいましょう。

スミス：はい、わかりました。じゃ、どようびに。

■はやしさんは　スミスさんと　にっこうに　スキーに　いきます。
　どようびの　あさ　7じに　とうきょうえきの　かいさつぐちで
　スミスさんに　あいます。

Hayashi:	Do-yōbi ni Nikkō ni sukī ni ikimasu. Sumisu-san, issho ni iki-masen ka.
Sumisu:	Ii desu ne. Ikimashō. Nan de ikimasu ka.
Hayashi:	Densha de ikimasu. Tōkyō Eki de aimasen ka.
Sumisu:	Hai. Nan-ji ni aimashō ka.
Hayashi:	Asa no 7-ji ni Tōkyō Eki no kaisatsuguchi de aimashō.
Sumisu:	Hai, wakarimashita. Ja, do-yōbi ni.

■ Hayashi-san wa Sumisu-san to Nikkō ni sukī ni ikimasu. Do-yōbi no asa 7-ji ni Tōkyō Eki no kaisatsuguchi de Sumisu-san ni aimasu.

Hayashi:	I'm going to Nikko on Saturday to ski. Mr. Smith, wouldn't you like to go with me?
Smith:	How nice! I'd love to go. (*lit.* "Let's go.") How do we get there?
Hayashi:	We'll go by train. Shall we meet at Tokyo Station?
Smith:	All right. What time shall we meet?
Hayashi:	Let's meet by the ticket gate in Tokyo Station at 7:00 in the morning.
Smith:	Sure. That's fine. Well, see you Saturday!

■ Mr. Hayashi is going skiing in Nikko with Mr. Smith. He is meeting Mr. Smith at 7:00 on Saturday morning by the ticket gate at Tokyo Station.

Vocabulary

にっこう	**Nikkō**	Nikko (city name)
スキー	**sukī**	skiing
に	**ni**	to (particle)
いっしょに	**issho ni**	together with
あいましょうか	**aimashō ka**	Shall we meet . . .
わかりました	**wakarimashita**	sure, certainly

GRAMMAR VII

Lessons 16–17   Inviting and Expressing Volition

1. verb **-MASHŌ**
2. verb **-MASHŌ KA**
3. verb **-MASEN KA**

● How to invite a person to do something with you.
  verb **-mashō ka**
  ex. **Issho ni Nikkō ni ikimashō ka.** "Shall we go to Nikko (together)?"
  verb **-masen ka**
  ex. **Issho ni Nikkō ni ikimasen ka.** "Won't you go to Nikko with me?"

● How to invite a person.
  verb **-masen ka**
  ex. **Uchi ni kimasen ka.** "Won't you come to my house?"

● How to offer to do something for a person.
  verb **-mashō ka**
  ex. **Chizu o kakimashō ka.** "Shall I draw you a map?"
  Replies to the above. The following English equivalents give an idea of the appropriate replies.
  Acceptance: 1. **Hai, zehi/yorokonde.** "I'd love to."
  2. **Hai,** verb **-mashō.** "Yes, let's . . ."
  3. **Hai,** verb **-masu.** "O.K."
  4. **Hai, onegaishimasu.** "Yes, please."
  Refusal: 5. **Zannen desu ga, tsugō ga warui desu.** "I'm sorry, I'm afraid I have another engagement." (*lit.* "Unfortunately conditions are unfavorable.")
  6. **Iie, kekkō desu.** "No, thank you." (*lit.* "No, I'm satisfied.")

NOTES

1. **Sukī ni ikimasu.**
   Sukī, "skiing," is a purpose, not a place. Therefore it takes the particle **ni**, not **e**.

2. **Sumisu-san, issho ni ikimasen ka.**
   Sumisu-san is simply being addressed by name and hence is not the topic of the sentence. In this case, the name, or title, usually comes at the beginning of the Japanese sentence.
   ex. **Tanaka-san, dōzo kochira ni.** "This way, please, Mr. Tanaka."

3. **Ja, do-yōbi ni.**
   Do-yōbi ni is short for **Do-yōbi ni aimashō,** "Let's meet on Saturday." Japanese often refer to the next meeting rather than saying "Goodbye."
   ex. **Ja, mata ashita.** "Well then, (see you) again tomorrow."

PRACTICE

KEY SENTENCES

1. **Do-yōbi ni issho ni tenisu o shimasen ka.**
2. **Issho ni shokuji ni ikimasen ka.**
3. **12-ji ni eki no mae de aimashō.**

1. Won't you play tennis with me on Saturday?
2. Won't you go out for a meal with me?
3. Let's meet at 12:00 in front of the station.

EXERCISES

I Verbs: Memorize the following **-mashō**, **-mashō ka**, and **-masen ka** forms.

	go	see	do	meet
V-masu	ikimasu	mimasu	shimasu	aimasu
V-mashō	ikimashō	mimashō	shimashō	aimashō
V-mashō ka	ikimashō ka	mimashō ka	shimashō ka	aimashō ka
V-masen ka	ikimasen ka	mimasen ka	shimasen ka	aimasen ka

II Practice the following patterns:

    ex. **eiga ni ikimasu** ⟶ **Eiga ni ikimashō.**
                            Eiga ni ikimashō ka.
                            Eiga ni ikimasen ka.

1. shokuji o shimasu
2. kōhī o nomimasu

III Make dialogues by changing the underlined parts as in the examples given.

A. *ex* A: B-san, ashita issho ni <u>shokuji</u> ni ikimasen ka.

B*a*: Ee, ikimashō.

B*n*: Zannen desu ga, tsugō ga warui desu.

1. kaimono
2. haikingu
3. doraibu

B. *ex*. A: B-san, issho ni <u>eiga o mimasen</u> ka.

B: Ee, <u>mimashō.</u>

1. sampo o shimasu
2. takushī de kaerimasu
3. ano resutoran de hiru-gohan o tabemasu

C. *ex*. A: Nan de kaerimashō ka.

B: <u>Takushī de kaerimasen ka.</u>

A: Ee, sō shimashō.

1. chikatetsu
2. basu

D. *ex*. A: Nan-ji ni aimashō ka.

B: <u>12-ji</u> goro wa dō desu ka.

A: Ee, ii desu.

1. 3-ji
2. 5-ji han

E. *ex*. A: Doko ni <u>doraibu</u> ni ikimashō ka.

B: <u>Umi no chikaku ni</u> ikimasen ka.

A: Ee, ikimashō.

1. kaimono, Ginza
2. sukī, Nikkō

F. *ex*. A: Nani o shimashō ka

B: <u>Tenisu o shimashō.</u>

1. sampo ni ikimasu
2. eiga o mimasu

Vocabulary

zannen desu ga ·	I'm sorry, but . . .	**doraibu**	driving
zannen	regret	**sampo o shimasu**	take a walk
tsugō ga warui	(I) am unable (*lit*. "Con-	**(sampo o suru)**	
desu	ditions are bad.")	**sampo**	a walk

tsugō	condition	**umi**	sea
haikingu	hiking		

SHORT DIALOGUES

1. Sumisu: **Hayashi-san, sampo ni ikimasen ka.**
   Hayashi: **Ee, ikimashō.**
   Sumisu: **Kono chikaku ni ōkii kōen ga arimasu. Kōen ni ikimashō.**

   Smith: Mr. Hayashi, wouldn't you like to go for a walk?
   Hayashi: Yes, let's go.
   Smith: There is a big park near here. Let's go to the park.

2. Discussing what to give the Tanakas for their new baby.
   Yamada: **Tanaka-san no akachan ni nani o agemashō ka.**
   Howaito: **Supūn to koppu wa dō desu ka.**
   Yamada: **Ii desu ne. Ashita depāto de kaimasen ka.**
   Howaito: **Ee, sō shimashō.**

   Yamada: What shall we give the Tanakas for their (new) baby?
   White: How about a spoon and a mug?
   Yamada: All right. Shall we buy them tomorrow at the department store?
   White: Yes, let's do that.

Vocabulary	
akachan	baby
supūn	spoon
koppu	mug

QUIZ ▰▰▰▰▰

I Read this lesson's opening dialogue and answer the following questions.

1. **Hayashi-san wa doko ni sukī ni ikimasu ka.**
2. **Hayashi-san wa hitori de sukī ni ikimasu ka.**
3. **Hayashi-san wa Sumisu-san ni doko de aimasu ka.**
4. **Hayashi-san wa Sumisu-san ni 7-ji ni aimasu ka, 8-ji ni aimasu ka.**
5. **Hayashi-san to Sumisu-san wa nan de ikimasu ka.**

II Complete the questions so that they fit the answers.

1. **Do-yōbi ni eiga ni ikimasen ka.**
   Ee, ikimashō. (   ) de aimashō ka.
   Tōkyō Eki no kaisatsuguchi de aimashō.

    (   ) ni aimashō ka.

    4-ji ni aimasen ka.

    Ee, ii desu. 4-ji ni aimashō.

2. Kinō tenisu ni ikimashita.

    Sō desu ka. (   ) to shimashita ka.

    Sumisu-san to shimashita.

III Put the appropriate particle in the parentheses. (If a particle is not required, put an X in the parentheses.)

1. Issho (   ) tenisu (   ) shimasen ka.

2. Issho (   ) tenisu (   ) ikimasen ka.

3. Raishū no do-yōbi (   ) doraibu (   ) ikimasen ka.

4. Shokuji (   ) ikimasen ka.

    Ee. Doko (   ) tabemashō ka.

IV Translate into Japanese.

1. I went shopping at a department store on Saturday.

2. Won't you have a meal with me?

    Yes, let's (do that). Where shall we go?

    Wouldn't you like to go to the new restaurant near the station?

    Yes, let's do that.

LESSON 17 INVITATION TO A PARTY

Mr. Tanaka invites Mr. Smith to a farewell party for Mr. Clark.

たなか：どようびの　ばん　うちで　クラークさんの　そうべつかいを
　　　　します。スミスさん、きませんか。

スミス：ええ、ぜひ。ありがとうございます。おたくは　どちらですか。

たなか：あざぶです。ちずを　かきましょうか。

スミス：ええ、おねがいします。

■スミスさんは　どようびの　ばん　クラークさんの　そうべつかいに
　いきます。

Tanaka: Do-yōbi no ban uchi de Kurāku-san no sōbetsukai o shimasu.
　　　　Sumisu-san, kimasen ka.
Sumisu: Ee, zehi. Arigatō gozaimasu. O-taku wa dochira desu ka.
Tanaka: Azabu desu. Chizu o kakimashō ka.
Sumisu: Ee, onegaishimasu.

■Sumisu-san wa do-yōbi no ban Kurāku-san no sōbetsukai ni ikimasu.

Tanaka: I'm giving a farewell party for Mr. Clark at my house on Saturday evening.
　　　　Won't you come, Mr. Smith?
Smith: Yes, I'd like to. Thank you very much. Where is your house?
Tanaka: It's in Azabu. Shall I draw you a map?
Smith: Yes, please.

■Mr. Smith is going to a farewell party for Mr. Clark on Saturday evening.

Vocabulary

そうべつかい	**sōbetsukai**	farewell party
ぜひ	**zehi**	I'd like to. (*lit.* "by all means")
どちら	**dochira**	where (polite word for **doko**)
あざぶ	**Azabu**	Azabu (place name)
かきましょうか	**kakimashō ka**	Shall (I) draw . . .

NOTES

1. Sōbetsukai o shimasu.

Since Mr. Tanaka is the host, he says **Sōbetsukai o shimasu,** "I'm giving a farewell party," rather than **sōbetsukai ga arimasu,** "There will be a farewell party." (See Grammar VIII, p. 124.)

PRACTICE

KEY SENTENCES

1. Nichi-yōbi ni uchi ni kimasen ka.

2. Mado o akemashō ka.

1. Won't you come to my house on Sunday?
2. Shall I open the window?

> **Vocabulary**

akemashō ka	Shall I open . . . ?
akemasu (akeru)	open

EXERCISES

I Verbs: Memorize the following verbs and their **-mashō** forms.

	open	close	turn on	turn off	make a copy
V-masu	akemasu	shimemasu	tsukemasu	keshimasu	kopī o shimasu
V-mashō	akemashō	shimemashō	tsukemashō	keshimashō	kopī o shi-mashō
V-mashō ka	akema-shō ka	shimema-shō ka	tsukema-shō ka	keshima-shō ka	kopī o shi-mashō ka

II Practice the following patterns.

> *ex.* **mado o akemasu ⟶ Mado o akemashō.**
> **Mado o akemashō ka.**

> 1. **rajio o keshimasu**
> 2. **doa o shimemasu**

III Make dialogues by changing the underlined parts as in the examples given.

> A. ex. **A: Do-yōbi ni uchi de <u>Kurāku-san no sōbetsukai</u> o shimasu. Uchi ni kimasen ka.**

B*a*: Ee, zehi.

B*n*: Zannen desu ga, tsugō ga warui desu.

1. **pātī**
2. **Kurāku-san no kangeikai**

B. *ex.* **A: Atsui desu ne. Mado o akemashō ka.**

B*a*: Ee, Onegaishimasu.

B*n*: Iie, kekkō desu.

1. **kurai, denki o tsukemasu**
2. **urusai, doa o shimemasu**
3. **atsui, hītā o keshimasu**

Vocabulary

keshimasu (kesu)	turn off	**denki**	(electric) light
doa	door	**tsukemasu (tsukeru)**	turn on
shimemasu (shimeru)	close	**urusai**	noisy (**-i** adj.)
kangeikai	welcome party	**hītā**	heater
kurai	dark (**-i** adj.)		

SHORT DIALOGUE

Yamada: Kopī o shimashō ka.
Sumisu: Hai, onegaishimasu.
Yamada: Nan-mai shimashō ka.
Sumisu: 3-mai onegaishimasu.

Yamada: Shall I make a copy?
Smith: Yes, please.
Yamada: How many copies shall I make?
Smith: Three copies, please.

Vocabulary

kopī photocopy

QUIZ

I Read this lesson's opening dialogue and answer the following questions.

1. **Kurāku-san no sōbetsukai wa itsu desu ka.**
2. **Sumisu-san wa Kurāku-san no sōbetsukai ni ikimasu ka, ikimasen ka.**
3. **Tanaka-san wa doko de Kurāku-san no sōbetsukai o shimasu ka.**
4. **Tanaka-san no uchi wa doko ni arimasu ka.**
5. **Tanaka-san wa Sumisu-san ni chizu o kakimasu ka.**

II Put the appropriate particles in the parentheses. (If a particle is not required, put an X in the parentheses.)

1. **Raishū no do-yōbi (   ) okusan to issho (   ) uchi (   ) kimasen ka.**
   Ee, zehi.
   Issho (   ) ban-gohan (   ) tabemashō.
2. **Tenisu (   ) ikimasen ka. Ii tenki desu kara.**
   Zannen desu (   ), tsugō (   ) warui desu.
3. **Atsui desu ne. Mado (   ) akemashō ka.**
   Hai, onegaishimasu.

III Translate into Japanese.

1. Won't you come to my house on Sunday?
2. We're having a farewell party for Mr. Clark at our house on Friday. Won't you come?
   Yes, I'd like to.
3. Won't you have a meal with me?
4. It's cold, isn't it? Shall I close the window?
   Yes, please.
5. Shall I draw you a map?

Mr. Hayashi and Mr. Smith are making a date to go to the movies.

はやし：わたしは　えいがの　きっぷが　2まい　あります。こんばん
　　　　いっしょに　いきませんか。

スミス：ざんねんですが、こんばん　7じに　たいしかんに　いきます。
　　　　たいしかんで　パーティーが　ありますから。

はやし：そうですか。あしたは　どうですか。

スミス：あしたは　じかんが　あります。

はやし：じゃ、あした　いきませんか。

スミス：ええ、あした　おねがいします。

■スミスさんは　こんばん　たいしかんで　パーティーが　あります
　ら、あした　はやしさんと　えいがに　いきます。

Hayashi:	Watashi wa eiga no kippu ga 2-mai arimasu. Komban issho ni ikimasen ka.
Sumisu:	Zannen desu ga, komban 7-ji ni taishikan ni ikimasu. Taishikan de pātī ga arimasu kara.
Hayashi:	Sō desu ka. Ashita wa dō desu ka.
Sumisu:	Ashita wa jikan ga arimasu.
Hayashi:	Ja, ashita ikimasen ka.
Sumisu:	Ee, ashita onegaishimasu.

■ Sumisu-san wa komban taishikan de pātī ga arimasu kara, ashita Hayashi-san to eiga ni ikimasu.

Hayashi:	I have two tickets for the movie. Wouldn't you like to go with me tonight?
Smith:	I'm sorry, but I'm going to the embassy tonight at 7:00. There's a party at the embassy.
Hayashi:	I see. What about tomorrow?
Smith:	I'm free tomorrow.
Hayashi:	Well then, would you like to go tomorrow?
Smith:	Yes, let's make it tomorrow.

■ There is a party at the embassy tonight, so Mr. Smith is going to the movie with Mr. Hayashi tomorrow.

Vocabulary

あります（ある）	**arimasu (aru)**	have
じかん	**jikan**	time

GRAMMAR VIII

Lesson 18   Ownership and Events

1. person **WA** noun **GA ARIMASU**
2. place **DE** event **GA ARIMASU**

● Grammar III covers the main uses of the verb **arimasu**. The following are additional uses.
    1. To have, to own
        ex. **Kuruma ga arimasu kara issho ni ikimashō.** "I have a car, so let's go together."
        ex. **Tanaka-san wa kodomo ga futari arimasu.** "Mr. Tanaka has two children."
    2. To take place, to happen
        ex. **Koko de 2-ji kara kaigi ga arimasu.** "There will be a meeting here from 2 o'clock."
Note: Remember that in the case of "giving a party" or "holding a meeting," etc., the verb **shimasu** is used. (See Note 1, p. 120.)
Note also, **koko de**. When **arimasu** means "take place" or "occur," the particle used with the place is **de**, rather than **ni**.

NOTES

1. **Sō desu ka.**
When **Sō desu ka** means "I see," as here, it is said with a falling intonation. It can also mean "Oh, really?" or "Is that so?" and be a question expecting an answer. In that case, it is said with a rising intonation.

2. **Ashita wa dō desu ka.**
The questioner is asking about his friend's arrangements for tomorrow. **Ashita** ("tomorrow"), though not the grammatical subject, is the topic in question, so it takes the topic marker **wa**.

PRACTICE

KEY SENTENCES

1. [Watashi wa] Kyō jikan ga arimasu.
2. [Watashi wa] Eiga no kippu ga 2-mai arimasu.
3. Sumisu-san wa kodomo ga futari arimasu.
4. Do-yōbi ni taishikan de pātī ga arimasu.

1. I have time today.
2. I have two tickets for the movie.
3. Mr. Smith has two children.
4. On Saturday there will be a party at the embassy.

EXERCISES

I Practice the following pattern by changing the underlined part as in the example given.

> ex. [Watashi wa] <u>Jikan</u> ga arimasu.
>
> 1. kaigi
> 2. eiga no kippu
> 3. kodomo
> 4. kyōdai

II Make dialogues by changing the underlined parts as in the examples given.

> A. ex. Q: [Anata wa] <u>Ima jikan</u> ga arimasu ka.
>
> Aa: Hai, arimasu.
>
> An: Iie, arimasen.
>
> 1. ima, o-kane
> 2. ashita, kaigi
> 3. kongetsu, yasumi
>
> B. ex. Q: [Anata wa] <u>Eiga no kippu</u> ga arimasu ka.
>
> A: Hai, arimasu.
>
> 1. kuruma
> 2. kyōdai
>
> C. ex. Q: Hayashi-san wa kyō <u>kaigi</u> ga arimasu ka.
>
> Aa: Hai, arimasu. 3-ji kara kaisha de arimasu.
>
> An: Iie, arimasen. Ashita arimasu.
>
> 1. Nihon-go no jugyō
> 2. pātī
>
> D. ex. Q: [Anata wa] Itsu <u>yasumi</u> ga arimasu ka.
>
> A: <u>Raigetsu</u> arimasu.
>
> 1. Nihon-go no jugyō, getsu-yōbi to ka-yōbi ni

2. kaigi, 9-ji kara 5-ji made

E. *ex.* A: Do-yōbi ni pātī ga arimasu.

B: Pātī wa doko de arimasu ka.

A: Taishikan de arimasu.

1. kaigi, kaisha

2. tomodachi no kekkon-shiki, hoteru

F. *ex.* Q: Sumisu-san wa kyōdai ga nan-nin arimasu ka.

A: 3-nin arimasu.

1. kodomo, futari

2. imōto-san, hitori

SHORT DIALOGUES

1. **Yamada:** **Hayashi-san, ima jikan ga arimasu ka.**
   Hayashi: **Iie, ima chotto isogashii desu. Ima kara kaigi ga arimasu kara.**

   Yamada: Mr. Hayashi, do you have time, now?
   Hayashi: No, I'm afraid I'm busy now. There's a conference (starting) now.

2. **Yamada:** **Kurāku-san no sōbetsukai wa doko de arimasu ka.**
   Howaito: **Hayashi-san no uchi de arimasu.**
   Yamada: **Itsu arimasu ka.**
   Howaito: **Kin-yōbi no gogo 7-ji kara desu.**

   Yamada: Where is the farewell party for Mr. Clark being held?
   White: It's being held at Mr. Hayashi's house.
   Yamada: When is it?
   White: On Friday evening, from 7 o'clock.

3. **Tanaka:** **Sumisu-san, okosan ga arimasu ka.**
   Sumisu: **Ee, futari arimasu. Musuko to musume desu.**
   Tanaka: **Musuko-san wa nan-sai desu ka.**
   Sumisu: **Musuko wa 15-sai desu.**
   Tanaka: **Ojō-san wa?**
   Sumisu: **13-sai desu.**

   Tanaka: Mr. Smith, do you have any children?
   Smith: Yes, I have two. A son and a daughter.

Tanaka: How old is your son?
Smith: My son is 15.
Tanaka: (And) Your daughter?
Smith: (She's) Thirteen.

Vocabulary

chotto	a little	nan-sai	how many years old
okosan	(your) child	-sai	years old (used only for
musuko	(my) son		people and pets)
musume	(my) daughter	ojō-san	(your) daughter
musuko-san	(your) son		

QUIZ

I Read this lesson's opening dialogue and answer the following questions.

1. **Hayashi-san wa nan no kippu ga arimasu ka.**
2. **Hayashi-san wa kippu ga nan-mai arimasu ka.**
3. **Sumisu-san wa komban eiga ni ikimasu ka, pātī ni ikimasu ka.**
4. **Komban taishikan de nani ga arimasu ka.**
5. **Hayashi-san wa komban hitori de eiga ni ikimasu ka.**
6. **Hayashi-san wa itsu, dare to eiga ni ikimasu ka.**

II Complete the questions so that they fit the answers.

1. **Hayashi-san wa kyōdai ga (   ) arimasu ka.**
   3-nin arimasu.
2. **Anata wa (   ) yasumi ga arimasu ka.**
   Raigetsu arimasu.
3. **Kyō taishikan de (   ) ga arimasu ka.**
   Pātī ga arimasu.
4. **Tomodachi no kekkon-shiki wa (   ) de arimasu ka.**
   Hoteru de arimasu.

III Put the appropriate particles in the parentheses. (If a particle is not required, put an X in the parentheses.)

1. **Tanaka-san wa kuruma (   ) arimasu.**
2. **Tanaka-san no kuruma wa asoko (   ) arimasu.**
3. **Kyō kaigi wa doko (   ) arimasu ka.**
4. **Sumisu-san wa kodomo (   ) futari (   ) arimasu.**
5. **Nichi-yōbi ni tomodachi no uchi (   ) pātī (   ) arimasu.**

6. **Eiga (   ) kippu (   ) 2-mai (   ) arimasu.**

   Ashita (   ) issho ni ikimasen ka.

   Tsugō ga warui desu. Shigoto (   ) takusan arimasu kara.

IV Translate into Japanese.

   1. I have three younger sisters. My sisters are in Tokyo and Osaka.
   2. Mr. Tanaka, will you have a vacation in August?

      No, I won't. I'll have (one) in September.
   3. There is a meeting at (our) Kyoto branch office next week.

LESSON 19 DOING THIS AND THAT

Mrs. Smith is telling Mr. Hayashi about her friend Linda who has just arrived in Japan.

スミス：きのう　アメリカから　ともだちの　リンダさんが　きました。

はやし：リンダさんは　いつまで　にほんに　いますか。

スミス：こんしゅうの　きんようびまで　とうきょうに　います。とう
きょうに　みっかだけ　います。しごとですから。それから
わたしと　いっしょに　りょこうを　します。

はやし：どこに　いきますか。

スミス：きょうとと　ならに　いって、ふるい　おてらや　にわを
みます。そして　リンダさんは　らいしゅうの　もくようびに
アメリカに　かえります。

■スミスさんの　ともだちの　リンダさんは　きのう　アメリカから
きました。らいしゅうの　もくようびまで　にほんに　います。

Sumisu: Kinō Amerika kara tomodachi no Rinda-san ga kimashita.
Hayashi: Rinda-san wa itsu made Nihon ni imasu ka.
Sumisu: Konshū no kin-yōbi made Tōkyō ni imasu. Tōkyō ni mikka dake
imasu. Shigoto desu kara. Sorekara watashi to issho ni ryokō o
shimasu.
Hayashi: Doko ni ikimasu ka.
Sumisu: Kyōto to Nara ni itte, furui o-tera ya niwa o mimasu. Soshite
Rinda-san wa raishū no moku-yōbi ni Amerika ni kaerimasu.

■ Sumisu-san no tomodachi no Rinda-san wa kinō Amerika kara kimashita.
Raishū no moku-yōbi made Nihon ni imasu.

Smith: My friend Linda came from America yesterday.
Hayashi: How long (*lit.* "until when") is Linda staying in Japan?
Smith: She'll be in Tokyo until this Friday. She'll only be in Tokyo three days, because
she is here on business. Then she's taking a trip with me.
Hayashi: Where are you going?
Smith: We'll go to Kyoto and Nara and see (things like) old temples and gardens. Then
Linda returns to America on Thursday of next week.

■ Mrs. Smith's friend Linda arrived yesterday from America. She is staying in Japan until Thursday of next week.

Vocabulary

リンダ	**Rinda**	Linda
います（いる）	**imasu (iru)**	stay
こんしゅう	**konshū**	this week
みっか	**mikka**	(for) 3 days
だけ	**dake**	only
それから	**sorekara**	after that
なら	**Nara**	Nara (city and prefecture)
おてら	**o-tera**	temple

GRAMMAR IX

Lessons 19–27   -TE Form, -NAI Form, and Model Verb Conjugation

• All the verbs presented so far have been in, or derived from, the **-masu** form. Here are two other important verb forms, the **-te** form and the **-nai** form.

1. **-te** Form

Regular I					
buy	**kai-masu**	**katte**	go	**iki-masu**	**itte***
return	**kaeri-masu**	**kaette**	read	**yomi-masu**	**yonde**
wait	**machi-masu**	**matte**	call	**yobi-masu**	**yonde**
write	**kaki-masu**	**kaite**	push	**oshi-masu**	**oshite**
Regular II					
eat	**tabe-masu**	**tabete**	see	**mi-masu**	**mite**
show	**mise-masu**	**misete**	get off	**ori-masu**	**orite**
Irregular					
come	**ki-masu**	**kite**	do	**shimasu**	**shite**

*iki-masu, irregular change

• As shown above, the **-te** form can be made from the **-masu** form, although most Regular I verbs undergo a phonetic change.

• Use of **-te** form: The **-te** form of the verb occurs in the middle of sentences or combined with **kudasai** to form the polite imperative. It is used extensively and has various meanings which should be learned. Particular uses are explained in Lessons 19–25.

2. -nai Form

Regular I					
buy return wait	**kai-masu** **kaeri-masu** **machi-masu**	**kawanai** **kaeranai** **matanai**	write go	**kaki-masu** **iki-masu**	**kakanai** **ikanai**
Regular II					
eat show	**tabe-masu** **mise-masu**	**tabenai** **misenai**	see get off	**mi-masu** **ori-masu**	**minai** **orinai**
Irregular					
come	**ki-masu**	**konai**	do	**shi-masu**	**shinai**

- Use of the **-nai** form: A negative verb when used in mid-sentence usually takes the **-nai** form, rather than the **-masen** form it has at the end of a sentence. In this book, only the following use of the **-nai** form is given: verb **-nai de kudasai,** "Please do not . . ."
  This verb **-nai** + **de** + **kudasai** is a polite prohibition. (While not included in this book, it should be noted that the **-nai** form does end negative sentences in familiar speech, which uses the dictionary form for present and future and the **-ta** form for the past tense.)

- Model Verb Conjugation
  As can be inferred from the above, the conjugation of Japanese verbs falls into the following three categories:
  Regular I: Five-vowel conjugation
  Regular II: Single-vowel conjugation
  Irregular: There are only two irregular verbs, **shimasu** and **kimasu.**

- Regular I verbs are conjugated according to the Japanese vowel order: **a, i, u, e, o.** Regular II verbs are based on the vowels **i** and **e** only. From the **-nai** form it can be seen whether a verb is Regular I or Regular II. If the vowel preceding **-nai** is **a,** it is a Regular I verb. If it is **i** or **e,** it is a Regular II verb.

	Regular I	Regular II
-nai form	**kaka-nai**	**tabe-nai**
-masu form	**kaki-masu**	**tabe-masu**
dictionary form	**kaku**	**taberu**
conditional form	**kake-ba**	**tabere-ba**
volitional form	**ka-kō**	**tabeyō**
-te form	**kaite**	**tabete**
-ta form	**kaita**	**tabeta**

- Of the seven forms above, this book includes the **-nai, -masu** and **-te** forms. These three forms, the dictionary form and the **-ta** form are given comprehensively in Appendix H.

NOTES

1. **Kinō Amerika kara Rinda-san ga kimashita.**
   Rinda-san wa itsu made Nihon ni imasu ka.
   Linda is the simple grammatical subject of the first sentence. Since we hear about her for the first time, she takes the subject marker **ga.** She becomes the topic of the second sentence, however, and then takes the topic marker **wa.** One might translate the second sentence, "Speaking of Linda, how long is she staying in Japan?"

2. **Kyōto to Nara ni itte, furui o-tera ya niwa o mimasu.**
   When one action is followed by another, the first clause is terminated by the verb **-te** form. The subject of the first clause and the second clause is the same. This cannot be done unless the mood and the tense of both sentences are the same. The following two sentences *cannot* be connected by the verb **-te** form.
   A. Statement: **Watashi wa kippu ga 2-mai arimasu.** "I have two tickets."
   B. Suggestion: **Ashita issho ni eiga ni ikimashō.** "Let's go to the movies tomorrow."

PRACTICE

KEY SENTENCES

1. **[Watashi wa] Kinō shigoto no ato de tomodachi to shokuji o shite, 9-ji ni uchi ni kaerimashita.**
2. **Kurāku-san wa kyonen no 5-gatsu kara Nihon ni imasu. Soshite rainen no 3-gatsu made [Nihon ni] imasu.**
3. **Tanaka-san wa mainichi 2-jikan benkyō o shimasu.**
4. **Hayashi-san wa asa-gohan no mae ni rajio de nyūsu o kikimasu. Shokuji no ato de shimbun o yomimasu.**

1. Yesterday, after work, I had a meal with my friends, and returned home at 9 o'clock.
2. Mr. Clark has been in Japan since last May and will stay until next March.
3. Mr. Tanaka studies two hours every day.
4. Mr. Hayashi listens to the news on the radio before breakfast. After the meal, he reads the newspaper.

Vocabulary			
shigoto no ato de	after work	**-kan**	for
no ato de	after	**asa-gohan no mae ni**	before breakfast

| 2-jikan | (for) 2 hours | **no mae ni** | before |
| -**jikan** | (counter) | | |

EXERCISES

I Verbs: Memorize the following **-te** forms:

meet	**ai-masu**	**atte**	see	**mi-masu**	**mite**
go	**iki-masu**	**itte**	do	**shi-masu**	**shite**
read	**yomi-masu**	**yonde**	come	**ki-masu**	**kite**
eat	**tabe-masu**	**tabete**			

II Connect the sentences using the **-te** form as in the example given.

   ex. **Hon-ya ni ikimasu. Jisho o kaimasu.**

   Hon-ya ni itte, jisho o kaimasu.

   1. **Tanaka-san ni aimasu. issho ni eiga ni ikimasu.**
   2. **kabuki o mimasu. shokuji o shimasu. takushī de kaerimasu.**
   3. **eiga o mimashō. shokuji o shimashō.**
   4. **uchi ni kimasen ka. o-cha o nomimasen ka.**
   5. **Sumisu-san ni aimashita. issho ni tenisu o shimashita.**

III Practice the following patterns by changing the underlined parts as in the examples given.

   A. *ex.* **Kurāku-san wa kyonen no 5-gatsu kara Nihon ni imasu. Soshite rainen no 3-gatsu made imasu.**

   1. **kotoshi no 1-gatsu, rainen no 8-gatsu**
   2. **senshū, raigetsu no 25-nichi**

   B. *ex.* **[Watashi wa] Shigoto no mae ni shimbun o yomimasu.**

   1. **kaigi**
   2. **shokuji**

   C. *ex.* **[Watashi wa] Shigoto no ato de Tanaka-san ni aimasu.**

   1. **pātī**
   2. **kaimono**

IV Make dialogues by changing the underlined parts as in the examples given.

   A. *ex.* **Q: [Anata wa] Do-yōbi ni donogurai shigoto o shimasu ka.**

   A: 3-jikan dake shimasu.

   1. **benkyō, shimasu, 30-pun**
   2. **hon, yomimasu, 1-jikan**

   B. *ex.* **Q: Kinō shigoto no ato de nani o shimashita ka.**

   A: Tanaka-san ni atte, issho ni ban-gohan o tabemashita.

1. hon-ya ni ikimasu. jisho o kaimasu.

2. tenisu o shimasu. uchi ni kaerimasu.

C. *ex.* Q: Nichi-yōbi ni nani o shimashō ka.

A: Ginza ni itte, kaimono o shimasen ka.

1. kabuki o mimasu. Ginza de shokuji o shimasu.

2. kōen ni ikimasu. hana o mimasu.

D. *ex.* Q: Howaito-san wa itsu kara Nihon ni imasu ka.

A: Kyonen no 8-gatsu kara imasu.

Q: Itsu made Nihon ni imasu ka.

A: Rainen no 10-gatsu made imasu.

1. 1980-nen, rainen

2. sengetsu no 15-nichi, asatte

Vocabulary

donogurai   how long

SHORT DIALOGUE

Yamada: Howaito-san wa donogurai Nihon-go no benkyō o shimashita ka.

Howaito: 4-shūkan dake shimashita. Mainichi 2-jikan shimashita.

Yamada: Nihon-go no benkyō wa dō deshita ka.

Howaito: Sukoshi muzukashikatta desu ga, omoshirokatta desu.

Yamada: How long did you study Japanese?

White: Only 4 weeks, 2 hours a day.

Yamada: How did you find Japanese?

White: It was a little difficult but fun.

Vocabulary

4-shūkan   4 weeks
-shūkan   (counter)
sukoshi   a little

QUIZ

I Read this lesson's opening dialogue and answer the following questions.

1. **Rinda-san wa Sumisu-san no tomodachi desu ka, Hayashi-san no tomodachi desu ka.**

2. **Rinda-san wa itsu Nihon ni kimashita ka.**

3. **Rinda-san wa itsu made Nihon ni imasu ka.**

4. **Rinda-san wa donogurai Tōkyō ni imasu ka.**

5. **Rinda-san wa Tōkyō kara doko ni ikimasu ka.**

6. **Rinda-san to Sumisu-san wa Kyōto ya Nara ni itte nani o shimasu ka.**

II Convert the following verbs into their **-te** form.

1. **tabemasu**	4. **kimasu**	7. **imasu**	10. **nomimasu**
2. **ikimasu**	5. **kakimasu**	8. **mimasu**	11. **aimasu**
3. **yomimasu**	6. **kaerimasu**	9. **shimasu**	12. **kikimasu**

III Complete the questions so that they fit the answers.

1. **Tanaka-san wa Amerika ni (   ) kara (   ) made imashita ka.**
   1979-nen no 5-gatsu kara 1982-nen no 3-gatsu made imashita.

2. **Ōsaka ni (   ) imashita ka.**
   1-shūkan imashita.

3. **(   ) Sumisu-san ni aimasu ka.**
   Shigoto no ato de aimasu.

IV Circle the correct words in the parentheses.

1. **Kyonen Nihon ni kimashita. (Soshite, To) rainen kaerimasu.**

2. **Ashita Kyōto ni (ikimasu to, itte), do-yōbi ni Tōkyō ni kaerimasu.**

3. **Tomodachi wa Tōkyō ni (donogurai, dō) imashita ka.**

4. **Kinō tenisu o 1-jikan (goro, gurai) shimashita.**

5. **Sono hon wa (donogurai, dō) desu ka.**
   Omoshiroi desu.

6. **Kaisha ni (nan, dō) de ikimasu ka.**
   Chikatetsu de ikimasu.
   Kaisha made (dō, donogurai) desu ka.
   25-fun (goro, gurai) desu.

V Translate into Japanese.

1. Every morning I listen to the news and then go to the office.

2. I met Mr. Tanaka and had dinner with him. And then I went home.

3. How long do you study Japanese at home?
   Only 30 minutes. (*lit.* "(I) only do it for 30 minutes.")

4. I didn't go anywhere yesterday. I was at home.

Mr. Hayashi telephones a liquor store and orders some beer to be delivered.

はやし：もしもし、はやしですが、ビールを　20ぽん　もってきて
　　　　ください。

さかや：なんじまでに　とどけましょうか。

はやし：3じまでに　うちに　とどけてください。

さかや：はい、わかりました。ごじゅうしょを　おねがいします。

はやし：あざぶ　2ちょうめ　2の1です。

さかや：すみません、もう　いちど　いってください。

はやし：あざぶ　2ちょうめ　2の1です。

さかや：まいど　ありがとうございます。

■はやしさんは　さかやに　でんわを　しました。さかやは　はやしさ
　んの　じゅうしょを　きいて、はやしさんの　うちに　ビールを
　とどけました。

Hayashi:	Moshi moshi, Hayashi desu ga, bīru o 20-pon mottekite ḳudasai.
Saka-ya:	Nanji made ni todokemashō ka.
Hayashi:	3-ji made ni uchi ni todokete kudasai.
Saka-ya:	Hai, wakarimashita. Go-jūsho o onegaishimasu.
Hayashi:	Azabu 2-chōme 2 no 1 desu.
Saka-ya:	Sumimasen, mō ichi-do itte kudasai.
Hayashi:	Azabu 2-chōme 2 no 1 desu.
Saka-ya:	Maido arigatō gozaimasu.

■Hayashi-san wa saka-ya ni denwa o shimashita. Saka-ya wa Hayashi-san no jūsho o kiite, Hayashi-san no uchi ni bīru o todokemashita.

Hayashi:	Hello, this is Mr. Hayashi. Please bring me 20 bottles of beer.
Clerk:	By what time should we deliver it?
Hayashi:	Please deliver it to my house by 3:00.
Clerk:	Certainly, sir. Please give me your address.

Hayashi: It's 2–1 Azabu 2-*chōme*.
Clerk: Excuse me, would you repeat that, please?
Hayashi: It's 2–1 Azabu 2-*chōme*.
Clerk: Thank you, sir.

■ Mr. Hayashi telephoned the liquor store. The liquor store clerk asked Mr. Hayashi for his address and delivered the beer to his house.

| Vocabulary |

もってきて　ください	mottekite kudasai	please bring
もってきます（もってくる）	mottekimasu (mottekuru)	bring
なんじまでに	nan-ji made ni	by what time
～までに	made ni	by
とどけましょうか	todokemashō ka	Shall we deliver?
とどけます（とどける）	todokemasu (todokeru)	deliver
とどけてください	todokete kudasai	Please deliver . . .
2ちょうめ2の1	2-chōme 2 no 1	2-*chōme* 2–1
2ちょうめ	2-chōme	2-*chōme*
～ちょうめ	-chōme	*chōme*
いちど	ichi-do	once (*lit.* "one time")
～ど	-do	time (counter)
いって　ください	itte kudasai	Please say
いいます（いう）	iimasu (iu)	say
まいど ありがとう ございます	maido arigatō gozaimasu	Thank you (for your patronage) each time.
まいど	maido	each time

NOTES

1. 3-ji made ni

Do not confuse **3-ji made** and **3-ji made ni**.
  ex. **15-nichi made Tokyo ni ite kudasai.** "Please stay in Tokyo until the 15."
  15-nichi made ni Tokyo ni kite kudasai. "Please come to Tokyo by the 15."

2. Uchi ni todokete kudasai.

Requests are formed by verb **-te** + **kudasai**.

3. Azabu 2-chōme 2 no 1

Japanese city addresses are typically made up of a place name (often combined with **machi** or **chō**, "town, community") + **chōme** + **banchi** + **gō**. **Chōme** are sections of the **machi**. They may be regular in shape, like a city block, or irregular, their borders being formed by streets or natural features such as rivers. **Chōme** are subdivided into **banchi,** and the **gō** is the individual house or building number. In the address above, 2 **no** 1 is **banchi** number 2, house number 1. The words **banchi** and **gō** are frequently omitted both in speaking and in writing (except in legal documents).

PRACTICE

KEY SENTENCES

1. **Chotto matte kudasai.**
2. **Tsugi no kado o migi ni magatte kudasai.**
3. **Taipu o onegaishimasu.**

1. Just a moment, please.
2. Turn right at the next corner.
3. Please type this.

| Vocabulary |

matte kudasai	please wait	**magatte kudasai**	please turn
tsugi	next	**magarimasu (magaru)**	turn
kado	corner	**taipu**	typing
migi	right		

EXERCISES

I Verbs: Memorize the following verbs and their **-te** form.

	-masu form	**-te** form		**-masu** form	**-te** form
wait	**machi-masu**	**matte**	deliver	**todoke-masu**	**todokete**
turn	**magari-masu**	**magatte**	show	**mise-masu**	**misete**
bring	**motteki-masu**	**mottekite**	stop, park	**tome-masu**	**tomete**
say	**ii-masu**	**itte**			

II Practice the following pattern by changing the **-masu** form to the **-te** form.

    ex. **Chotto machimasu.** ⟶ **Chotto matte kudasai.**

       1. **Menyū o misemasu.**

       2. **Yukkuri iimasu.**

       3. **Bīru to jūsu o todokemasu.**

III Practice the following patterns by changing the underlined parts as in the examples given.

    A. *ex.* **Taipu o onegaishimasu.**

1. kopī
2. kēki
3. sandoitchi to sarada

B. *ex.* <u>Kopī</u> o <u>3-mai</u> onegaishimasu.

1. kēki, yottsu
2. bīru, 2-hon

C. *ex.* Tsugi no <u>kado</u> o <u>migi</u> ni magatte kudasai.

1. shingo, migi
2. kōsaten, hidari

IV Make dialogues by changing the underlined parts as in the examples given.

A. *ex.* A: <u>Mado</u> o <u>akemashō</u> ka.

B: Hai, <u>akete</u> kudasai.

1. doa, shimemasu
2. terebi, tsukemasu
3. rajio, keshimasu
4. jūsho to namae, kakimasu
5. denwa-bangō, iimasu

B. *ex.* A: Ashita denwa o <u>shite</u> kudasai.

B: Doko ni denwa o <u>shimashō</u> ka.

A: Kaisha ni [denwa o] <u>shite</u> kudasai.

B: Nan-ji ni [denwa o] <u>shimashō</u> ka.

A: 10-ji made ni onegaishimasu.

1. hana o todokemasu

Vocabulary

menyū	menu	shingō	traffic light
yukkuri	slowly	kōsaten	intersection
kēki	cake	hidari	left

SHORT DIALOGUE

Ueitoresu: Irasshaimase.
Yamada: Kōcha to kēki o onegaishimasu.
Ueitoresu: Hai, shōshō omachi kudasai.

Waitress: Good afternoon, madam.
Yamada: (A cup of) Tea and some cake, please.
Waitress: Certainly, madam. (Wait) Just a moment, please.

Vocabulary

ueitoresu   waitress

QUIZ

I Read this lesson's opening dialogue and answer the following questions.

1. **Hayashi-san wa doko ni denwa o shimashita ka.**
2. **Saka-ya wa doko ni bīru o todokemasu ka.**
3. **Saka-ya wa bīru o nan-bon todokemasu ka.**
4. **Saka-ya wa nan-ji made ni bīru o todokemasu ka.**
5. **Hayashi-san wa saka-ya ni jūsho o oshiemashita ka.**

II Convert the following verbs into their **-te** form.

1. iimasu
2. imasu
3. machimasu
4. **kikimasu**
5. **magarimasu**
6. **misemasu**
7. **mottekimasu**
8. **ikimasu**
9. **shimemasu**
10. **aimasu**
11. **nomimasu**
12. **shimasu**

III Put the appropriate particles in the parentheses. (If a particle is not required put an X in the parentheses.)

1. **Kore (　　) kudasai.**
2. **Bīru (　　) 5-hon (　　) kudasai.**
3. **Ashita 8-ji han made (　　) kite kudasai.**
4. **Kopī (　　) onegaishimasu.**
5. **Jūsu (　　) 5-hon (　　) bīru (　　) 12-hon uchi (　　) mottekite kudasai.**
6. **Tsugi no kado (　　) hidari (　　) magatte kudasai.**

IV Translate into Japanese.

1. Please show me the menu.
   Certainly. Here you are.
2. Excuse me, but could you please deliver 12 bottles of beer to my house.
   Yes, certainly. It's Mr. Clark, isn't it?
   Yes, that's right.
3. Please give me this small TV set.
   Yes, certainly, sir. Shall I deliver it?
   No, that's all right. (Because) I came by car.

LESSON 21 HAVING THINGS DONE

Giving directions to a taxi driver.

はやし： 　　とうきょうえきの　ちかくに　いってください。
うんてんしゅ：はい。

はやし： 　　つぎの　しんごうを　みぎに　まがって、まっすぐ
　　　　　　　いってください。

はやし： 　　あの　こうさてんの　てまえで　とめてください。

うんてんしゅ：1,200えんです。
はやし： 　　5,000えんで　おねがいします。
うんてんしゅ：3,800えんの　おつりです。
はやし： 　　どうも。

Hayashi: **Tōkyō Eki no chikaku ni itte kudasai.**
Untenshu: **Hai.**

Hayashi: **Tsugi no shingō o migi ni magatte, massugu itte kudasai.**

Hayashi: **Ano kōsaten no temae de tomete kudasai.**

Untenshu: **1,200-en desu.**
Hayashi: **5,000-en de onegaishimasu.**
Untenshu: **3,800-en no otsuri desu.**
Hayashi: **Dōmo.**

Hayashi: (I want to) go to the neighborhood of Tokyo Station, please.
Driver: Yes, sir.

Hayashi: Please turn right at the next traffic light and go straight ahead.

Hayashi: Please stop just before that crossing.

Driver: That's ¥1,200.
Hayashi: Please take it out of this ¥5,000.
Driver: Here's (your) change, ¥3,800.
Hayashi: Thanks.

うんてんしゅ	untenshu	driver
まっすぐ	massugu	straight ahead
てまえ	temae	just before
とめてください	tomete kudasai	Please stop.
とめます（とめる）	tomemasu (tomeru)	stop
おつり	otsuri	change
どうも	dōmo	thanks (colloquial)

Making a reservation at a restaurant by telephone.

レストランの　ひと：レストランとうきょうでございます。

はやし：　　　　　　よやくを　おねがいします。

レストランの　ひと：はい、ありがとうございます。いつですか。

はやし：　　　　　　あしたの　ばんです。7じごろ　おねがいします。

レストランの　ひと：なんにんさまですか。

はやし：　　　　　　6にんです。

レストランの　ひと：はい、わかりました。おなまえと　おでんわばん
　　　　　　　　　　ごうを　どうぞ。

Resutoran no hito:	Resutoran Tōkyō de gozaimasu.
Hayashi:	Yoyaku o onegaishimasu.
Resutoran no hito:	Hai, arigatō gozaimasu. Itsu desu ka.
Hayashi:	Ashita no ban desu. 7-ji goro onegaishimasu.
Resutoran no hito:	Nan-nin-sama desu ka.
Hayashi:	6-nin desu.
Resutoran no hito:	Hai, wakarimashita. O-namae to o-denwa-bangō o dōzo.

Restaurant employee:	This is Restaurant Tokyo.
Hayashi:	I'd like to make a reservation.
Restaurant employee:	Thank you. When would you like it for?
Hayashi:	Tomorrow evening, about 7 o'clock.
Restaurant employee:	For how many?
Hayashi:	Six.
Restaurant employee:	Certainly, sir. May I have your name and telephone number, please?

レストランとうきょう	Resutoran Tōkyō	Restaurant Tokyo

よやく	**yoyaku**	reservation
なんにんさま	**nan-nin-sama**	how many people (shopkeeper's expression)
～さま	**-sama**	politer form of **-san**

Having things cleaned.

はやし：　　　　クリーニングを　おねがいします。いつ　できますか。
クリーニングや：すいようびの　ごご　できます。

■はやしさんは　すいようびの　ごご　クリーニングやに　いきました。

はやし：　　　　もう　できましたか。
クリーニングや：すみません。まだです。4じごろ　できます。
はやし：　　　　じゃ、また　きます。

Hayashi: **Kurīningu o onegaishimasu. Itsu dekimasu ka.**
Kurīningu-ya: **Sui-yōbi no gogo dekimasu.**

■ **Hayashi-san wa sui-yōbi no gogo kurīningu-ya ni ikimashita.**

Hayashi: **Mō dekimashita ka.**
Kurīningu-ya: **Sumimasen. Mada desu. 4-ji goro dekimasu.**
Hayashi: **Ja, mata kimasu.**

Hayashi:　I'd like to have this (these) cleaned. When will it (they) be done?
Clerk:　　It (they) will be done on Wednesday afternoon.

■ Mr. Hayashi went to the cleaner's on Wednesday afternoon.

Hayashi:　Is it (are they) ready?
Clerk:　　I'm sorry, it's (they're) not finished yet. It (they) will be ready about 4:00.
Hayashi:　I'll come back, then.

Vocabulary

クリーニング	**kurīningu**	dry cleaning
できます（できる）	**dekimasu (dekiru)**	be ready (finished, done)
クリーニングや	**kurīningu-ya**	dry cleaner
まだです	**mada desu**	not yet
まだ	**mada**	yet

LESSON 22 PUBLIC TRANSPORTATION

Mrs. Tanaka went to visit Haruko at the hospital. Mrs. Hayashi is going to visit her tomorrow and is asking how to get to Tokyo Hospital.

たなか：せんしゅう　とうきょうびょういんに　いきました。

はやし：はるこさんは　どうでしたか。

たなか：あまり　げんきでは　ありませんでした。

はやし：どうやって　とうきょうびょういんに　いきましたか。わたし　　　　も　あした　いきます。

たなか：とうきょうえきで　80ばんの　バスに　のりました。あざぶ　　　　で　おりて、びょういんまで　5ふんぐらい　あるきました。

はやし：そうですか。とうきょうえきから　あざぶまで　どのぐらい　　　　かかりますか。

たなか：バスで　30ぷん　かかります。

■たなかさんの　おくさんは　せんしゅう　とうきょうびょういんに　いきました。たなかさんの　おくさんは　とうきょうえきで　バスに　のって、あざぶで　おりました。とうきょうえきから　あざぶまで　30ぷん　かかりました。それから　びょういんまで　5ふんぐらい　あるきました。

Tanaka:	Senshū Tōkyō Byōin ni ikimashita.
Hayashi:	Haruko-san wa dō deshita ka.
Tanaka:	Amari genki dewa arimasendeshita.
Hayashi:	Dōyatte Tōkyō Byōin ni ikimashita ka. Watashi mo ashita iki-masu.
Tanaka:	Tōkyō Eki de 80-ban no basu ni norimashita. Azabu de orite, byōin made 5-fun gurai arukimashita.
Hayashi:	Sō desu ka. Tōkyō Eki kara Azabu made donogurai kakarimasu ka.
Tanaka:	Basu de 30-pun kakarimasu.

■ Tanaka-san no okusan wa senshū Tōkyō Byōin ni ikimashita. Tanaka-san no okusan wa Tōkyō Eki de basu ni notte, Azabu de orimashita. Tōkyō Eki kara Azabu made 30-pun kakarimashita. Sorekara byōin made 5-fun gurai arukimashita.

Tanaka: I went to Tokyo Hospital last week.
Hayashi: How was Haruko?
Tanaka: She wasn't feeling very well.
Hayashi: How did you get to Tokyo Hospital? I'm going, too, tomorrow.
Tanaka: I took a No. 80 bus from Tokyo Station. I got off at Azabu and walked about 5 minutes to (get to) the hospital.
Hayashi: I see. How long does it take from Tokyo Station to Azabu?
Tanaka: It takes 30 minutes by bus.

■ Mrs. Tanaka went to Tokyo Hospital last week. She took a bus from Tokyo Station and got off at Azabu. It took 30 minutes from Tokyo Station to Azabu. Then she walked about 5 minutes to Tokyo Hospital.

Vocabulary		
とうきょうびょういん	**Tōkyō Byōin**	Tokyo Hospital
どうやって	**dōyatte**	how
に	**ni**	on (particle)
のりました	**norimashita**	took, got on
のります（のる）	**norimasu (noru)**	take, get on
おりて	**orite**	get/got off (and)
おります（おりる）	**orimasu (oriru)**	get off
まで	**made**	to, as far as
あるきました	**arukimashita**	walked
あるきます（あるく）	**arukimasu (aruku)**	walk
かかります（かかる）	**kakarimasu (kakaru)**	(it) takes

NOTES

1. **Tōkyō Eki de basu ni norimashita. Azabu de (basu o) orimashita.**

   Note the particles used: **basu NI norimasu,** "take/get on a bus"
   basu O orimasu, "get off the bus"
   Tōkyō Eki DE, "at Tokyo Station"
   Azabu DE, "at Azabu"

2. **5-fun gurai**

   An approximate time period is expressed by the suffix **-gurai.**
   ex. **5-fun gurai,** "about 5 minutes"
   2-jikan gurai, "about 2 hours"
   3-shūkan gurai, "about 3 weeks"

Do not confuse with **goro,** which expresses an approximate specific time. (See Note 5, p. 89.)

3. **Nan-pun, nan-jikan, nan-nichi**
   How many minutes, hours, days.
   ex. **Nan-jikan kakarimasu ka.** "How long (*lit.* "how many hours") does it take?"
   To ask in a more general way, **donogurai,** "how long," may be used.
   ex. **Donogurai kakarimasu ka.** "How long does/will it take?"
   Donogurai is also used to ask how much something will cost.
   ex. **Donogurai/Ikura kakarimasu ka.** "How much will it cost?"

PRACTICE

KEY SENTENCES

1. **Hikōki wa gozen 8-ji 10-pun ni Narita Kūkō o demasu.**
2. **Sumisu-san wa gogo 3-ji ni Narita Kūkō ni tsukimashita.**
3. **Tōkyō Eki de basu ni notte, Ginza de basu o orite kudasai.**
4. **[Watashi no] Uchi kara eki made basu de 10-pun kakarimasu.**

1. The airplane leaves Narita Airport at 8:10 A.M.
2. Mr. Smith arrived at Narita Airport at 3:00 P.M.
3. Take the bus from Tokyo Station and get off at the Ginza.
4. It takes 10 minutes by bus from my house to the station.

Vocabulary

o	from (particle)
demasu (deru)	leave
tsukimashita	arrived
tsukimasu (tsuku)	arrive

EXERCISES

I Verbs: Memorize the following verbs and their **-te** form.

	-masu form	**-te** form		**-masu** form	**-te** form
go out, leave	**de-masu**	**dete**	get off	**ori-masu**	**orite**
arrive	**tsuki-masu**	**tsuite**	walk	**aruki-masu**	**aruite**
take, get on	**nori-masu**	**notte**	take	**kakari-masu**	**kakatte**

II Practice the following patterns by changing the underlined parts as in the examples given.

  A. *ex.* **[Watashi wa] <u>Densha</u> ni norimasu. <u>Densha</u> o orimasu.**

1. basu

2. takushī

B. *ex.* Tanaka-san wa <u>hiru</u> Ōsaka o demashita. <u>Yūgata</u> Tōkyō ni tsukimashita.

    1. 6-ji ni, uchi, 7-ji ni, kaisha

    2. asa, Kyōto, 11-ji goro, Tōkyō no uchi

III Make dialogues by changing the underlined parts as in the examples given.

A. *ex.* Q: <u>Hikōki</u> wa nan-ji ni Ōsaka o demasu ka.

    A: <u>Gozen 7-ji</u> ni demasu.

    Q: [Hikōki wa] Nan-ji ni Tōkyō ni tsukimasu ka.

    A: <u>Gozen 8-ji</u> ni tsukimasu.

    1. Shinkansen, gogo 1-ji, gogo 4-ji 10-pun

    2. Tanaka-san, gozen 10-ji, gogo 1-ji han

B. *ex.* Q: <u>Ueno Eki</u> de nani ni norimashita ka.

    A: <u>Densha</u> ni norimashita.

    Q: Doko de <u>densha</u> o orimashita ka.

    A: <u>Tōkyō Eki</u> de orimashita.

    1. basu, kōen no mae

    2. takushī, uchi no chikaku

Vocabulary

yūgata   late afternoon, early evening
Ueno   Ueno (place name)

SHORT DIALOGUE

Howaito: Yamada-san wa dōyatte kaisha ni ikimasu ka.

Yamada: Azabu de basu ni notte, Aoyama 1-chōme de orimasu. Aoyama 1-chōme kara chikatetsu ni notte, Nihombashi de orimasu. Soshite kaisha made 5-fun gurai arukimasu.

Howaito: O-taku kara kaisha made donogurai kakarimasu ka.

Yamada: 1-jikan gurai kakarimasu.

White: How do you go to (your) office?

Yamada: I take a bus from Azabu and get off at Aoyama 1-*chōme*. I take the subway from Aoyama 1-*chōme* and get off at Nihombashi and walk about 5 minutes to my office.

White: How long does it take from your house to your office?

Yamada: It takes about one hour.

Vocabulary

Aoyama   Aoyama (place name)
Nihombashi   Nihombashi (place name)

QUIZ

I Read this lesson's opening dialogue and answer the following questions.

1. **Tanaka-san no okusan wa itsu Tōkyō Byōin ni ikimashita ka.**
2. **Hayashi-san no okusan wa Tanaka-san no okusan to issho ni Tōkyō Byōin ni ikimashita ka.**
3. **Hayashi-san no okusan wa itsu Tōkyō Byōin ni ikimasu ka.**
4. **Tanaka-san no okusan wa doko de basu o orimashita ka.**
5. **Tōkyō Eki kara Azabu made basu de 1-jikan gurai kakarimashita ka.**

II Complete the questions so that they fit the answers.

1. **Kaisha ni (   ) de ikimasu ka.**
   Chikatetsu de ikimasu.
2. **(   ) de basu o orimasu ka.**
   Tōkyō Eki no mae de orimasu.
3. **(   ) ni norimashō ka.**
   Takushī ni norimasen ka. Tenki ga warui desu kara.
4. **Tōkyō kara Ōsaka made Shinkansen de (   ) kakarimasu ka.**
   3-jikan gurai kakarimasu.
5. **(   ) koko ni kimashita ka.**
   Tōkyō Eki de densha o orite, basu ni norimashita. Soshite kōen no chikaku de orite, aruite kimashita.

III Put the appropriate particles in the parentheses. (If a particle is not required, put an X in the parentheses.)

1. **Tōkyō Eki (   ) basu (   ) notte, Ginza (   ) basu (   ) orite kudasai.**
2. **Asa Kyōto (   ) dete, 5-ji (   ) Tōkyō (   ) tsukimashita. Nan (   ) kimashita ka.**
   Kuruma de kimashita.
3. **Uchi kara eki (   ) basu (   ) 15-fun (   ) kakarimasu.**

IV Translate into Japanese.

1. There was a farewell party for a friend (of mine) at a hotel in the Ginza yesterday.
2. I left the office at 6 o'clock, took a bus, and got off at the Ginza.
3. How long did it take you from the office to the hotel?
   It took about 35 minutes.

LESSON **23** ASKING PERMISSION

Mr. Smith went to an electrical appliance store.

スミス：　この　テレビを　つけても　いいですか。

でんきや：はい、どうぞ。つけてください。

スミス：　この　テレビの　カタログは　ありますか。

でんきや：はい、その　ケースの　うえに　あります。

スミス：　もらっても　いいですか。

でんきや：はい、どうぞ。

スミス：　どうも　ありがとう。

■スミスさんは　でんきやで　テレビの　カタログを　もらいました。

Sumisu:	Kono terebi o tsukete mo ii desu ka.
Denki-ya:	Hai, dōzo tsukete kudasai.
Sumisu:	Kono terebi no katarogu wa arimasu ka.
Denki-ya:	Hai, sono kēsu no ue ni arimasu.
Sumisu:	Moratte mo ii desu ka.
Denki-ya:	Hai, dōzo.
Sumisu:	Dōmo arigatō.

■Sumisu-san wa denki-ya de terebi no katarogu o moraimashita.

Smith:	May I turn this TV set on?
Salesman:	Certainly, sir. (Please turn it on.)
Smith:	Do you have a brochure about this set?
Salesman:	Yes. (They're) On top of that showcase.
Smith:	May I have one?
Salesman:	Certainly, sir.
Smith:	Thank you very much.

■Mr. Smith got a TV set brochure at an electrical appliance store.

Vocabulary

つけても　いいですか	**tsukete mo ii desu ka**	May I turn it on?

でんきや	denki-ya	electrical appliance store or clerk
カタログ	katarogu	catalogue, brochure
ケース	kēsu	showcase

NOTES

1. **Terebi o tsukete mo ii desu ka.**

   (Terebi no katarogu o) Moratte mo ii desu ka.

   Asking permission to do something is done using the following sentence construction.

      Verb **-te** form + **mo ii desu ka**

   Permission is given as follows. The first is politer than the second.
      1. **Hai, dōzo.** "Yes, please (do)."
      2. **Hai, ii desu.** "Yes, you may."
   For refusal of permission, see Note 1, p. 155.

PRACTICE

KEY SENTENCES

1. **Koko de shashin o totte mo ii desu ka.**
2. **Kono heya o tsukatte mo ii desu.**

1. May (I) take a photograph here?
2. You may use this room.

Vocabulary

shashin o totte mo ii desu ka	May (I) take a photograph?
shashin o torimasu (toru)	take a photograph
tsukatte mo ii desu	You may use it.
tsukaimasu (tsukau)	use

EXERCISES

I Verbs: Memorize the following verbs and their **-te** form.

	-masu form	**-te** form
take (a photograph)	**(shashin o) tori-masu**	**totte**
use	**tsukai-masu**	**tsukatte**
go in, enter	**hairi-masu**	**haitte**

II Practice the following patterns.

    A. *ex.* **Shashin o torimasu.** ──────→ **Shashin o totte mo ii desu.**

                                  ──────→ **Shashin o totte mo ii desu ka.**

        1. **kono heya o tsukaimasu**

        2. **kono mizu o nomimasu**

        3. **rajio o tsukemasu**

        4. **mado o akemasu**

        5. **daidokoro ni hairimasu**

III Make dialogues by changing the underlined parts as in the examples given.

    A. *ex.* A: <u>Kono katarogu o moratte</u> mo ii desu ka.

           B: **Hai, dōzo.**

        1. **kamera no katarogu o moraimasu**

        2. **kono pen o tsukaimasu**

        3. **o-tearai o tsukaimasu**

        4. **koko de shashin o torimasu**

        5. **kono mizu o nomimasu**

        6. **daidokoro ni hairimasu**

    B. *ex.* A: <u>Mado o akete</u> mo ii desu ka.

           B: **Hai, dōzo. <u>Akete</u> kudasai.**

        1. **rajio, tsukemasu**

        2. **doa, shimemasu**

Vocabulary

pen pen

SHORT DIALOGUES

1. **Yamada:**   **Ashita 2-ji goro denwa o shite mo ii desu ka.**

   Hayashi: **Sumimasen ga, [watashi wa] 2-ji goro uchi ni imasen kara, 6-ji goro onegaishimasu.**

   Yamada: **Hai, wakarimashita.**

   Yamada: May I call you about 2 o'clock tomorrow?

   Hayashi: I'm sorry, but I won't be at home about 2:00, so call me about 6:00.

   Yamada: I see.

2. **Ten'in:**   **Go-jūsho to o-namae o onegaishimasu.**

   Hayashi: **Sumimasen. Pen ga arimasen. Kono pen o tsukatte mo ii desu ka.**

   Ten'in: **Hai, dōzo.**

   Clerk: Your name and address, please.

Hayashi: I'm afraid I don't have a pen. May I use this pen?
Clerk: Certainly. Please do.

3. **Tanaka:** **Koko wa yūmeina o-tera desu. Naka ni hairimashō.**
   Sumisu: **Subarashii niwa desu ne. Kono niwa no shashin o totte mo ii desu ka.**
   Tanaka: **Sā, wakarimasen. Ano hito ni kikimashō.**

Tanaka: This is a famous temple. Let's go inside.
Smith: What a wonderful garden. May I take a picture of this garden?
Tanaka: Well, I don't know. Let's ask that man over there.

Vocabulary

subarashii   wonderful (-i adj.)
sā   well . . .

QUIZ

I Read this lesson's opening dialogue and answer the following questions.

1. **Sumisu-san wa doko de katarogu o moraimashita ka.**
2. **Sumisu-san wa nan no katarogu o moraimashita ka.**
3. **Katarogu wa kēsu no naka ni arimashita ka.**
4. **Katarogu wa doko ni arimashita ka.**

II Convert the following verbs into their **-te** form.

1. **hairimasu**	4. **mimasu**	7. **shimasu**	10. **ikimasu**
2. **kimasu**	5. **tsukaimasu**	8. **torimasu**	11. **imasu**
3. **tabemasu**	6. **nomimasu**	9. **kikimasu**	12. **iimasu**

III Complete the sentences with the appropriate form of the verbs indicated.

1. **Koko de shashin o (   ) mo ii desu ka.**   (torimasu)
2. **Issho ni tenisu o (   ) masen ka.**   (shimasu)
   Ee, (   ) mashō.   (shimasu)
3. **Mado o (   ) mashō ka.**   (akemasu)
   Hai, (   ) kudasai.   (akemasu)
4. **Kono denwa o (   ) mo ii desu ka.**   (tsukaimasu)
   Sumimasen, chotto (   ) kudasai.   (machimasu)
5. **Ashita nan-ji ni (   ) mashō ka.**   (kimasu)
   8-ji han ni (   ) kudasai.   (kimasu)
6. **Kono katarogu o (   ) mo ii desu ka.**   (moraimasu)
7. **Hon o (   ), uchi ni kaerimashita.**   (kaimasu)

IV Translate into Japanese.

1. Shall I turn on the light?
   Yes, please.
2. May I use this telephone?
   Yes, of course. (*lit.* "please.")
3. Is it O.K. to stay here till 3 o'clock?

LESSON 24 REFUSAL

A man parked his car in a "No Parking" area.

けいかん： もしもし、ここは　ちゅうしゃきんしですから、くるま
　　　　　　を　とめないでください。

おとこのひと：すみません。この　ちかくに　ちゅうしゃじょうが
　　　　　　ありますか。

けいかん： ええ、つぎの　かどを　ひだりに　まがって　ください。
　　　　　　ひだりがわに　ちゅうしゃじょうが　あります。

おとこのひと：どうも　ありがとう。

■けいかんは　おとこのひとに　ちゅうしゃじょうを　おしえました。

Keikan:	Moshi moshi, koko wa "Chūsha Kinshi" desu kara, kuruma o tomenaide kudasai.
Otoko no hito:	Sumimasen. Kono chikaku ni chūshajō ga arimasu ka.
Keikan:	Ee, tsugi no kado o hidari ni magatte kudasai. Hidari-gawa ni chūshajō ga arimasu.
Otoko no hito:	Dōmo arigatō.

■ **Keikan wa otoko no hito ni chūshajō o oshiemashita.**

Policeman:	I say, this is a "No Parking" (area), so don't park (your) car here.
Man:	I'm sorry. Is there a place to park nearby?
Policeman:	Yes. Turn left at the next corner. There's a parking lot on the left-hand side.
Man:	Thank you very much.

■ A policeman directed the man to a parking lot.

Vocabulary

けいかん	**keikan**	policeman
もしもし	**moshi moshi**	I say
ちゅうしゃきんし	**chūsha kinshi**	No Parking
とめないで　ください	**tomenaide kudasai**	Do not park.
とめます（とめる）	**tomemasu (tomeru)**	park

154

| ちゅうしゃじょう | **chūshajō** | parking lot |
| ひだりがわ | **hidari-gawa** | left-hand side |

NOTE

1. **Tomenaide kudasai**

   The "please do not . . ." construction is formed as follows: verb **nai** + **de** + **kudasai**

   (For explanation of the **-nai** form, see Grammar IX, p. 130).

   For refusal of permission, **Iie, dame desu,** "No, you can't," is sometimes used. **Dame,** "no good, useless, hopeless, out of the question," is a frequently used word in Japanese. Straightforward prohibitive requests such as this are seldom used in politer society. Instead, one says, **Sumimasen, ga,** "Excuse me, but . . ." "I'm sorry, but . . ." and simply gives the reason for not wanting something done,

   ex. **O-taku ni kuruma de itte mo ii desu ka.** "Is it all right to go to your house by car?"

   Sumimasen ga, chūshajō ga arimasen kara . . . "I'm sorry, but there's no parking place."

PRACTICE

KEY SENTENCES

1. **Koko de tabako o suwanaide kudasai.**
2. **Koko wa "Chūsha Kinshi" desu kara, kuruma o tomenaide kudasai.**

1. Please don't smoke here.
2. This is a "No Parking" (area), so don't park (your) car here.

Vocabulary	
tabako	tobacco, cigarette
suwanaide kudasai	Do not smoke.
suimasu (suu)	smoke, inhale

EXERCISES

I Verbs: Memorize the following verbs and their **-nai** form.

	-masu form	**-te** form	**-nai** form
inhale	**sui-masu**	sutte	suwanai
stop, park	**tome-masu**	tomete	tomenai

take (a photograph)	(shashin o) tori-masu	totte	toranai
use	tsukai-masu	tsukatte	tsukawanai
open	ake-masu	akete	akenai
close	shime-masu	shimete	shimenai

II Practice the following pattern.

    ex. **tabako o suimasu** ⟶ **Tabako o suwanaide kudasai.**

        1. **kuruma o tomemasu**

        2. **shashin o torimasu**

        3. **kono heya o tsukaimasu**

        4. **mado o akemasu**

        5. **doa o shimemasu**

III Make dialogues by changing the underlined part as in the examples given.

    A. *ex.* **A: Doa o shimete mo ii desu ka.**

          B: Iie, shimenaide kudasai. Atsui desu kara.

        1. **mado**

        2. **kono doa**

    B. *ex.* **A: Koko wa iriguchi desu kara, kuruma o tomenaide kudasai.**

          B: Dōmo sumimasen.

        1. **deguchi**

        2. **mise no mae**

Vocabulary

deguchi   exit

SHORT DIALOGUES

1. **Otoko no hito:** **Koko de tabako o sutte mo ii desu ka.**
   Sumisu: **Sumimasen ga, suwanaide kudasai.**

   Man: May I smoke here?
   Smith: I'm afraid not. (*lit.* "I'm sorry, please don't.")

2. **Onna no hito:** **Denki o keshimashō ka.**
   Tanaka: **Iie, ima kara kono heya o tsukaimasu kara, kesanaide kudasai.**

   Woman: Shall I turn off the light?
   Tanaka: No, we are going to use this room (from now), so don't turn it off.

QUIZ ▓▓▓▓▓▓▓

I Read this lesson's opening dialogue and answer the following questions.

1. **Dare ga otoko no hito ni chūshajō o oshiemashita ka.**
2. **Otoko no hito wa doko o hidari ni magarimasu ka.**
3. **Otoko no hito wa tsugi no kado o hidari ni magatte, doko ni ikimasu ka.**

II Convert the following verbs into their **-nai** form.

1. tabemasu	6. yomimasu	11. keshimasu
2. mimasu	7. shimasu	12. tsukemasu
3. ikimasu	8. suimasu	13. tsukaimasu
4. kimasu	9. akemasu	14. shimemasu
5. iimasu	10. magarimasu	15. torimasu

III Complete the sentences with the appropriate form of the verbs indicated.

1. **Koko de tabako o (   ) mo ii desu ka.** (suimasu)
   Iie, sumimasen ga, (   ) kudasai. (suimasu)
2. **Mado o (   ) mo ii desu ka.** (akemasu)
   Hai, (   ) mo ii desu. (akemasu)
3. **Ashita o-taku ni (   ) mo ii desu ka.** (ikimasu)
   Hai, dōzo (   ) kudasai. (kimasu)
4. **Doa o (   ) mashō ka.** (shimemasu)
   Iie, (   ) kudasai. Atsui desu kara. (shimemasu)

IV Put the appropriate particles in the parentheses. (If a particle is not required, put an X in the parentheses.)

1. **Koko (   ) "Chūsha Kinshi" desu (   ), kuruma (   ) tome-naide kudasai.**
2. **Tsugi no kado (   ) hidari (   ) magatte kudasai.**
3. **Densha (   ) tabako (   ) suwanaide kudasai.**
4. **Kinō no asa 8-ji goro uchi (   ) dete, yoru 10-ji (   ) kaerimashita.**

V Translate into Japanese.

1. Please do not go into that room now.
2. Please do not smoke here.
3. Turn right at the next traffic light.

LESSON  NOW IN PROGRESS

Mr. Hayashi is looking for Mr. Smith. He knocks on the door.

はやし：すみません、スミスさんは　いますか。

ひしょ：いいえ、いません。3がいの　かいぎしつに　います。

はやし：かいぎを　していますか。

ひしょ：いいえ、スライドを　みています。

はやし：どうも。

■スミスさんは　かいぎしつで　スライドを　みています。

Hayashi: Sumimasen, Sumisu-san wa imasu ka.
Hisho: Iie, imasen. 3-gai no kaigi-shitsu ni imasu.
Hayashi: Kaigi o shite imasu ka.
Hisho: Iie, suraido o mite imasu.
Hayashi: Dōmo.

■Sumisu-san wa kaigi-shitsu de suraido o mite imasu.

Hayashi: Excuse me, is Mr. Smith here?
Secretary: No, he isn't. He's in the conference room on the third floor.
Hayashi: Is he in conference?
Secretary: No. He's looking at (some) slides.
Hayashi: Thanks.

■Mr. Smith is looking at slides in the conference room.

Vocabulary

かいぎしつ	**kaigi-shitsu**	conference room
～しつ	**-shitsu**	room
かいぎをしています	**kaigi o shite imasu**	is in conference
（している）	**(shite iru)**	
スライド	**suraido**	slide
みています（みている）	**mite imasu (mite iru)**	is looking

NOTES

1. Kaigi o shite imasu.
Suraido o mite imasu.

The present progressive is expressed as follows: verb **-te** + **imasu**.

This construction expresses either action that is presently going on or action that regularly takes place.

ex. **Sumisu-san wa maishū Taimu o yonde imasu.** "Mr. Smith reads *Time* every week."

There is also the past progressive.

ex. **Kinō no gogo nani o shite imashita ka.** "What were you doing yesterday afternoon?"

2. Dōmo

A colloquial shortening of **dōmo arigatō**, "Thank you so much." It is also widely used as an abbreviation of **dōmo sumimasen**, "I'm sorry." It is not especially polite.

PRACTICE

KEY SENTENCES

1. **Yamada-san wa ima denwa o shite imasu.**
2. **Howaito-san wa ima shigoto o shite imasu.**

1. Mr. Yamada is making a telephone call now.
2. Miss White is working now.

Vocabulary

denwa o shite imasu	is telephoning
shigoto o shite imasu	is working

EXERCISES

I Verbs: Memorize the following **-te imasu** forms.

		Present Progressive	
		aff.	*neg.*
	-masu form	**-te imasu**	**-te imasen**
talk	**hanashi o shi-masu**	**hanashi o shite imasu**	**hanashi o shite imasen**
read	**yomi-masu**	**yonde imasu**	**yonde imasen**
listen	**kiki-masu**	**kiite imasu**	**kiite imasen**
write	**kaki-masu**	**kaite imasu**	**kaite imasen**

Past Progressive		
	aff.	*neg.*
	-te imashita	**-te imasendeshita**
talk	hanashi o shite imashita	hanashi o shite imasendeshita
read	yonde imashita	yonde imasendeshita
listen	kiite imashita	kiite imasendeshita
write	kaite imashita	kaite imasendeshita

II Practice the following pattern.

   ex. hon o yomimasu ⟶ Tanaka-san wa hon o yonde imasu.

     1. rajio o kikimasu   Tanaka-san wa
     2. tegami o kakimasu   Tanaka-san wa
     3. tomodachi to hanashi o shimasu   Tanaka-san wa

III Make dialogues by changing the underlined parts as in the examples given.

  A. *ex.* Q: Ima hon o yonde imasu ka.

        A*a*: Hai, yonde imasu.

        A*n*: Iie, yonde imasen.

      1. kōhī, nomimasu

      2. tegami, kakimasu

      3. shigoto, shimasu

  B. *ex.* Q: Dare ga denwa o shite imasu ka.

        A: Howaito-san ga [denwa o] shite imasu.

      1. terebi o mimasu, Yamada-san

      2. tegami o kakimasu, Sumisu-san

  C. *ex.* Q: Yamada-san wa nani o shite imasu ka.

        A: Shimbun o yonde imasu.

      1. Howaito-san, denwa o shimasu

      2. Ichirō-san, terebi o mimasu

      3. Tanaka-san, bīru o nomimasu

  D. *ex.* Q: Yamada-san wa doko de shashin o totte imasu ka.

        A: Niwa de [shashin o] totte imasu.

      1. denwa o shimasu, tonari no heya

      2. hon o yomimasu, ima

  E. *ex.* Q: Yamada-san wa ima kōhī o nonde imasu ka.

        A: Iie, shimbun o yonde imasu.

      1. denwa o shimasu, tegami o kakimasu

      2. kaigi o shimasu, shokuji o shimasu

      3. shashin o torimasu, Howaito-san to hanashi o shimasu

hanashi o shimasu (suru)   talk
Ichirō   a given name (male)

SHORT DIALOGUE ─────────────────────────

Hayashi: **Yamada-san wa ima doko ni imasu ka.**
Howaito: **Tonari no heya ni imasu.**
Hayashi: **[Yamada-san wa] Ima nani o shite imasu ka.**
Howaito: **Okyaku-san to hanashi o shite imasu.**

Hayashi: Where is Miss Yamada now?
White: [She's] In the next room.
Hayashi: What's she doing now?
White: [She's] Talking with a client.

Vocabulary

o-kyaku-san   client

QUIZ ▰▰▰▰▰▰

I Read this lesson's opening dialogue and answer the following questions.

1. **Sumisu-san wa 2-kai ni imasu ka, 3-gai ni imasu ka.**
2. **Sumisu-san wa 3-gai no doko ni imasu ka.**
3. **Sumisu-san wa nani o shite imasu ka.**

II Complete the questions so that they fit the answers.

1. **Tanaka-san wa ima (   ) ni imasu ka.**
   2-kai ni imasu.
   2-kai de (   ) o shite imasu ka.
   Tegami o kaite imasu.
2. **Hayashi-san wa (   ) de shashin o totte imasu ka.**
   Asoko de totte imasu.
3. **Sumisu-san wa (   ) to hanashi o shite imasu ka.**
   Sumisu-san no hisho to hanashi o shite imasu.
4. **Howaito-san wa (   ) ni denwa o shite imasu ka.**
   Kaisha ni shite imasu.

III Translate into Japanese.

1. Mr. Hayashi will telephone Mr. Smith.

2. Mr. Hayashi is telephoning Mr. Smith.
3. What is that girl over there doing?
   She is waiting for a friend.
4. Miss White is not working now.

■すずきさんが ブラウンさんの うちに でんわを しました。すず
　きさんは ブラウンさんの ともだちです。

すずき： もしもし、すずきですが、ブラウンさんの おたくですか。
ブラウン：あ、すずきさん、こんばんは。
すずき： ブラウンさん、らいしゅうの どようびの ばん、わたしの
　　　　　うちで パーティーを します。わたしの たんじょうびの
　　　　　パーティーです。おくさんと いっしょに きませんか。
ブラウン：どうも ありがとうございます。よろこんで いきます。
すずき： では、どようびに。
ブラウン：おでんわ どうも ありがとうございました。

■きょうは パーティーの ひです。
　ブラウンさんと おくさんが すずきさんの うちに つきました。

すずき： よく いらっしゃいました。こちらに どうぞ。
ブラウン：おまねき ありがとうございます。これを どうぞ。
すずき： きれいな はなですね。どうも ありがとうございます。
ブラウン：この ワインも どうぞ。
すずき： みなさんに ごしょうかい しますから、どうぞ こちらに。

■とても にぎやかな パーティーです。

■12じです。みんなは かえります。

すずきさんの ともだち：ブラウンさん、くるまで きましたか。
ブラウン：　　　　　　　　いいえ、でんしゃで きました。

163

すずきさんの　ともだち：おそいですから　わたしの　くるまで　かえ
　　　　　　　　　　　　りませんか。

ブラウン：　　　　　　　そうですか。ありがとうございます。おねが
　　　　　　　　　　　　いします。

みんな：　　　　　　　　とても　たのしかったです。きょうは　どう
　　　　　　　　　　　　も　ありがとう　ございました。

すずき：　　　　　　　　どういたしまして。わたしも　たのしかった
　　　　　　　　　　　　です。また　きてください。

すずきさんの　おくさん：どうぞ　きをつけて。

みんな：　　　　　　　　おやすみなさい。

すずき：　　　　　　　　おやすみなさい。

■ Suzuki-san ga Buraun-san no uchi ni denwa o shimashita. Suzuki-san wa
　Buraun-san no tomodachi desu.

Suzuki:　Moshi moshi, Suzuki desu ga, Buraun-san no o-taku desu ka.
Buraun:　A, Suzuki-san, kombanwa.
Suzuki:　Buraun-san, raishū no do-yōbi no ban, watashi no uchi de pātī o
　　　　　shimasu. Watashi no tanjōbi no pātī desu. Okusan to issho ni ki-
　　　　　masen ka.
Buraun:　Dōmo arigatō gozaimasu. Yorokonde ikimasu.
Suzuki:　Dewa, do-yōbi ni.
Buraun:　O-denwa dōmo arigatō gozaimashita.

■ Kyō wa pātī no hi desu. Buraun-san to okusan ga Suzuki-san no uchi ni
　tsukimashita.

Suzuki:　Yoku irasshaimashita. Kochira ni dōzo.
Buraun:　Omaneki arigatō gozaimasu. Kore o dōzo.
Suzuki:　Kireina hana desu ne. Dōmo arigatō gozaimasu.
Buraun:　Kono wain mo dōzo.
Suzuki:　Mina-san ni go-shōkai shimasu kara, dōzo kochira ni.

■ Totemo nigiyakana pātī desu.

■ 12-ji desu. Minna wa kaerimasu.

Suzuki-san no tomodachi:　Buraun-san, kuruma de kimashita ka.
Buraun:　　　　　　　　　 Iie, densha de kimashita.
Suzuki-san no tomodachi:　Osoi desu kara, watashi no kuruma de kaeri-
　　　　　　　　　　　　　masen ka.

Buraun:	Sō desu ka. Arigatō gozaimasu. Onegaishimasu.
Minna:	Totemo tanoshikatta desu. Kyō wa dōmo arigatō gozaimashita.
Suzuki:	Dō itashimashite. Watashi mo tanoshikatta desu. Mata kite kudasai.
Suzuki-san no okusan:	Dōzo ki o tsukete.
Minna:	Oyasumi nasai.
Suzuki:	Oyasumi nasai.

■ Mr. Suzuki telephoned the Browns' house. Mr. Suzuki is a friend of Mr. Brown's.

Suzuki:	Hello. This is Suzuki. Is this the Browns' residence?
Brown:	Ah, Mr. Suzuki! Good evening.
Suzuki:	Mr. Brown, we're having a party at my house next Saturday evening. It's my birthday party. Won't you come, together with Mrs. Brown?
Brown:	Thank you very much. We'll be happy to come.
Suzuki:	Well then, (see you) on Saturday.
Brown:	Thank you for your telephone call.

■ Today is the day of the party. Mr. and Mrs. Brown have arrived at Mr. Suzuki's house.

Suzuki:	How nice of you to come. This way, please.
Brown:	Thank you for your invitation. These are for you.
Suzuki:	What lovely flowers! Thank you very much.
Brown:	This wine is for you, too.
Suzuki:	Come this way and I'll introduce you to everybody.

■ It is a very lively party.

■ (Now) It is 12 o'clock. Everyone is leaving.

Mr. Suzuki's friend:	Mr. Brown, did you come by car?
Brown:	No, we came by train.
Mr. Suzuki's friend:	Since it's late, can't I drive you home? (*lit.* "Won't you go home in my car?")
Brown:	Oh, would you (do that)? Thank you. (*lit.* "I'm happy to accept your offer.")
All:	It was very enjoyable. Thank you very much for today.
Suzuki:	You're welcome. I enjoyed it too. Please come again.
Mrs. Suzuki:	Please be careful (on your way home).
All:	Good-night!
The Suzukis:	Good-night!

Vocabulary

| すずき | **Suzuki** | a surname |
| あ | **a** | Ah! |

よろこんで	**yorokonde**	(I'd) be happy to.
ひ	**hi**	day
おまねき　ありがとう　ございます	**omaneki arigatō gozaimasu**	Thank you for your invitation.
ワイン	**wain**	wine
みなさん	**mina-san**	everyone (excluding the speaker and his or her group)
みんな	**minna**	everyone
おそい	**osoi**	late (**-i** adj.)
きを　つけて	**ki o tsukete**	take care, be careful

Mr. Smith tells Mr. Hayashi that his brother has arrived in Japan.

スミス：せんしゅう　あにが　アメリカから　にほんに　きました。

はやし：おにいさんは　おくさんと　いっしょに　きましたか。

スミス：いいえ、しごとですから　ひとりで　きました。いま　きょうとに　いっています。あには　りょこうがいしゃに　つとめています。

はやし：おにいさんは　いつまで　きょうとに　いますか。

スミス：こんしゅうの　すいようびまで　います。それから　ホンコンに　いって、アメリカに　かえります。

はやし：アメリカの　どこに　すんでいますか。

スミス：ニューヨークに　すんでいます。

■スミスさんの　おにいさんは　りょこうがいしゃに　つとめています。
　せんしゅう　にほんに　きました。いま　きょうとに　いっています。

Sumisu:　Senshū ani ga Amerika kara Nihon ni kimashita.
Hayashi:　O-niisan wa okusan to issho ni kimashita ka.
Sumisu:　Iie, shigoto desu kara, hitori de kimashita. Ima Kyōto ni itte i-masu. Ani wa ryokō-gaisha ni tsutomete imasu.
Hayashi:　O-niisan wa itsu made Kyōto ni imasu ka.
Sumisu:　Konshū no sui-yōbi made imasu. Sorekara Honkon ni itte, Ame-rika ni kaerimasu.
Hayashi:　Amerika no doko ni sunde imasu ka.
Sumisu:　Nyū Yōku ni sunde imasu.

■Sumisu-san no o-niisan wa ryokō-gaisha ni tsutomete imasu. Senshū Nihon ni kimashita. Ima Kyōto ni itte imasu.

Smith:　My (older) brother came to Japan from America last week.
Hayashi:　Did your brother come with his wife?

Smith:	No, he came on business, so he came alone. He's in Kyoto now. My brother works for a travel agency.
Hayashi:	How long will your brother be in Kyoto?
Smith:	He'll be there until this week Wednesday. After that he'll go to Hong Kong, then return to America.
Hayashi:	Where does he live in America?
Smith:	He lives in New York (City).

■ Mr. Smith's (older) brother works for a travel agency. He came to Japan last week. Now he is in Kyoto.

Vocabulary

あに	**ani**	(my) older brother
おにいさん	**o-niisan**	(your) older brother
りょこうがいしゃ	**ryokō-gaisha**	travel agency
つとめて います	**tsutomete imasu**	be employed, work for
つとめます（つとめる）	**tsutomemasu (tsutomeru)**	serve, hold a post
ホンコン	**Honkon**	Hong Kong
すんで います	**sunde imasu**	live (*lit.* "is living")
すみます（すむ）	**sumimasu (sumu)**	live
ニューヨーク	**Nyū Yōku**	New York

NOTES

1. Ima Kyoto ni itte imasu.

Verb **-te imasu** is used here. The sentence literally means, "Having gone to Kyoto, he is there now." Other common examples of this usage are, **Tanaka-san wa kekkon shite imasu.** "Mr. Tanaka is married." (*lit.* "Mr. Tanaka, having got married, is married.") And **Bengoshi wa mō kimashita ka.** "Has the lawyer come yet?" **Hai, kite imasu.** "Yes, he has."

2. Ani wa ryokō-gaisha ni tsutomete imasu.

The particle used with the verb **tsutomeru** is **ni.** Here again the verb **-te** form is used.

When asked what kind of work they do, Japanese usually reply by giving their place of work rather than the type of work. Note also that in Japanese siblings are always referred to as older or younger brothers or sisters, for which there are separate words. I.e., **ani,** "my older brother," **otōto,** "my younger brother," **o-nii-san,** "your older brother," **otōto-san,** "your younger brother," etc. Note the following terms for one's own and for other person's relatives.

	Related to the Speaker	Related to Others
family	kazoku	go-kazoku
husband	shujin	go-shujin
wife	kanai	okusan
child	kodomo	kodomo-san/okosan
son	musuko	musuko-san/botchan
daughter	musume	musume-san/ojō-san
parents	ryōshin	go-ryōshin
father	chichi	o-tōsan
mother	haha	o-kāsan
grandfather	sofu	ojī-san
grandmother	sobo	obā-san
brothers and sisters	kyōdai	go-kyōdai
older brother	ani	o-nii-san
older sister	ane	o-nē-san
younger brother	otōto	otōto-san
younger sister	imōto	imōto-san
grandchild	mago	o-mago-san
uncle	oji	oji-san
aunt	oba	oba-san
nephew	oi	oigo-san
niece	mei	meigo-san
cousin	itoko	o-itoko-san

3. **Nyū Yōku ni sunde imasu.**

In describing where people live, the verb **-te** form is used. **Uru**, the verb meaning "sell" and **shiru**, "know," similarly use the **-te** form.

PRACTICE

KEY SENTENCES

1. **Sumisu-san no o-niisan wa ima Nihon ni kite imasu.**
2. **Kurāku-san wa Tōkyō ni sunde imasu.**
3. **Hayashi-san wa Nihon Ginkō ni tsutomete imasu.**
4. **Watashi wa Tanaka-san o yoku shitte imasu.**
5. **Chika 1-kai de niku ya sakana o utte imasu.**

1. Mr. Smith's older brother is in Japan now.
2. Mr. Clark lives in Tokyo.
3. Mr. Hayashi works for the Bank of Japan.
4. I know Mr. Tanaka well.
5. They sell meat, fish (and other things) in the first basement.

shitte imasu (shiru)	know
chika 1-kai	first basement
chika	basement (*lit.* "underground")
utte imasu	sell (*lit.* "is selling")
urimasu (uru)	sell

EXERCISES

I Verbs: Memorize the following verbs and their **-te imasu** forms.

	-masu form	**-te imasu** form	
		aff.	*neg.*
live	**sumi-masu**	**sunde imasu**	**sunde imasen**
work for	**tsutome-masu**	**tsutomete imasu**	**tsutomete imasen**
know	*	**shitte imasu**	**shirimasen****
sell	**uri-masu**	**utte imasu**	**utte imasen**

*The form **shirimasu** is never used; **shitte imasu** replaces it.

The negative of **shitte imasu is the irregular **shirimasen**.

II Practice the following pattern by changing the underlined part as in the example given.

   ex. **[Watashi wa] <u>Tōkyō ni</u> sunde imasu.**

     1. **Tōkyō no Azabu**

     2. **kaisha no chikaku**

III Make dialogues by changing the underlined parts as in the examples given.

  A *ex.* **Q: Howaito-san wa ima <u>Nihon ni kite imasu</u> ka.**

      A*a*: Hai, <u>kite imasu</u>. Sengetsu <u>[Nihon ni] kimashita</u>.

      A*n*: Iie, <u>kite imasen</u>. Raigetsu <u>[Nihon ni] kimasu</u>.

     1. **Tōkyō, kimasu**

     2. **gaikoku, ikimasu**

  B. *ex.* **Q: <u>Tanaka-san</u> o shitte imasu ka.**

      A*a*: Hai, shitte imasu.

      A*n*: Iie, shirimasen.

     1. **Howaito-san**

     2. **Yamada-san no jūsho**

     3. **Hayashi-san no atarashii denwa-bangō**

     4. **ii niku-ya**

C. *ex.* Q: Tanaka-san no tomodachi wa doko ni tsutomete imasu ka.

A: <u>Taishikan</u> ni tsutomete imasu.

1. depāto
2. gakkō
3. ryokō-gaisha

D. *ex.* Q: Doko de <u>kasa</u> o utte imasu ka.

A: <u>1-kai</u> de utte imasu.

1. sētā, 4-kai
2. kutsu, 6-kai
3. kitte, ano mise

Vocabulary

gaikoku   foreign country
sētā   sweater

SHORT DIALOGUE

Suzuki: Sumisu-san wa doko ni tsutomete imasu ka.
Sumisu: ABC ni tsutomete imasu.
Suzuki: Jā, Kyōto shisha no Satō-san o shitte imasu ka.
Sumisu: Ee, shitte imasu.

Suzuki: Where do you work, Mr. Smith?
Smith: I work for ABC.
Suzuki: Then, do you know Mr. Satō in the Kyoto branch?
Smith: Yes, I do.

Vocabulary

Satō   a surname

QUIZ

I Read this lesson's opening dialogue and answer the following questions.

1. **Dare to dare ga hanashi o shite imasu ka.**
2. **Senshū dare ga Amerika kara Nihon ni kimashita ka.**
3. **Sumisu-san no o-niisan wa ima Tōkyō ni imasu ka.**
4. **Sumisu-san no o-niisan wa doko ni tsutomete imasu ka.**
5. **Sumisu-san no o-niisan wa doko ni sunde imasu ka.**

II Complete the questions so that they fit the answers.

1. (   ) de kitte o utte imasu ka.
   Ano mise de utte imasu.
2. Ano hito wa (   ) ni tsutomete imasu ka.
   Depāto ni tsutomete imasu.
3. (   ) ga Hayashi-san no atarashii denwa-bangō o shitte imasu ka.
   Hayashi-san no hisho ga shitte imasu.
4. Howaito-san wa ima (   ) ni itte imasu ka.
   Ginkō ni itte imasu.

III Put the appropriate particles in the parentheses. (If a particle is not required, put an X in the parentheses.)

1. Kochira wa Tōkyō Denki (   ) Tanaka-san desu.
2. Tanaka-san wa doko (   ) tsutomete imasu ka.
   Tōkyō Denki (   ) tsutomete imasu.
3. Sumisu-san wa ima Tōkyō (   ) shigoto o shite imasu.
4. Buraun-san wa doko (   ) sunde imasu ka.
   Ueno Eki (   ) chikaku (   ) sunde imasu.
5. Doko (   ) Ei-go (   ) shimbun (   ) utte imasu ka.
   Asoko (   ) utte imasu.

IV Translate into Japanese.

1. Do you know Mr. Tanaka?
   No, I don't know (him).
2. I live near (my) office. It's a 15-minute walk.
3. Mr. Smith works for ABC.

Mr. Smith wants to buy some antique furniture. He is asking Miss Yamada where to find some.

スミス：わたしは　にほんの　ふるい　かぐが　すきです。せんげつ
　　　　たんすを　かいました。つぎは　つくえを　かいたいです。
　　　　いい　みせを　しっていますか。

やまだ：さあ、しりません。はやしさんは　いろいろな　ことを　よく
　　　　しっていますから　はやしさんに　きいてください。

■スミスさんは　ふるい　かぐが　すきです。スミスさんは　やまださ
んに　ふるい　かぐの　みせについて　ききました。

Sumisu:　Watashi wa Nihon no furui kagu ga suki desu. Sengetsu tansu o
　　　　kaimashita. Tsugi wa tsukue o kaitai desu. Ii mise o shitte imasu
　　　　ka.
Yamada:　Sā, shirimasen. Hayashi-san wa iroirona koto o yoku shitte imasu
　　　　kara Hayashi-san ni kiite kudasai.

■Sumisu-san wa furui kagu ga suki desu. Sumisu-san wa Yamada-san ni
furui kagu no mise ni tsuite kikimashita.

Smith:　　I like antique Japanese furniture. Last month I bought a *tansu*. Next, I want to
　　　　buy a table. Do you know a good store?
Yamada:　Let me see . . . No, I don't. Mr. Hayashi knows a lot about various things, so
　　　　ask him.

■Mr. Smith likes antique furniture. Mr. Smith asked Miss Yamda about stores that sell
antique furniture.

かぐ	**kagu**	furniture
たんす	**tansu**	*tansu* (chest of drawers)
つくえ	**tsukue**	table
いろいろな こと	**iroirona koto**	various things
いろいろな	**iroirona**	various (**-na** adj.)
こと	**koto**	thing
みせに ついて	**mise ni tsuite**	about stores
～に ついて	**ni tsuite**	about, concerning

GRAMMAR X

Desire, Preference, Like and Dislike

1. person **WA** noun **GA SUKI desu**
2. person **WA** noun **GA II desu**
   (person **WA**) noun **WA** noun **GA II desu**
3. Watashi wa verb **-TAI desu**

- Particle **ga** is used with   **suki desu (-na** adj.)
                              ii desu (-i adj.)

- In "I like bananas," "like" is a verb and "bananas" is the object, but in Japanese, "bananas" takes the particle **ga**, and they are described as being "likable," using an adjective rather than a verb.
  ex. **Banana ga suki desu.** "I like bananas." (*lit.* "Bananas are likable.")
  Anata ga suki desu. "I love you." (*lit.* "You are lovable.")

- The same construction is used with the adjective **ii**, "good, preferable," etc.
  ex. **Kōhī ga ii desu.** "I'd like coffee." (*lit.* "Coffee is preferable.") Note the following constructions, all of which mean "I'd like coffee."
  1. **Watashi wa kōhī ga ii desu.** (*lit.* "As far as I'm concerned, coffee is preferable.")
  2. **Nomimono wa kōhī ga ii desu.** (*lit.* "As for something to drink, coffee is my choice.")
  3. **Watashi wa nomimono wa kōhī ga ii desu.** (*lit.* "As for me, regarding something to drink, coffee is my choice.")

- The verb **wakarimasu** also takes **ga** (see Note 2, p. 104.), as does the verb **dekimasu**, expressing possibility, ability, etc.
  ex. **Watashi wa taipu ga dekimasu.** "I can type." (*lit.* "As far as I'm concerned, typing (is something) I can do.")
  Note: **Dekimasu** also has the meaning "be done" or "be ready." (See Lesson 21.)

- Verb -**tai desu**

  Constructions expressing desire can be made from the **-masu** form as follows:

  iki-masu   iki-tai

  tabe-masu   tabe-tai

  The verb -**tai** form is inflected like an **-i** adjective.

  ex. **Ikitai desu.** "(I) want to go."

  Ikitakunai desu. "(I) don't want to go."

  Ikitakatta desu. "(I) wanted to go."

  Ikitakunakatta desu. "(I) didn't want to go."

- Verb -**tai** expresses the speaker's desire, and it can be made into a question asking a person what he wishes to do by adding the question marker **ka**.

  ex. **Takushī de ikitai desu.** "(I) want to go by taxi."

  Takushī de ikitai desu ka. "Do (you) want to go by taxi?"

  It cannot be used referring to a third person.

  The particle **ga** is sometimes used instead of **o**.

  Suraido o/ga mitai desu. "(I) want to see the slides."

NOTES

1. **Shitte imasu**, "(I) know," always takes the verb **-te** form. The reply is irregular:

   A*a*: **Hai, shitte imasu.** "Yes, (I) know."

   A*n*: **Iie, shirimasen.** "No, (I) don't know."

2. **Sā, shirimasen.**

   Sā . . . ("Let me see . . .") is an expression often used in Japanese when thinking about an answer.

PRACTICE

KEY SENTENCES

1. **Tanaka-san wa gorufu ga jōzu desu.**

2. **[Watashi wa] Ringo ga suki desu.**

3. **[Watashi wa] Taipu ga dekimasu.**

4. **[Watashi wa] Atama ga itai desu.**

5. **[Watashi wa] Yōroppa ni ikitai desu.**

6. **[Watashi wa] Ima nani mo tabetakunai desu.**

1. Mr. Tanaka is good at golf.

2. I like apples.

3. I can type.

4. I have a headache.

5. I'd like to go to Europe.

6. I don't want to eat anything now.

Vocabulary

jōzuna	good at (**-na** adj.)	**atama**	head
dekimasu	can (do)	**itai**	aching (**-i** adj.)
(dekiru)		**Yōroppa**	Europe

EXERCISES

I Memorize the following adjectives and verb.

		Present Form		Past Form	
		aff.	*neg.*	*aff.*	*neg.*
-na adj.	skilled in	**jōzu desu**	**jōzu dewa arimasen**	**jōzu de-shita**	**jōzu dewa arimasen-deshita**
	like, love	**suki desu**	**suki dewa arimasen**	**suki de-shita**	**suki dewa arimasen-deshita**
verb	be able to (do)	**dekimasu**	**dekimasen**	**dekima-shita**	**dekimasen deshita**
-i adj.	be painful	**itai desu**	**itakunai desu**	**itakatta desu**	**itakuna-katta desu**

II Practice the following patterns by changing the underlined part as in the examples given.

    A. *ex.* **Tanaka-san wa <u>gorufu</u> ga jōzu desu.**

        1. **Doitsu-go**

        2. **ryōri**

    B. *ex.* **[Watashi wa] <u>Atama</u> ga itai desu.**

        1. **nodo**

        2. **onaka**

        3. **ha**

III Make dialogues by changing the underlined parts as in the examples given.

    A. *ex.* **Q: [Anata wa] <u>Kudamono</u> ga suki desu ka.**

        A*a*: Hai, totemo suki desu.

        A*n*: Iie, amari suki dewa arimasen.

        1. **eiga**

        2. **ryokō**

        3. **Haruko-san**

B. *ex.* Q: [Anata wa] <u>Nihon-go</u> ga dekimasu ka.

    A*a*: Hai, sukoshi dekimasu.

    A*n*: Iie, zenzen dekimasen.

    1. Furansu-go

    2. taipu

C. *ex.* Q: [Anata wa] <u>Atama</u> ga itai desu ka.

    A*a*: Hai, itai desu.

    A*n*: Iie, itakunai desu.

    1. nodo

    2. onaka

    3. ha

D. *ex.* Q: [Anata wa] Donna <u>kudamono</u> ga suki desu ka.

    A: <u>Ringo</u> ga suki desu.

    1. yasai, tomato

    2. ryōri, niku no ryōri

IV Memorize the following **-tai desu** form.

	Present Form		Past Form	
	aff.	*neg.*	*aff.*	*neg.*
want to go	ikitai desu	ikitakunai desu	ikitakatta desu	ikitakunakatta desu
want to send	okuritai desu	okuritakunai desu	okuritakatta desu	okuritakunakatta desu

V Practice the following **-tai desu** form.

    1. **eiga ni ikimasu**

       [Watashi wa] Eiga ni ikitai desu.

                          ikitakunai desu.

                          ikitakatta desu.

                          ikitakunakatta desu.

    2. **terebi o mimasu**

       [Watashi wa] Terebi o mitai desu.

                          mitakunai desu.

                          mitakatta desu.

                          mitakunakatta desu.

    3. **Tanaka-san ni aimasu**

       [Watashi wa] Tanaka-san ni aitai desu.

                              aitakunai desu.

                              aitakatta desu.

                              aitakunakatta desu.

VI Practice the following pattern by changing the underlined part as in the example given.

    ex. **[Watashi wa] <u>Yama</u> ni ikitai desu.**

      1. **toshokan**

      2. **Yōroppa**

      3. **onsen**

VII Make dialogues by changing the underlined parts as in the examples given.

    A. *ex.* **Q: [Anata wa] <u>Terebi</u> o mitai desu ka.**

        A*a*: Hai, mitai desu.

        A*n*: Iie, mitakunai desu.

      1. **eiga**

      2. **Nihon no matsuri**

    B. *ex.* **Q: [Anata wa] Doko ni ikitai desu ka.**

        A: <u>Yama</u> ni ikitai desu.

      1. **umi**

      2. **onsen**

    C. *ex.* **Q: [Anata wa] Nani o kaitai desu ka.**

        A: <u>Kagu</u> o kaitai desu.

      1. **nekutai**

      2. **kutsushita**

      3. **tsukue**

    D. *ex.* **Q: [Anata wa] Ima nani o shitai desu ka.**

        A: <u>Tenisu</u> o shitai desu.

      1. **hon o yomimasu**

      2. **eiga ni ikimasu**

      3. **ryokō o shimasu**

    E. *ex.* **Q: [Anata wa] Nani o <u>shitai</u> desu ka.**

        A: Nani mo <u>shitakunai</u> desu.

      1. **tabemasu**

      2. **nomimasu**

      3. **kaimasu**

    F. *ex.* **Q: [Anata wa] Doko ni <u>ikitai</u> desu ka.**

        A: <u>Doko ni mo ikitakunai</u> desu.

      1. **dare ni, aimasu**

Vocabulary

Doitsu-go	German language	**okuritai**	want to send
nodo	throat	**okurimasu (okuru)**	send
onaka	stomach	**yama**	mountain
ha	tooth	**toshokan**	library

kudamono	fruit	**onsen**	hot spring
Furansu-go	French language	**matsuri**	festival
tomato	tomato	**kutsushita**	socks

SHORT DIALOGUES

1. **Tanaka:** Kono ryōri wa totemo oishii desu.
   Howaito: Sō desu ka. Mō sukoshi ikaga desu ka.
   Tanaka: Arigatō gozaimasu. Itadakimasu. Howaito-san wa ryōri ga jōzu desu ne.

   Tanaka: This dish is very good.
   White: Is it? Would you like some more?
   Tanaka: Thank you. I'd love some more. You're a good cook.

2. **Isha:** Dō shimashita ka.
   Yamada: Kinō kara kibun ga warui desu.
   Isha: Netsu ga arimasu ka.
   Yamada: Ee, 39-do arimasu. Atama mo itai desu.
   Isha: Nodo mo itai desu ka.
   Yamada: Hai, itai desu.
   Isha: Kusuri o agemasu kara shokuji no ato de nonde kudasai. Dōzo o-daiji ni.

   Doctor: What's the matter?
   Yamada: I haven't felt well since yesterday.
   Doctor: Do you have a fever?
   Yamada: Yes. My temperature is 39 degrees (C.). I have a headache.
   Doctor: Do you have a sore throat too?
   Yamada: Yes, I do.
   Doctor: (*After the examination.*) I'll give you some medicine. Take it after meals.
   Look after yourself.
   (Note: Parts of the body are given in Appendix F.)

3. **Tanaka:** Tsugi no nichi-yōbi ni nani o shitai desu ka.
   Hayashi: Tenisu o shitai desu. Hon mo yomitai desu. Tanaka-san wa nani o shitai desu ka.
   Tanaka: [Watashi wa] Eiga ni ikitai desu.

   Tanaka: What would you like to do next Sunday?
   Hayashi: I'd like to play tennis. I'd like to read a book, too. What would you like to do?
   Tanaka: I'd like to go to a movie.

4. **Howaito:** Kono nimotsu o Amerika ni okuritai desu. Donogurai kaka-rimasu ka.
   Yūbinkyoku no hito: Kōkūbin desu ka, funabin desu ka.
   Howaito: Funabin de onegaishimasu.

Yūbinkyoku no hito: Sō desu ne. Ikkagetsu gurai kakarimasu.

White:	I'd like to send this parcel to the United States. How long will it take?
Post office clerk:	By airmail or sea mail?
White:	By sea mail, please.
Post office clerk:	Let me see . . . It'll take about one month.

5. **Hayashi:** Senshū no nichi-yōbi ni haikingu ni ikimashita ka.

   Tanaka: Iie, ikitakatta desu ga, atama ga itakatta desu kara ikimasen deshita.

Hayashi:	Did you go hiking last week Sunday?
Tanaka:	No. I wanted to, but I had a headache, so I didn't go.

Vocabulary

isha	doctor	**nimotsu**	parcel
dō shimashita ka	What's the matter?	**kōkūbin**	airmail
kibun	feeling	**funabin**	sea mail
netsu	fever	**sō desu ne**	Let me see . . .
39-do	39 degrees (Centigrade)	**ikkagetsu**	(for) one month
-do	degree	**-kagetsu**	month (see Appendix
dōzo o-daiji ni	Look after yourself.		G.)

QUIZ ▰▰▰▰▰.

I Read this lesson's opening dialogue and answer the following questions.

1. **Sumisu-san wa donna kagu ga suki desu ka.**
2. **Sumisu-san wa mō tansu o kaimashita ka.**
3. **Yamada-san wa Nihon no furui kagu no ii mise o shitte imasu ka.**
4. **Sumisu-san wa Hayashi-san ni nani ni tsuite kikimasu ka.**

II Complete the questions so that they fit the answers.

1. **Shūmatsu ni (　　) o shitai desu ka.**
   Eiga o mitai desu.
2. **Tsugi no nichi-yōbi ni (　　) ni ikitai desu ka.**
   Doko ni mo ikitakunai desu. Uchi ni itai desu.
3. **(　　) kudamono ga suki desu ka.**
   Ringo ga suki desu.
4. **Issho ni shokuji ni ikimasen ka.**
   Zannen desu ga, [watashi wa] ima (　　) mo tabetakunai desu.

III Put the appropriate particles in the parentheses. (If a particle is not required, put an X in the parentheses.)

1. **Kurāku-san (   ) tenisu (   ) jōzu desu (   ), watashi (   ) jōzu dewa arimasen.**
2. **Ano hito (   ) Nihon-go (   ) dekimasu. Totemo jōzu desu.**
3. **Kinō kara nodo (   ) itai desu kara, hiru-yasumi (   ) byōin (   ) ikitai desu.**
4. **Ima nani (   ) nomitakunai desu.**
5. **Kyō doko ni (   ) ikitakunai desu. Uchi (   ) itai desu. Uchi (   ) hon (   ) yomitai desu.**

IV Translate into Japanese.

1. Miss White likes apples.
2. Can you ski?
   Yes, I can.
3. I want to meet a friend tomorrow and play tennis (together).
4. I wanted to write a letter yesterday, but there wasn't time.
5. My throat is sore, so I don't want to eat anything.

Mr. Tanaka has invited Mr. Brown to a meal. They are in a restaurant looking at the menu and conversing.

たなか：　　　すみません、メニューを　みせてください。

ウェイトレス：はい、どうぞ。

たなか：　　　のみものは　なにが　いいですか。

ブラウン：　　ビールが　いいです。

たなか：　　　りょうりは　すきやきが　いいですか、しゃぶしゃぶが
　　　　　　　いいですか。

ブラウン：　　すきやきは　せんしゅう　たべましたから、しゃぶしゃ
　　　　　　　ぶが　いいです。

たなか：　　　しょくじの　あとで　コーヒーは　いかがですか。

ブラウン：　　はい、いただきます。

たなか：　　　ビールを　2ほんと　しゃぶしゃぶを　おねがいします。
　　　　　　　デザートは　メロンが　いいです。

ウェイトレス：はい、わかりました。

■ たなかさんと　ブラウンさんは　レストランで　しょくじを　しまし
　た。ビールを　のんで、しゃぶしゃぶを　たべました。しょくじの
　あとで　コーヒーを　のみました。

Tanaka:　　Sumimasen, menyū o misete kudasai.
Ueitoresu:　Hai, dōzo.
Tanaka:　　Nomimono wa nani ga ii desu ka.
Buraun:　　Bīru ga ii desu.
Tanaka:　　Ryōri wa sukiyaki ga ii desu ka, shabushabu ga ii desu ka.
Buraun:　　Sukiyaki wa senshū tabemashita kara, shabushabu ga ii desu.
Tanaka:　　Shokuji no ato de kōhī wa ikaga desu ka.
Buraun:　　Hai, itadakimasu.
Tanaka:　　Bīru o 2-hon to shabushabu o onegaishimasu. Dezāto wa meron
　　　　　　ga ii desu.

Ueitoresu: Hai, wakarimashita.

■ Tanaka-san to Buraun-san wa resutoran de shokuji o shimashita. Bīru o nonde shabushabu o tabemashita. Shokuji no ato de kōhī o nomimashita.

Tanaka: Excuse me, could we see the menu, please? (*lit*. "Please show us the menu.")
Waitress: Certainly, sir. Here you are.
Tanaka: What would you like to drink?
Brown: I'd like some beer.
Tanaka: As for dinner, would you like sukiyaki or (would you like) *shabushabu*?
Brown: I had sukiyaki last week, so I'd like *shabushabu*.
Tanaka: After the meal, how about some coffee?
Brown: Yes, I'd love some.
Tanaka: Two bottles of beer and some *shabushabu*, please. For dessert, we'd like some melon.
Waitress: I see.

■ Mr. Tanaka and Mr. Brown had a meal in a restaurant. They drank beer and ate *shabushabu*. After the meal they had coffee.

Vocabulary

のみもの	**nomimono**	beverage
すきやき	**sukiyaki**	sukiyaki
しゃぶしゃぶ	**shabushabu**	*shabushabu*
デザート	**dezāto**	dessert
メロン	**meron**	melon

NOTES

1. **Nomimono wa nani ga ii desu ka.**
   Bīru ga ii desu.
   See Grammar X (p. 174) for replies when a choice is offered.

2. **Ryōri wa sukiyaki ga ii desu ka, shabushabu ga ii desu ka.**
   When offering a choice between two possibilities, the key word is replaced and the predicate is repeated. Note the difference between this and the usual English construction.
   ex. **Kyōto ni ikimasu ka, Ōsaka ni ikimasu ka.** "Are you going to Kyoto or (are you going to) Osaka?"

3. **Sukiyaki wa senshū tabemashita kara**
   Although **sukiyaki** is the object, it is also the topic and therefore takes the particle **wa**.

PRACTICE

KEY SENTENCES

1. **Watashi wa jūsu ga ii desu.**
2. **Nomimono wa jūsu ga ii desu.**

1. I'll have fruit juice.
2. (As for something) to drink, I'll have fruit juice.

EXERCISES

I Practice the following pattern by changing the underlined part as in the example given.

   ex. [Watashi wa] Ryokō wa <u>Kyōto</u> ga ii desu.

     1. getsu-yōbi
     2. raigetsu
     3. onsen

II Make dialogues by changing the underlined parts as in the examples given.

   A. *ex.* A: <u>Bīru</u> ga ii desu ka, <u>wain</u> ga ii desu ka.
         B: <u>Bīru</u> ga ii desu.

     1. kōhī, kōcha
     2. niku no ryōri, sakana no ryōri
     3. yama, umi
     4. do-yōbi, nichi-yōbi

   B. *ex.* A: Nomimono wa <u>kōhī</u> ga ii desu ka, <u>kōcha</u> ga ii desu ka.
         B: <u>Kōcha</u> ga ii desu.

     1. dezāto, o-kashi, kudamono
     2. doraibu, konshū, raishū
     3. kaigi, 9-ji kara, 10-ji kara

   C. *ex.* A: <u>Dezāto</u> wa nani ga ii desu ka.
         B: <u>Aisukurīmu</u> ga ii desu.

     1. ryōri, sukiyaki
     2. hiru-gohan, sandoitchi

Vocabulary

aisukurīmu ice cream

SHORT DIALOGUES

1. **Hayashi:** Ryōri wa niku ga ii desu ka, sakana ga ii desu ka.
   Howaito: Niku ga ii desu.

Hayashi:	Dewa, sukiyaki wa ikaga desu ka.
Howaito:	Ee, sukiyaki o onegaishimasu.

Hayashi:	(As for the meal) Would you like meat or fish?
White:	I'd like meat.
Hayashi:	Then how about sukiyaki?
White:	Yes, sukiyaki please.

2.
Tanaka:	Shokuji wa nan-ji goro ga ii desu ka.
Howaito:	6-ji ga ii desu.
Tanaka:	Dewa, shokuji no mae ni niwa de shashin o torimasen ka.
Howaito:	Ee, torimashō.

Tanaka:	What time would you like to eat? (*lit.* "What time would you like the meal?")
White:	Six o'clock would be nice.
Tanaka:	Well then, wouldn't you like to take some pictures in the garden before dinner?
White:	Yes, let's take some.

3.
Hayashi:	Shūmatsu ni doraibu ni ikimasen ka.
Howaito:	Ee, ii desu ne.
Hayashi:	Do-yōbi ga ii desu ka, nichi-yōbi ga ii desu ka.
Howaito:	Do-yōbi ga ii desu.
Hayashi:	Doko ni ikimashō ka. Umi wa dō desu ka.
Howaito:	Ee, watashi wa umi ga suki desu. Umi ni ikitai desu.

Hayashi:	Wouldn't you (like to) go for a drive this weekend?
White:	Yes. How nice.
Hayashi:	Would you like to go on Saturday or (would you prefer) Sunday?
White:	Saturday would be fine.
Hayashi:	Where shall we go? What about the seaside?
White:	Yes. I like the sea. I'd like to go to the seaside.

QUIZ ▰▰▰▰

I Read this lesson's opening dialogue and answer the following questions.

1. **Tanaka-san to Buraun-san wa ima doko ni imasu ka.**
2. **Tanaka-san to Buraun-san wa nani o nomimasu ka.**
3. **Tanaka-san to Buraun-san wa sukiyaki o tabemasu ka, shabushabu o tabemasu ka.**

II Complete the questions so that they fit the answers.

1. **Nomimono wa (   ) ga ii desu ka.**
   Kōhī ga ii desu.

2. **Ryōri wa sakana ga ii desu ka, (   ) ga ii desu ka.**
   Niku ga ii desu.
3. **Shokuji wa (   ) kara ga ii desu ka.**
   11-ji kara ga ii desu.
4. **Ryokō wa (   ) ga ii desu ka.**
   Kyōto ga ii desu.

III Put the appropriate particles in the parentheses. (If a particle is not required, put an X in the parentheses.)

1. **Raigetsu no yasumi ni Kyōto (   ) ikitai desu. Anata (   )?**
   Watashi (   ) Ōsaka (   ) ii desu.
2. **Dezāto (   ) kudamono (   ) ii desu (   ), aisukurīmu (   ) ii desu (   ).**
   Aisukurīmu (   ) ii desu.
3. **Shokuji (   ) ato de, kudamono (   ) onegaishimasu.**
4. **Kaigi (   ) mae (   ), watashi (   ) heya (   ) kite kudasai.**

IV Translate into Japanese.

1. What would you like for dessert?
   Some fruit, please.
2. I wanted to drink some coffee before the meeting, but there wasn't time, so I drank some after the meeting.

■ブラウンさんと　おくさんは　アメリカで　にほんごの　べんきょう
を　していました。そして　きょう　ブラウンさんは　アメリカの
さとうせんせいに　にほんごで　てがみを　かきました。

さとうせんせい、おげんきですか。
　とうきょうは　とても　あついですが、わたしたちは　げんきです。
わたしは　まいにち　ちかてつで　かいしゃに　いきます。うちから
かいしゃまで　20ぷんぐらいです。とうきょうの　ちかてつは　べんり
ですが、あさ　8じごろから　9じごろまでと　ごご　5じごろから　6じは
んごろまで、とても　こんでいます。しゅうまつには　ドライブを
したいですが、わたしたちは　くるまが　ありませんから、でんしゃで
おもしろい　ところに　いきます。
　しごとは　とても　いそがしいです。せんしゅう　おおさかと
きょうとの　ししゃに　いきました。きょうとの　かいぎの　あとで
ちいさい　おてらに　いきました。しずかでした。にわが　きれい
でした。ほかの　おてらも　みたかったですが、じかんが　ありません
でした。　ざんねんでした。
　かないは　にほんじんの　ともだちや　アメリカじんの　ともだちと
ちいさい　べんきょうの　グループを　つくりました。グループの
ひとは　まいつき　15にちに　あって、にほんと　アメリカの
しゃかいや　ぶんかや　かんがえかたや　けいざいや　せいじについて
はなしを　します。
　かないは　じかんが　ありますから、いろいろな　べんきょうを
しています。そして　にほんじんの　ともだちが　たくさん　あります。
かないは　にほんごが　じょうずです。かんじも　よみます。さいきん
かないは　まいあさ　にほんごの　べんきょうを　しています。わたし
は　かようびにだけ　にほんごの　べんきょうを　しています。

らいげつから　きんようびにも　したいです。いまの　テキストは
もうすぐ　おわりますから、らいげつから　あたらしいのを　つかいま
す。わたしは　あたらしい　テキストを　たのしみに　しています。
　では　また　てがみを　かきます。
　みなさまに　どうぞ　よろしく。おげんきで。さようなら。

　　8がつ　いつか

　　　　　　　　　　　　　　　ジョン・ブラウン

■ Buraun-san to okusan wa Amerika de Nihon-go no benkyō o shite imashita. Soshite kyō Buraun-san wa Amerika no Satō-sensei ni Nihon-go de
tegami o kakimashita.

Satō-sensei, o-genki desu ka.
　　Tōkyō wa totemo atsui desu ga, watashi-tachi wa genki desu. Watashi
wa mainichi chikatetsu de kaisha ni ikimasu. Uchi kara kaisha made
20-pun gurai desu. Tōkyō no chikatetsu wa benri desu ga, asa 8-ji goro
kara 9-ji goro made to gogo 5-ji goro kara 6-ji han goro made, totemo
konde imasu. Shūmatsu ni wa doraibu o shitai desu ga, watashi-tachi wa
kuruma ga arimasen kara, densha de omoshiroi tokoro ni ikimasu.
　　Shigoto wa totemo isogashii desu. Senshū Ōsaka to Kyōto no shisha ni
ikimashita. Kyōto no kaigi no ato de chiisai o-tera ni ikimashita. Shizuka
deshita. Niwa ga kirei deshita. Hoka no o-tera mo mitakatta desu ga, jikan
ga arimasendeshita. Zannen deshita.
　　Kanai wa Nihon-jin no tomodachi ya Amerika-jin no tomodachi to
chiisai benkyō no gurūpu o tsukurimashita. Gurupu no hito wa maitsuki
15-nichi ni atte, Nihon to Amerika no shakai ya bunka ya kangaekata ya
keizai ya seiji ni tsuite hanashi o shimasu.
　　Kanai wa jikan ga arimasu kara, iroirona benkyō o shite imasu. Soshite
Nihon-jin no tomodachi ga takusan arimasu. Kanai wa Nihon-go ga jōzu
desu. Kanji mo yomimasu. Saikin kanai wa maiasa Nihon-go no benkyō o
shite imasu. Watashi wa ka-yōbi ni dake Nihon-go no benkyō o shite i-
masu. Raigetsu kara kin-yōbi ni mo shitai desu. Ima no tekisuto wa mō
sugu owarimasu kara, raigetsu kara atarashii no o tsukaimasu. Watashi wa atarashii tekisuto o tanoshimi ni shite imasu.
　　Dewa mata tegami o kakimasu.
　　Mina-sama ni dōzo yoroshiku. O-genki de. Sayōnara.

8-gatsu itsuka

　　　　　　　　　　　　　　　Jon Buraun

■ Mr. and Mrs. Brown studied Japanese in America. And today Mr. Brown wrote a letter in Japanese to their teacher in America, Satō Sensei.

Dear Satō Sensei,

How are you? It is very hot in Tokyo, but we are well.

I go to my office every day by subway. It takes (*lit.* is) about 20 minutes from my house to the office. Tokyo subways are convenient, but they are very crowded from about 8:00 in the morning till about 9:00 and from about 5:00 in the afternoon till about 6:30. On weekends, we'd like to go driving, but since we don't have a car, we visit interesting places by train.

I'm very busy with work. I visited our Osaka and Kyoto branches last week. After a meeting in Kyoto I went to a small temple. It was quiet, and the garden was beautiful. I wanted to see other temples but, sorry to say, did not have time.

My wife has formed a small study group with Japanese and American friends. The people in the group meet on the 15 of each month and talk about Japanese and American community life and social conditions, culture, ways of thinking, economy, politics, etc.

My wife has time, so she is studying various things. And she has many Japanese friends. My wife's Japanese is good. She reads *kanji,* too. Nowadays my wife has a Japanese lesson every morning. I have a Japanese lesson only on Tuesday. From next month, I want to have one on Friday, too. I'll soon finish my present textbook, so I will use a new one from next month. I am looking forward to the new **textbook**. I'll write a letter again (soon).

Please give my best regards to everyone. Take care of yourself.

Good-bye,

August 5

John Brown

Vocabulary

さとうせんせい	**Satō-sensei**	Professor Satō
せんせい	**sensei**	(term of respect for professors, doctors, lawyers, etc.)
こんで　います	**konde imasu**	be crowded
こみます（こむ）	**komimasu (komu)**	be crowded
ところ	**tokoro**	place
ほか	**hoka**	other
グループ	**gurūpu**	group
つくりました	**tsukurimashita**	formed
つくります（つくる）	**tsukurimasu (tsukuru)**	form
まいつき	**maitsuki**	every month
しゃかい	**shakai**	society, social conditions
ぶんか	**bunka**	culture
かんがえかた	**kangaekata**	way of thinking
けいざい	**keizai**	economy
せいじ	**seiji**	politics

さいきん	saikin	nowadays
テキスト	tekisuto	text
もう　すぐ	mō sugu	very soon
おわります（おわる）	owarimasu (owaru)	finish
あたらしいの	atarashii no	new one
の	no	one
たのしみに　して　います	tanoshimi ni shite imasu	be looking forward to
みなさまに　どうぞ　よろしく	mina-sama ni dōzo yoroshiku	Best regards to everyone.
みなさま	mina-sama	everyone (politer than **minna-san**)
〜に　よろしく	ni yoroshiku	Best regards to . . .
おげんきで	o-genki de	Take care of yourself. (*lit.* "(Keep) well.")
ジョン	Jon	John

APPENDICES

A. Adjectives

Included in the following list of adjectives are some which do not appear in the text.

-i adjectives

abunai, dangerous
akarui, bright
amai, sweet
atarashii, new, fresh
atatakai, warm
atsui, hot
chiisai, small
chikai, near
furui, old
hayai, fast, early
hikui, low
hiroi, wide
ii, good
isogashii, busy
itai, painful

karai, hot, spicy
karui, light
kitanai, dirty
kurai, dark
mijikai, short
muzukashii, difficult
nagai, long
ōi, many, much
oishii, delicious
ōkii, large
omoi, heavy
omoshiroi, interesting
osoi, slow, late
samui, cold
semai, narrow

shiokarai, salty
sukanai, few, a little
suppai, sour
suzushii, cool
tadashii, correct
takai, high, expensive
tanoshii, pleasant
tōi, far
tsumaranai, boring
tsumetai, cold
wakai, young
warui, bad
yasashii, easy
yasui, cheap

-na adjectives

anzenna, safe
benrina, convenient
daijina, important
damena, no good
fubenna, inconvenient
fushinsetsuna, unkind
genkina, well, healthy

hetana, unskillful
himana, free
iroirona, various
jōzuna, skillful
kiraina, unlikeable
kireina, clean, pretty
nigiyakana, lively

shinsetsuna, kind
shitsureina, rude
shizukana, quiet
sukina, likeable
teineina, polite
yūmeina, famous

Color words

akai, red
aoi, green, blue
chairoi, chairo no,* brown
kiiroi, kiiro no,* yellow

kuroi, black
midoriiro no,* green
murasaki no,* purple
shiroi, white

*Note that these words are nouns and are followed by the particle **no**.

B. Common Japanese Names (Source: Nippon Univac Kaisha, Ltd., 1975.)

Family Names	Male Given Names	Female Given Names
1. Katō	1. Hiroshi	1. Yoshiko
2. Suzuki	2. Toshio	2. Keiko
3. Watanabe	3. Yoshio	3. Kazuko
4. Tanaka	4. Kazuo	4. Hiroko
5. Itō	5. Akira	5. Yōko

C. Counters

The abstract numbers (**ichi**, **ni**, **san**) are given on p. 28 (0–20), p. 33 (20, 30, . . .) and p. 41 (100, 200, . . .). The **hitotsu**, **futatsu**, **mittsu** system is given on p. 48. Two counters (**-mai** and **-hon**) appear on p. 45. Below are other counters used in this book.

1. Floors of a house or building: **-kai**. Which/how many floors, **nan-kai/nan-gai**.

ikkai, 1st floor	**go-kai**, 5th floor	**kyū-kai**, 9th floor
ni-kai, 2nd floor	**rokkai**, 6th floor	**jukkai**, 10th floor
san-gai, 3rd floor	**nana-kai**, 7th floor	**jūikkai**, 11th floor
yon-kai, 4th floor	**hachi-kai**, 8th floor	**jūni-kai**, 12th floor

   Also: **chika ikkai**, (1st) basement, **chika ni-kai**, 2nd basement, etc.

2. Liquid measure (cupful, glassful): **-hai**, **-bai**, **-pai**. How many, **nam-bai**.

ippai, 1 cupful	**go-hai**, 5 cupfuls	**kyū-hai**, 9 cupfuls
ni-hai, 2 cupfuls	**roppai**, 6 cupfuls	**juppai**, 10 cupfuls
san-bai, 3 cupfuls	**nana-hai**, 7 cupfuls	**jūippai**, 11 cupfuls
yon-hai, 4 cupfuls	**happai**, 8 cupfuls	**jūni-hai**, 12 cupfuls

3. People: **-nin**. How many people, **nan-nin**.

hitori, 1 person	**roku-nin**, 6 people	**ku-nin**, 9 people
futari, 2 people	**shichi-nin**, 7 people	**jū-nin**, 10 people
san-nin, 3 people	**nana-nin**, 〃 〃	**jūichi-nin**, 11 people
yo-nin, 4 people	**hachi-nin**, 8 people	**jūni-nin**, 12 people
go-nin, 5 people	**kyū-nin**, 9 people	

4. Times: **-kai**, **-do**. Generally speaking, these two counters may be used interchangeably. How many times, **nan-kai**. How many times/degrees, **nan-do**.

ikkai, **ichi-do**, once	**nana-kai**, **nana-do**, 7 times
ni-kai, **ni-do**, twice	**hachi-kai**, **hachi-do**, 8 times
san-kai, **san-do**, 3 times	**kyū-kai**, **kyū-do**, 9 times
yon-kai, **yon-do**, 4 times	**jukkai**, **jū-do**, 10 times
go-kai, **go-do**, 5 times	**jūikkai**, **jūichi-do**, 11 times
rokkai, **roku-do**, 6 times	**jūni-kai**, **jūni-do**, 12 times

D. Country, Nationality, Language

	Country	Nationality	Language
Australia	**Ōsutoraria**	**Ōsutoraria-jin**	**Ei-go**
Brazil	**Burajiru**	**Burajiru-jin**	**Porutogaru-go**
Canada	**Kanada**	**Kanada-jin**	**Ei-go/Furansu-go**
China	**Chūgoku**	**Chūgoku-jin**	**Chūgoku-go**
Egypt	**Ejiputo**	**Ejiputo-jin**	**Arabia-go**
France	**Furansu**	**Furansu-jin**	**Furansu-go**
Germany	**Doitsu**	**Doitsu-jin**	**Doitsu-go**
Indonesia	**Indoneshia**	**Indoneshia-jin**	**Indoneshia-go**
Italy	**Itaria**	**Itaria-jin**	**Itaria-go**
Japan	**Nihon**	**Nihon-jin**	**Nihon-go**
New Zealand	**Nyūjīrando**	**Nyūjīrando-jin**	**Ei-go**
Spain	**Supein**	**Supein-jin**	**Supein-go**

Switzerland	**Suisu**	**Suisu-jin**	**Doitsu-go/Furansu-go/Itaria-go**
Thailand	**Tai**	**Tai-jin**	**Tai-go**
United Kingdom	**Igirisu**	**Igirisu-jin**	**Ei-go**
United States	**Amerika**	**Amerika-jin**	**Ei-go**
USSR	**Soren**	**Roshia-jin**	**Roshia-go**

The question words are: **Doko no kuni**, belonging to or coming from "What country." (This is often shortened to **doko?) Nani-go**, "What language," and **nani-jin**, "What nationality."

E. Extent, Frequency, Quantity

1. Extent

100%	**totemo**	very, extremely
	amari . . . -nai/-masen	not very
0%	**zenzen . . . -nai/-masen**	not at all

ex. **Kono nomimono wa totemo oishii desu**. "This drink is very good."
Kono nomimono wa amari oishikunai desu. "This drink is not very good."
Kono nomimono wa zenzen oishikunai desu. "This drink is not good at all."

2. Frequency

100%	**itsumo**	always
	yoku	often
	tokidoki	sometimes
	tamani	occasionally
	amari . . . -masen	not very often
0%	**zenzen . . . -masen**	never

ex. **Ban-gohan no ato de itsumo terebi o mimasu**. "(I) always watch TV after supper."
Ban-gohan no ato de yoku terebi o mimasu. "(I) often watch TV after supper."
Ban-gohan no ato de tokidoki terebi o mimasu. "(I) sometimes watch TV after supper."

Ban-gohan no ato de <u>tamani</u> terebi o mimasu. "(I) occasionally watch TV after supper."

Ban-gohan no ato de <u>amari</u> terebi o <u>mimasen</u>. "(I) don't often watch TV after supper."

Ban-gohan no ato de <u>zenzen</u> terebi o <u>mimasen</u>. "(I) never watch TV after supper."

3. Quantity

```
100% ┬
     │   takusan              a lot, many
     │
     ┼
     │
     │   sukoshi              few, a little
  0% ┴   zenzen . . . -masen  none at all
```

ex. **Mise ga <u>takusan</u> <u>arimasu</u>.** "There are a lot of stores."

Mise ga <u>sukoshi</u> arimasu. "There are a few stores."

Mise ga <u>zenzen</u> <u>arimasen</u>. "There are no stores."

F. Parts of the Face and Body

1. Face, **kao**, and head, **atama**

ago, chin, jaw	**kami**, hair	**mayu/mayuge**, eyebrow
ha, tooth	**kuchi**, mouth	**me**, eye
hana, nose	**kuchibiru**, lip	**mimi**, ear
hitai, forehead	**mabuta**, eyelid	**shita**, tongue
hoho, cheek	**matsuge**, eyelash	

2. Body, **karada**

ashi, foot, leg	**mune**, chest	**te**, hand
hifu, skin	**nodo**, throat	**tsume**, nail
kata, shoulder	**onaka**, stomach, abdomen	**ude**, arm
koshi, hip	**oshiri**, buttock	**yubi**, finger, toe
kubi, neck	**senaka**, back	

G. Time Expressions

The days of the week and month and the months are given on p. 35.

1. Every, **mai-**

mai-nichi, every day	**mai-shū**, every week
mai-asa, every morning	**mai-nen/mai-toshi**, every year
mai-ban, every evening, every night	**mai-tsuki/mai-getsu**, every month

2. Period of Time

Minutes, **-fun**, **-pun**. How many minutes, **nam-pun (kan)**.

ippun (kan), (for) 1 minute
ni-fun (kan), (for) 2 minutes
sam-pun (kan), (for) 3 minutes
yom-pun (kan), (for) 4 minutes
go-fun (kan), (for) 5 minutes
roppun (kan), (for) 6 minutes
nana-fun (kan), (for) 7 minutes

happun (kan), (for) 8 minutes
hachi-fun (kan), ″ ″   ″
kyū-fun (kan), (for) 9 minutes
juppun (kan), (for) 10 minutes
jūippun (kan), (for) 11 minutes
jūni-fun (kan), (for) 12 minutes

Hours, **-jikan**. How many hours, **nan-jikan**.

ichi-jikan, (for) 1 hour
ni-jikan, (for) 2 hours
san-jikan, (for) 3 hours
yo-jikan, (for) 4 hours
go-jikan, (for) 5 hours
roku-jikan, (for) 6 hours
nana-jikan, (for) 7 hours

shichi-jikan, (for) 7 hours
hachi-jikan, (for) 8 hours
ku-jikan, (for) 9 hours
ju-jikan, (for) 10 hours
jūichi-jikan, (for) 11 hours
jūni-jikan, (for) 12 hours

Days, **-nichi (kan)**. How many days, **nan-nichi (kan)**.

ichinichi (kan), (for) 1 day
futsuka (kan), (for) 2 days
mikka (kan), (for) 3 days
yokka (kan), (for) 4 days
itsuka (kan), (for) 5 days
muika (kan), (for) 6 days

nanoka (kan), (for) 7 days
yōka (kan), (for) 8 days
kokonoka (kan), (for) 9 days
tōka (kan), (for) 10 days
jūichi-nichi (kan), (for) 11 days
jūni-nichi (kan), (for) 12 days

Weeks, **-shūkan**. How many weeks, **nan-shūkan**.

isshūkan, (for) 1 week
ni-shūkan, (for) 2 weeks
san-shūkan, (for) 3 weeks
yon-shūkan, (for) 4 weeks
go-shūkan, (for) 5 weeks
roku-shūkan, (for) 6 weeks

nana-shūkan, (for) 7 weeks
hasshūkan, (for) 8 weeks
kyū-shūkan, (for) 9 weeks
jusshūkan, (for) 10 weeks
jūisshūkan, (for) 11 weeks
jūni-shūkan, (for) 12 weeks

Months, **-kagetsu (kan)**. How many months, **nan-kagetsu (kan)**.

ikkagetsu (kan), (for) 1 month
ni-kagetsu (kan), (for) 2 months
san-kagetsu (kan), (for) 3 months
yon-kagetsu (kan), (for) 4 months
go-kagetsu (kan), (for) 5 months
rokkagetsu (kan), (for) 6 months
nana-kagetsu (kan), (for) 7 months

shichi-kagetsu (kan), (for) 7 months
hakkagetsu (kan), (for) 8 months
kyū-kagetsu (kan), (for) 9 months
jukkagetsu (kan), (for) 10 months
jūikkagetsu (kan), (for) 11 months
jūni-kagetsu (kan), (for) 12 months

Years, **-nen (kan)**. How many years, **nan-nen (kan)**.

ichi-nen (kan), (for) 1 year
ni-nen (kan), (for) 2 years
san-nen (kan), (for) 3 years
yo-nen (kan), (for) 4 years
go-nen (kan), (for) 5 years
roku-nen (kan), (for) 6 years
nana-nen (kan), (for) 7 years

shichi-nen (kan), (for) 7 years
hachi-nen (kan), (for) 8 years
kyū-nen (kan), (for) 9 years
jū-nen (kan), (for) 10 years
jūichi-nen (kan), (for) 11 years
jūni-nen (kan), (for) 12 years

Note: Except for **-jikan** and **-shūkan** the suffix **kan** may be considered optional and need be added only when specificity is called for.

3. Relative Time

Day

ototoi, day before yesterday
kinō, yesterday
kyō, today
ashita, tomorrow
asatte, day after tomorrow

Week

sensen-shū, week before last
sen-shū, last week
kon-shū, this week
rai-shū, next week
sarai-shū, week after next

Morning

ototoi no asa, morning before last
kinō no asa, yesterday morning
kesa, this morning
ashita no asa, tomorrow morning
asatte no asa, morning of the day
    after tomorrow

Month

sensen-getsu, month before
    last
sen-getsu, last month
kon-getsu, this month
rai-getsu, next month
sarai-getsu, month after next

Evening

ototoi no ban/yoru, evening/night
    before last
kinō no ban/yoru, yesterday evening/last
    night
komban, tonight
ashita no ban/yoru, tomorrow evening/
    night
asatte no ban/yoru, evening/night of the
    day after tomorrow

Year

ototoshi, year before last
kyonen, last year
kotoshi, this year
rai-nen, next year
sarai-nen, year after next

4. Seasons

haru, spring   **natsu**, summer   **aki**, autumn   **fuyu**, winter

H. Verb Conjugation

The following are the **-masu**, **-te**, **-nai**, plain dictionary and **-ta** forms of Regular I, Regular II and Irregular verbs. (See also Model Verb Conjugation in Lesson 19.)

Regular I					
-masu	**-te**	**-nai**	plain	**ta**	
aimasu	atte	awanai	au	atta	meet
arimasu	atte	nai	aru	atta	be, have
arukimasu	aruite	arukanai	aruku	aruita	walk
chigaimasu	chigatte	chigawanai	chigau	chigatta	be wrong
gambarimasu	gambatte	gambaranai	gambaru	gambatta	do one's best
hairimasu	haitte	hairanai	hairu	haitta	enter
iimasu	itte	iwanai	iu	itta	say
ikimasu	itte	ikanai	iku	itta	go
irasshaimasu	irasshatte	irassharanai	irassharu	irasshatta	go, be
itadakimasu	itadaite	itadakanai	itadaku	itadaita	accept
kaerimasu	kaette	kaeranai	kaeru	kaetta	return
kaimasu	katta	kawanai	kau	katta	buy

kakarimasu	kakatte	kakaranai	kakaru	kakatta	(it) takes
kakimasu	kaite	kakanai	kaku	kaita	write
keshimasu	keshite	kesanai	kesu	keshita	turn off
kikimasu	kiite	kikanai	kiku	kiita	listen
komimasu	konde	komanai	komu	konda	be crowded
machimasu	matte	matanai	matsu	matta	wait
magarimasu	magatte	magaranai	magaru	magatta	turn
mochimasu	motte	motanai	motsu	motta	have, hold
moraimasu	moratte	morawanai	morau	moratte	receive
nomimasu	nonde	nomanai	nomu	nonda	drink
norimasu	notte	noranai	noru	notta	ride, get on
okurimasu	okutte	okuranai	okuru	okutta	send
oshimasu	oshite	osanai	osu	oshita	push
owarimasu	owatte	owaranai	owaru	owatta	finish
suimasu	sutte	suwanai	suu	sutta	smoke (tobacco)
sumimasu	sunde	sumanai	sumu	sunda	live
torimasu	totte	toranai	toru	totta	take (a picture)
tsukaimasu	tsukatte	tsukawanai	tsukau	tsukatta	use
tsukimasu	tsuite	tsukanai	tsuku	tsuita	arrive
tsukurimasu	tsukutte	tsukuranai	tsukuru	tsukutta	make
urimasu	utte	uranai	uru	utta	sell
wakarimasu	wakatte	wakaranai	wakaru	wakatta	understand
yomimasu	yonde	yomanai	yomu	yonda	read

Regular II					
-masu	**-te**	**-nai**	plain	**-ta**	
agemasu	agete	agenai	ageru	ageta	give
akemasu	akete	akenai	akeru	aketa	open
dekimasu	dekite	dekinai	dekiru	dekita	be able
demasu	dete	denai	deru	deta	leave
imasu	ite	inai	iru	ita	be
kakemasu	kakete	kakenai	kakeru	kaketa	sit down
mimasu	mite	minai	miru	mita	see
misemasu	misete	misenai	miseru	miseta	show
orimasu	orite	orinai	oriru	orita	get off
oshiemasu	oshiete	oshienai	oshieru	oshieta	tell
shimemasu	shimete	shimenai	shimeru	shimeta	close
tabemasu	tabete	tabenai	taberu	tabeta	eat
todokemasu	todokete	todokenai	todokeru	todoketa	deliver
tomemasu	tomete	tomenai	tomeru	tometa	stop, park
tsukemasu	tsukete	tsukenai	tsukeru	tsuketa	turn on
(ki o) tsu-kemasu	tsukete	tsukenai	tsukeru	tsuketa	be careful
tsutomemasu	tsutomete	tsutomenai	tsutomeru	tsutometa	work for

Irregular					
-masu	**-te**	**-nai**	plain	**-ta**	
kimasu	kite	konai	kuru	kita	come
mottekimasu	mottekite	mottekonai	mottekuru	mottekita	bring
shimasu	shite	shinai	suru	shita	do
onegaishi-masu	onegaishi-te	onegaishi-nai	onegai-suru	onegai-shita	beg a favor
shitsurei-shimasu	shitsurei-shite	shitsurei-shinai	shitsu-reisuru	shitsurei-shita	be rude
benkyō o shimasu	shite	shinai	suru	shita	study

The following is a selection of compounds that are formed with **suru** and are conjugated in the same way as **benkyō o shimasu**.

denwa o shimasu, telephone
doraibu o shimasu, go driving
gorufu o shimasu, play golf
hanashi o shimasu, talk
kaigi o shimasu, have a meeting
kaimono o shimasu, shop
kopī o shimasu, make a copy
kurīningu o shimasu, dry clean
pātī o shimasu, give a party
ryokō o shimasu, take a trip

setsumei o shimasu, explain
shigoto o shimasu, work
shōkai o shimasu, introduce
sōbetsukai o shimasu, give a farewell party
sukī o shimasu, ski
taipu o shimasu, type
tenisu o shimasu, play tennis
unten o shimasu, drive
yoyaku o shimasu, make a reservation

QUIZ ANSWERS ▰▰▰▰▰▰

Lesson 1

I   1. Sumisu desu.   2. Iie, Nihon-jin dewa arimasen.   3. Bengoshi desu.
II 1. Sumisu-san   2. Doitsu-jin   3. bengoshi   4. donata
III 1. wa   2. ka, ka   3. no   4. wa
IV 1. Sumisu desu.   2. Hajimemashite. Dōzo yoroshiku.   3. Yamada-san, kochi-ra wa Tōkyō Denki no Tanaka-san desu.   4. Sumisu-san wa Amerika-jin desu ka, Doitsu-jin desu ka.

Lesson 2

I   1. Meishi desu.   2. Hai, kaisha no namae desu.   3. Kaisha no [jūsho] desu.
    4. Iie, uchi no denwa-bangō dewa arimasen.   5. Zero-san no yon-zero-zero no kyū-zero-san-ichi desu.
II 1. kaisha   2. dare/donata   3. nan   4. nan-ban
III 1. wa   2. wa, ka, no, wa, no   3. wa, no, no
IV 1. Kochira wa Tanaka-san desu.   2. Kore wa Tanaka-san no meishi desu.
    3. Kore wa Tanaka-san no uchi no denwa-bangō dewa arimasen. Kaisha no desu.
    4. [Anata no] Kaisha no denwa-bangō wa nan-ban desu ka.

Lesson 3

I   1. Iie, 10-ji dewa arimasen.   2. 10-ji kara desu.   3. Iie, 7-ji made dewa arima-sen.
II 1. nan-ji   2. nan-yōbi   3. nan-nichi
III 1. wa   2. no, wa   3. wa, kara, made
IV 1. Dōmo arigatō.   2. Dō itashimashite.   3. Sumimasen. Yūbinkyoku wa nan-ji made desu ka.   4. Kyō wa 15-nichi desu. Ashita wa 16-nichi desu.   5. Kyō wa moku-yōbi desu. Kinō wa sui-yōbi deshita.

Lesson 4

I   1. Iie, [kore wa] tokei dewa arimasen.   2. [Are wa] Terebi desu.   3. [Are wa] 50,000-en desu.   4. Iie, [sore wa] 50,000-en dewa arimasen.   5. [Sore wa] 5,000-en desu.   6. Hai, [kore mo] 5,000-en desu.
II 1. nan   2. ikura   3. donata   4. Are
III 1. o   2. wa, mo, mo, mo, wa, wa
IV 1. Sore o misete kudasai.   2. Kore o kudasai.   3. Kore wa ikura desu ka.
    4. Irasshaimase.

Lesson 5

I   1. [Sono Doitsu no kamera wa/Sore wa] 50,000-en desu.   2. Iie, [kono kamera wa/kore wa] Doitsu no dewa arimasen.   3. [Kono kamera wa/Kore wa] 35,000-en desu.   4. [Ano chiisai rajio wa/Are wa] Nihon no desu.
II 1. ikura   2. Are   3. Igirisu, Doko
III 1. wa, no, mo, no   2. o   3. o, x   4. wa   5. x, wa, x
IV 1. Kore wa ikura desu ka.   2. Kono rajio wa ikura desu ka.   3. Watashi no tokei wa Nihon no dewa arimasen. Amerika no desu.   4. Sono chiisai tēpurēkō-dā o misete kudasai.   5. Fuirumu o mittsu kudasai. Dono fuirumu desu ka. Sono fuirumu desu.

Lesson 6

I   1. Kyōto no shisha ni/e ikimasu.   2. Kaisha no hito to ikimasu.   3. Asatte kaerimasu.

II   1. Ginkō, Yūbinkyoku   2. Itsu   3. Doko, Dare/Donata

III   1. x, ni/e   2. to, ni/e   3. wa, x   4. de   5. ni/e, mo, wa   6. ga

IV   1. Sumimasen, kono basu wa Tōkyō Eki ni/e ikimasu ka.   2. Tanaka-san wa kinō kaisha no hito to Ōsaka ni/e ikimashita. Soshite asatte Tōkyō ni/e kaerimasu. 3. Sumisu-san wa kyonen hitori de Nihon ni/e kimashita.   4. Dare/Donata ga kūkō ni/e ikimashita ka. Tanaka-san no hisho ga ikimashita.

Lesson 7

I   1. Sumisu-san ga ikimashita.   2. Nichi-yōbi ni ikimashita.   3. Iie, densha de ikimasen deshita.   4. Takushī de ikimashita.

II   1. doko   2. itsu   3. nan-nichi, Nan, Dare/Donata

III   1. de, ni/e, mo   2. x, ni

IV   1. Konnichiwa.   2. Yoku irasshaimashita.   3. Dōzo okake kudasai.

V   1. Dōzo kochira ni/e.   2. Dōzo ohairi kudasai.   3. Tanaka-san wa kinō takushī de uchi ni/e kaerimashita.   4. Howaito-san wa kin-yōbi ni Ōsaka no shisha ni/e ikimasu.

Lesson 8

I   1. Ima ni arimasu.   2. Shimbun to hana ga arimasu.   3. Tanaka-san no oku-san ga imasu.   4. Dare mo imasen.

II   1. dare/donata   2. nani   3. dare/donata   4. nani

III   1. arimasu   2. imasu   3. imasen   4. arimasen

IV   1. no, ni, ga   2. no, to, ga   3. ya, ga   4. ga, mo

V   1. Ima ni isu ya tēburu ga arimasu.   2. Niwa ni Tanaka-san to otoko no ko ga imasu.   3. Daidokoro ni dare ga imasu ka. Dare mo imasen.   4. Isu no ue ni nani mo arimasen.

Lesson 9

I   1. Iie, sūpā no mae dewa arimasen.   2. 12-ji made desu.   3. Kyō wa do-yōbi desu kara.

II   1. doko   2. nani   3. doko   4. Dōshite   5. ikutsu   6. nan-nin

III   1. wa, x, no, ni   2. ni, x, x   3. ni/e, kara   4. wa, ni

IV   1. Saka-ya wa yaoya no tonari desu./Saka-ya wa yaoya no tonari ni arimasu. 2. Sumimasen, o-tearai wa doko desu ka./Sumimasen, o-tearai wa doko ni arimasu ka. Asoko desu./Asoko ni arimasu.   3. Howaito-san wa Ōsaka ni/e ikimashita kara, kyō kaisha ni imasen.   4. Dōshite kyō yūbinkyoku wa 12-ji made desu ka. Do-yōbi desu kara.   5. Hon-ya no mae ni kodomo ga 5-nin imasu.

Lesson 10

I   1. Kabuki o mimasu.   2. Iie, hitori de mimasen.   3. Senshū kaimashita. 4. Ginza no pureigaido de kaimashita.

II   1. Nan-yōbi   2. doko   3. nani   4. nani

III   1. ni   2. de, ni/e   3. de, o   4. de, mo   5. o   6. x, de, o

IV   1. Nichi-yōbi ni depāto de kamera o kaimashita. 45,000-en deshita.   2. Kinō nani o shimashita ka. Asa, uchi de Nihon-go no tēpu o kikimashita. Gogo Ginza ni/e ikimashita. Soshite, Ginza de kamera o kaimashita.   3. Howaito-san wa asa nani mo tabemasen.

Lesson 12

I   1. Katō-san ga shimashita.   2. Imasen deshita.   3. 9-ji goro kaerimasu.
    4. Hai, shimasu.

II   1. nani, Dare/Donata   2. dare/donata   3. Dare/Donata

III   1. Iie, kimasen   2. mimasu, Iie, mimasen   3. yoku   4. yomimasu, yomi-masen

IV   1. ni   2. ni   3. x, to   4. ni, o   5. ga, wa

V   1. Moshi-moshi, Tanaka-san no o-taku desu ka.   2. Tōkyō Denki no Tanaka desu. Hayashi-san wa irasshaimasu ka.   3. Mata ato de denwa o shimasu.
    4. Sumisu-san wa tokidoki densha de Nihon-go no tēpu o kikimasu.   5. Kurāku-san ni kaisha no denwa-bangō o kikimashita.   6. Kurāku-san wa amari tomodachi ni tegami o kakimasen ga, Howaito-san wa yoku kakimasu.

Lesson 13

I   1. Hai, tabemashita.   2. Nihon no o-kashi o tabemashita.   3. O-cha o nomi-mashita.

II   1. genki   2. omoshiroi   3. donata/dare   4. donna

III   1. oishikunai desu   2. kireina   3. omoshirokunai desu   4. yokunai desu
    5. yūmeina   6. chikai desu

IV   1. Kōhī wa ikaga desu ka. Arigatō gozaimasu. Itadakimasu.   2. Kōhī o mō ip-pai ikaga desu ka. Iie, mō kekkō desu.   3. Watashi-tachi wa yūmeina resutoran de ban-gohan o tabemashita.   4. Ano kissaten wa kirei desu ga, shizuka dewa arimasen.   5. [Watashi wa] Kyō isogashii desu.

Lesson 14

I   1. Kabuki o mimashita.   2. Omoshirokatta desu.   3. Iyahōn de kikimashita.

II   1. yasashii   2. chikai   3. tsumaranai   4. ōkii   5. takai   6. isogashii
    7. atsui   8. shizukana   9. furui   10. warui

III   1. nani, dō, yokatta   2. Dōshite   3. donna

IV   1. yokatta desu   2. dō   3. nigiyaka deshita   4. kirei dewa arimasen
    5. omoshirokunakatta desu.   6. genki deshita

V   1. Kinō no kaigi wa dō deshita ka.   2. Kinō no tenki wa yokatta desu.
    3. Ano resutoran no ryōri wa amari oishikunakatta desu.

Lesson 15

I   1. Tanjōbi ni moraimashita.   2. Kurāku-san ni/kara moraimashita.   3. Kurāku-san ga agemashita.   4. Tanaka-san ni agemashita.

II   1. dare/donata   2. dare/donata   3. nani

III   1. ni/kara   2. ga, o   3. ni, o   4. ni, o, mo

IV   1. Tanaka-san wa Kurāku-san ni kireina kabin o moraimashita.   2. Hayashi-san wa Sumisu-san ni Kyōto no chizu o agemashita.   3. Ano hito ni meishi o agema-shita ka. Hai, agemashita.

Lesson 16

I   1. Nikkō ni ikimasu.   2. Iie, hitori de ikimasen.   3. Tōkyō Eki (no kaisatsugu-chi) de aimasu.   4. 7-ji ni aimasu.   5. Densha de ikimasu.

II   1. Doko, Nan-ji   2. Dare/Donata

III   1. ni, o   2. ni, ni   3. ni, ni   4. ni, de

IV   1. Do-yōbi ni depāto ni/e kaimono ni ikimashita.   2. Issho ni shokuji o shima-sen ka. Ee, shimashō. Doko ni/e ikimashō ka. Eki no chikaku no atarashii resuto-ran ni/e ikimasen ka. Ee, sō shimashō.

Lesson 17

I 1. Do-yōbi [no ban] desu.   2. Ikimasu.   3. Tanaka-san no uchi de shimasu.
4. Azabu ni arimasu.   5. Hai, kakimasu.

II 1. ni, ni, ni/e, ni, o   2. ni, ga, ga   3. o

III 1. Nichi-yōbi ni uchi ni/e kimasen ka.   2. Kin-yōbi ni uchi de Kurāku-san no sō-betsukai o shimasu. Kimasen ka. Ee, zehi.   3. Issho ni shokuji o shimasen ka.
4. Samui desu ne. Mado o shimemashō ka. Hai, onegaishimasu.   5. Chizu o ka-kimashō ka.

Lesson 18

I 1. Eiga no kippu ga arimasu.   2. 2-mai arimasu.   3. Pātī ni ikimasu.
4. Pātī ga arimasu.   5. Iie, ikimasen.   6. Ashita Sumisu-san to ikimasu.

II 1. nan-nin   2. itsu   3. nani   4. doko

III 1. ga   2. ni   3. de   4. ga, x   5. de, ga   6. no, ga, x, x, ga

IV 1. Watashi wa imōto ga 3-nin arimasu. Imōto wa Tōkyō to Ōsaka ni imasu.
2. Tanaka-san. 8-gatsu ni yasumi ga arimasu ka. Iie, arimasen. 9-gatsu ni arimasu.
3. Raishū, Kyōto no shisha de kaigi ga arimasu.

Lesson 19

I 1. Sumisu-san no tomodachi desu.   2. Kinō kimashita.   3. Raishū no moku-yōbi made imasu.   4. Mikka (kan) imasu.   5. Kyōto ya Nara ni/e ikimasu.
6. Furui o-tera ya niwa o mimasu.

II 1. tabete   4. kite   7. ite   10. nonde
2. itte   5. kaite   8. mite   11. atte
3. yonde   6. kaette   9. shite   12. kiite

III 1. itsu/nan-nen no nan-gatsu, itsu/nan-nen no nan-gatsu   2. donogurai/nan-nichi
(kan) gurai/nan-shūkan gurai   3. Itsu

IV 1. Soshite   2. itte   3. donogurai   4. gurai   5. dō   6. nan, donogurai,
gurai

V 1. Maiasa nyūsu o kiite, kaisha ni/e ikimasu.   2. Tanaka-san ni atte, issho ni
ban-gohan o tabemashita. Soshite uchi ni kaerimashita.   3. Donogurai uchi de
Nihon-go no benkyō o shimasu ka. 30-pun dake shimasu.   4. Kinō doko ni/e
mo ikimasen deshita. Uchi ni imashita.

Lesson 20

I 1. Sakaya ni (denwa o) shimashita.   2. Hayashi-san no uchi ni todokemasu.
3. 20-pon todokemasu.   4. 3-ji made ni todokemasu.   5. Hai, oshiemashita.

II 1. itte   4. kiite   7. mottekite   10. atte
2. ite   5. magatte   8. itte   11. nonde
3. matte   6. misete   9. shimete   12. shite

III 1. o   2. o, x   3. ni   4. o   5. o, to, o, ni/e   6. o, ni/e

IV 1. Menyū o misete kudasai. Hai, dōzo.   2. Sumimasen ga, uchi ni bīru o 12-hon
todokete kudasai. Hai, wakarimashita. Kurāku-san desu ne. Ee, sō desu.   3. Ko-no chiisai terebi o kudasai. Hai, wakarimashita. Todokemashō ka. Iie, kekkō desu.
Kuruma de kimashita kara.

Lesson 22

I 1. Senshū ikimashita.   2. Iie, (issho ni) ikimasen deshita.   3. Ashita ikimasu.
4. Azabu de orimashita.   5. Iie, kakarimasen deshita.

II 1. nan   2. Doko   3. Nani   4. donogurai/nan-jikan gurai   5. Dōyatte

III 1. de, ni, de, o   2. o, ni, ni, de   3. made, de, x

IV 1. Kinō Ginza no hoteru de tomodachi no sōbetsukai ga arimashita. 2. Kaisha o 6-ji ni dete, basu ni notte, Ginza de orimashita. 3. Kaisha kara hoteru made donogurai kakarimashita ka. 35-fun gurai kakarimashita.

Lesson 23

I   1. Denki-ya de moraimashita. 2. Terebi no katarogu o moraimashita.
    3. Iie, kēsu no naka ni arimasen deshita. 4. Kēsu no ue ni arimashita.
II 1. haitte   4. mite   7. shite   10. itte
    2. kite   5. tsukatte   8. totte   11. ite
    3. tabete   6. nonde   9. kiite   12. itte
III 1. totte   2. shi, shi   3. ake, akete   4. tsukatte, matte   5. ki, kite
    6. moratte   7. katte
IV 1. Denki o tsukemashō ka. Hai, onegaishimasu. 2. Kono denwa o tsukatte mo ii desu ka. Hai, dōzo. 3. 3-ji made koko ni ite mo ii desu ka.

Lesson 24

I   1. Keikan ga oshiemashita. 2. Tsugi no kado o hidari ni magarimasu.
    3. Chūshajō ni/e ikimasu.
II 1. tabenai   5. iwanai   9. akenai   13. tsukawanai
    2. minai   6. yomanai   10. magaranai   14. shimenai
    3. ikanai   7. shinai   11. kesanai   15. toranai
    4. konai   8. suwanai   12. tsukenai
III 1. sutte, suwanaide   2. akete, akete   3. itte, kite   4. shime, shimenaide
IV 1. wa, kara, o   2. o, ni/e   3. de, o   4. o, ni
V   1. Ima ano heya ni hairanaide kudasai. 2. Koko de tabako o suwanaide kudasai. 3. Tsugi no shingō o migi ni/e magatte kudasai.

Lesson 25

I   1. 3-gai ni imasu. 2. Kaigishitsu ni imasu. 3. Suraido o mite imasu.
II 1. doko/nan-gai, nani   2. doko   3. dare/donata   4. doko
III 1. Hayashi-san wa Sumisu-san ni denwa o shimasu. 2. Hayashi-san wa Sumisu-san ni denwa o shite imasu. 3. Ano onna no ko wa nani o shite imasu ka. Tomodachi o matte imasu. 4. Howaito-san wa ima shigoto o shite imasen.

Lesson 27

I   1. Sumisu-san to Hayashi-san ga hanashi o shite imasu. 2. Sumisu-san no o-nii-san ga kimashita. 3. Iie, imasen. 4. Ryokō-gaisha ni tsutomete imasu.
    5. Nyū Yōku ni sunde imasu./Amerika ni sunde imasu.
II 1. Doko   2. doko   3. Dare/Donata   4. doko
III 1. no   2. ni, ni   3. de   4. ni, no, ni   5. de, no, o, de
IV 1. Tanaka-san o shitte imasu ka. Iie, shirimasen. 2. Watashi wa kaisha no chikaku ni sunde imasu. Aruite 15-fun desu. 3. Sumisu-san wa ABC ni tsutomete imasu.

Lesson 28

I   1. Nihon no furui kagu ga suki desu. 2. Hai, mō kaimashita. 3. Iie, shirimasen. 4. Furui kagu no mise ni tsuite kikimasu.
II 1. nani   2. doko   3. Donna   4. nani
III 1. wa, ga, ga, wa   2. wa, ga   3. ga, ni, ni/e   4. mo   5. mo, ni, de, o/ga
IV 1. Howaito-san wa ringo ga suki desu. 2. Sukī ga dekimasu ka. Hai, dekimasu.

3. Ashita tomodachi ni atte, issho ni tenisu o/ga shitai desu.   4. Kinō tegami o/ga kakitakatta desu ga, jikan ga arimasen deshita.   5. [Watashi wa] Nodo ga itai desu kara, nani mo tabetakunai desu.

Lesson 29

I   1. Resutoran ni imasu.   2. Bīru o nomimasu.   3. Shabushabu o tabemasu.

II   1. nani   2. niku   3. nan-ji   4. doko

III   1. ni/e, wa, wa, ga   2. wa, ga, ka, ga, ka, ga   3. no, o   4. no, ni, no, ni/e

IV   1. Dezāto wa nani ga ii desu ka. Kudamono o onegaishimasu.   2. Kaigi no mae ni kōhī o/ga nomitakatta desu ga, jikan ga arimasen deshita kara, kaigi no ato de nomimashita.

GLOSSARY

a, Ah, 165

achira, over there, that person over there, 46

agemashita, gave; *agemasu*, *ageru*, give, 109

aimashō ka, shall (we) meet, 114; *aimasu*, *au*, meet, 89

aisukurīmu, ice cream, 184

akachan, baby, 117

akai, red, 49

akemashō ka, shall (I) open; *akemasu*, *akeru*, open, 120

amari . . . -masen, does not . . . often, 89

amari . . . -nai/-masen, not very . . . , 97

Amerika, America, 22

Amerika-jin, an American, 23

Amerika Taishikan, American Embassy, 22

anata, you, 21, 23

ane, (my) older sister, 110

ani, (my) older brother, 168

ano, that (over there), 46, 49

aoi, blue, 50

are, that (one) over there, 40, 46

arigatō gozaimasu, (I am) grateful, 26

arimasen, do/does not have, 20

arimasendeshita, was/were not, 33

arimasu, *aru*, is/are (inanimate), 20, 66

arimasu, *aru*, have, 124

arukimashita, walked; *arukimasu*, *aruku*, walk, 145

asa, morning, 83

asa-gohan, breakfast, morning meal, 83

asatte, the day after tomorrow, 53

ashita, tomorrow, 33

asoko, over there, that place (over there), 46, 70

atama, head, 176

atarashii, new, fresh, 100

ato de, afterwards, later, 88

atsukunakatta, was not hot; *atsui*, hot, 104

-ban, number, 29

ban, evening, 83

banana, banana, 20

banchi, 137

bangō, number, 26

ban-gohan, dinner, evening meal, 83

basu, bus, 57

basu-noriba, bus terminal, 76

bengoshi, lawyer, 19

benkyō o shimasu (suru), study, 80

benri(na), 100

biru, building, 70

bīru, beer, 49

botchan, (your) son, 169

bun, part, 41

bunka, culture, 189

byōin, hospital, 76

cha, tea, 83

chichi, (my) father, 110

chigaimasu, *chigau*, That's/It's wrong (different), 92

chiisai, small, 44

chika, basement, underground, 170

chika 1-kai (ikkai), first basement, 170

chikai, near, close to, 98

chikaku, neighborhood, vicinity; *no chikaku ni/de*, near, close to, 68

chikatetsu, subway, underground (railway), 57

chizu, map, 83

chō, town, community, 137

-chōme, chome, 137

chotto, a little, 127

Chūgoku-jin, a Chinese, 23

chūshajō, parking lot, 155

chūsha kinshi, no parking, 154

daidokoro, kitchen, 66

dake, only, 130

dame, no good, useless, hopeless, out of the question, 155

dare, who, 21, 46

dare mo . . . -masen, nobody is, 66

dare no, whose, 29

de, at, 79

de, by, 61

de gozaimasu, This is . . . , 92

deguchi, exit, 156

dekimasu, *dekiru*, be able to, can (do), be ready (finished, done), 143, 174, 176

demasu, *deru*, leave, start, 146

denchi, battery, 47

denki, (electric) light, 121

denki-ya, electrical appliance store/clerk, 150

densha, (electric) train, 56

denwa, telephone, 26

denwa-bangō, telephone number, 26

denwa o shimasu (suru), make a phone call, telephone, 79, 89

depāto, department store, 32

deshita, was/were, 20, 33

desu, is/are, 19, 54, 67

dewa, well then, 39, 42

dewa/ja arimasen, is/are not, 20

dezāto, dessert, 183

-do, times, 137

-do, degree, 180

dō, how, 103

doa, door, 121

dochira, where, 46, 119

dō deshita ka, How was it, 103, 104

dō desu ka, How is it, 96

dō itashimashite, Don't mention it, You're welcome, 32

Doitsu, Germany, 48

Doitsu-go, German language, 178

Doitsu-jin, a German, 23

doko, where, belonging to or coming from what place, 46, 49, 80

doko ni mo, nowhere, 67

dōmo, very much, 26

dōmo, thanks, 142, 159

dōmo arigatō gozaimasu, Thank you very much, 26

donata, who, 21, 23, 46

donna, what kind of, 96, 100

dono, which, 46, 50

donogurai, how long, 134; how much, 146

doraibu, driving, a drive, 116

dore, which (one), 44, 46

dō shimashita ka, What's the matter, 180

dōshite, why, 73, 76

dōyatte, how, 145

do-yōbi, Saturday, 35

dōzo, please (accept, do), 26, 96

dōzo o-daijini, Look after yourself, 180

dōzo yoroshiku, Please favor me, 19, 21

e, picture, 83

e, to, 53

ee, yes, 26

eiga, movie, film, 36

Ei-go, English language, 104

eki, station, 56

en, yen, 39

fuirumu, film, 39, 45

-fun, minute, 32

funabin, sea mail, 61, 180

Furansu, France, 49

Furansu-go, French language, 179

furui, old, not fresh, 100

futari, 2 people, 76

futatsu, two, 49

futsuka, 2 day of the month, 35

ga, (subject marker, particle), 57

ga, but (particle), 86

ga, (particle), 88

gaikoku, foreign country, 171

gakkō, school, 29

gakusei, student, 23

-gatsu, month, 33

genkan, entrance hall, 68

genki(na), well, healthy, 100

getsu-yōbi, Monday, 35

ginkō, bank, 23

go, five, 28

-go, language, 49

go-, (honorific), 88

gō, number, 137

gochisōsama, Thank you for a lovely meal, 96

gogo, P.M., afternoon, 32

gohan, meal, 80

gojuppun, gojippun, 50 minutes, 32

5(go)-nin, 5 people, 74

goro, about, 86, 89

gorufu, golf, 106

go-ryōshin, (your) parents, 169

go-shōkai shimasu, Let me introduce you, 23

go-shujin, (your) husband, 88

gozen, A.M., morning, 33

gurai, about, approximately, 101, 145

gurūpu, group, 189

gyū-niku, beef, 100

ha, tooth, 179

hachi, eight, 28

hagaki, postcard, 45, 68

haha, (my) mother, 91, 169

hai, yes, certainly, 20, 23

-hai, measureful (counter), 95

haikingu, hiking, 117

hairimasu, hairu, enter, go/come in, 61, 150

haizara, ashtray, 42

hajimemashite, How do you do, 19, 21; *hajimeru*, begin, 21

hako, box, 68

han, half, 30 minutes after the hour, 33

hana, flower, 66

hanashi o shimasu (suru), talk, 161

hana-ya, flower shop, florist, 45

hatsuka, 20 day of the month, 35

heya, room, 76

hi, day, 166

hidari, left, 139

hidarigawa, left-hand side, 155

higashi, east, 53

hikōki, airplane, 76

hima(na), free, 100

hiragana, (Japanese script), 111

hirakimasu, hiraku, open, 32
hiru, noon, daytime, 33
hiru-gohan, lunch, noon meal, 80
hiru-yasumi, lunch time, noon recess, 33
hisho, secretary, 23
hītā, heater, 121
hito, person, 32
hitori, 1 person, 76
hitori de, alone, 53
hitotsu, one, 47
hoka, other, 189
hon, book, 29
-hon, (counter), 45, 49
hontō ni, really, truly, 101
hon-ya, book store/seller, 45, 74
hoteru, hotel, 91
hyaku, one hundred, 33, 41

ichi, one, 28
ichi-do, once, one time, 137
1(ichi)-ji han, half past one, 33
ichiman, ten thousand, 41
ichioku, one hundred million, 41
Igirisu, United Kingdom, 49
ii, good, 79
ii desu ne, It's/That's nice (good, all right), 79
iie, no, 20, 23
iie, dame desu, No, you can't, 155
iie, mō kekkō desu, No, (thank you). That was enough, 96
iimasu, iu, say, speak, 137
ikaga, how, 95
ikaga desu ka, How is it, 95, 96
ikimasu, iku, go, is going, will go, 53
ikkagetsu, (for) one month, 180
1-kai (ikkai), first floor, ground floor, 68
ikura, how much, 39, 146
ikutsu, how many, 46, 76
ima, living room, 66
ima, now, 32
imasu, iru, is/are (animate), 66
imasu, iru, stay, 130
imōto, (my) younger sister; imōto-san, (your) younger sister, 126, 169
ippai, 1 cupful/glassful/bottleful, 95
irasshaimase, Come in, Welcome, 39
irasshaimashita, came, 61
irasshaimasu, irassharu, is/are, 61, 88
iriguchi, entrance, 76
iro, color, 108
iroiro(na), various, 174
isha, doctor, 180
isogashii, busy, 100
issho ni, together (with), 114
isu, chair, 66
itadakimasu, itadaku, eat, 95, 96

itai, aching, painful, 176
Itaria, Italy, 49
itoko, (my) cousin, 169
itsu, when, 32, 36
itsuka, 5 day of the month, 35
itsutsu, five, 49
itte kudasai, Please say/speak, 137
iyahōn, earphones, 61, 104

ja, well then, 39
-ji, o'clock, 32
jikan, time, 124
-jikan, (for) . . . hours, 133
-jin, person (suffix), 23
jisho, dictionary, 110
jogingu o shimasu (suru), jog, 92
jōzu(na), good at, skillful, 176
jū, ten, 28
jugyō, class, lesson, 126
18(jūhachi)-nichi, 18 day of the month, 33, 35
11(jūichi)-nichi, 11 day of the month, 35
10(jū)-ji, 10 o'clock, 32
10(jū)-mai, 10 (sheets), 49
12(jūni)-hon, 12 (bottles), 49
jūsho, address, 29
jūsu, juice, 83
jūyokka, 14 day of the month, 35

ka, (question marker, particle), 20, 23
kabin, vase, 108
kabuki, Kabuki (Japanese theater), 78
kado, corner, 138
kaerimasu, kaeru, return, come/go back, 53
-kagetsu, (for) . . . month, 180
kagi, key, 29
kagu, furniture, 174
-kai, floor (counter), 68
kaigi, conference, meeting, 36
kaigi o shimasu (suru), hold a meeting/conference, 86; kaigi o shite imasu, be holding a meeting, be in conference, 158, 159
kaigi-shitsu, conference/meeting room, 158
kaimashita, bought; kaimasu, kau, buy, 79
kaimono, shopping, 83
kaimono o shimasu (suru), shop, 81
kaisatsuguchi, ticket gate, 76
kaisha, company, 26
kaishain, company employee, 23
kakarimasu, kakaru, (it) takes/costs, 145, 146
kakemasu, kakeru, sit, 61
kakimasu, kaku, write, draw, 89
kamera, camera, 44

kamera-ya, camera store/clerk, camera seller, 44

-kan, for (a period of time), 132

Kanada, Canada, 62

kanai, (my) wife, 111, 169

kangaekata, way of thinking, 189

kangeikai, welcome party, 121

kanji, (Chinese characters), 111

kanrinin, superintendent, 73

kara, from, 32, 56

kara, since, because, 73

kasa, umbrella, 39, 42

katarogu, catalogue, 150

ka-yōbi, Tuesday, 35

kazoku, (my) family, 83, 169

keikan, policeman, 154

keizai, economy, 189

kēki, cake, 139

kekkon, marriage, 126; *kekkon shite imasu*, be married, 168

kekkon-shiki, wedding, 126

keshimasu, kesu, turn/switch off, 121

kēsu, show case, 150

ki, tree, 101

kibun, feeling, 180

kikimasu, kiku, listen, hear, 83; ask, 90, 91

kimashita, came, 54, 56; *kimasu, kuru*, come, 56

kinō, yesterday, 33

kin-yōbi, Friday, 33, 35

ki o tsukete, Take care, Be careful, 166

kippu, ticket, 76

kippu-uriba, ticket office, 76

kirei(na), pretty, clean, neat, 95

-kiro, kilogram, 49

kissaten, cafe, coffee shop, tea shop, 83

kitte, postage stamp, 49

ko, child, 66

kōban, police box, 76

kōcha, black tea, 83

kochira, this one, this person, 19, 21, 46

kochira, here, this way, this direction, 46, 61

kodomo, child, 69, 169

kōen, park, 95, 100

kōhī, coffee, 83

kōkanshu, switchboard/telephone operator, 92

koko, here, this place, 46, 76

kokonoka, 9 day of the month, 35

kokonotsu, nine, 48

kōkūbin, airmail, 180

komban, this evening, tonight, 83

konde imasu, komimasu, komu, be crowded, 189

kongetsu, this month, 126

kono, this, 46, 47

konshū, this week, 130

kopī, photocopy, 121; *kopī o shimasu (suru)*, 120

koppu, mug, glass, cup, 117

kore, this (one), 26, 39, 46

kōsaten, intersection, 139

koto, thing, 174

kotoshi, this year, 86

ku, nine, 28

kudamono, fruit, 179

kudasai, Please give (me) . . . , 39

9(ku)-ji, 9 o'clock, 32

kukkī, cookie, 96

kūkō, airport, 57

kurai, dark, 121

kuremasu, kureru, give, 109

kurīningu, dry cleaning; *kurīningu-ya*, dry cleaner, 143

kurisumasu kādo, Christmas card, 91

kuroi, black, 50

kuruma, car, vehicle, 29

kusuri, medicine, 76

kusuri-ya, pharmacy, drug store, 76

kutsu, shoe, 83

kutsushita, sock, 179

kyō, today, 33

kyōdai, brothers, sisters, siblings, 126, 169

kyonen, last year, 54, 56

kyū, nine, 28

machi, town, street, community, 106, 137

machimasu, matsu, wait, 92

mada desu, not yet, 143

made, to, as far as, 145

made, until, 32

made ni, by, 137

mado, window, 68

mae, in front of, before, 68

magatte kudasai, Please turn; *magarimasu, magaru*, turn, 138

mago, grandchild, 169

-mai, (counter), 45, 49

mai-, every, 80

maiasa, every morning, 83

maiban, every evening/night, 83

maido, each (every) time, 137; *maido arigatō gozaimasu*, Thank you (for your patronage) each time, 137

mainen, every year, 91

mainichi, every day, 54, 80

maishū, every week, 83

maitsuki, every month, 189

massugu, straight, straight ahead, 142

mata, again, 88

matsuri, festival, 179

matte kudasai, Please wait; *matsu*, wait, 130, 138

megane, (eye)glasses, 76
mei, (my) niece, 169
meigo-san, (your) niece, 169
meishi, business card, name card, 26
menyū, menu, 139
meron, melon, 183
meshiagatte kudasai, Please eat/have (some), 95
migi, right, 138
mikan, tangerine, 49
mikka, 3 day of the month, 35
mikka, (for) 3 days, 130
mimasu, *miru*, see, watch, look at, 78, 130
mina-sama, everyone, 190
mina-sama ni dōzo yoroshiku, Best regards to everyone, 190
minna, *mina-san*, everyone, 166
miruku, milk, 83
mise, store, shop, 91
misete kudasai, Please show me; *misemasu*, *miseru*, show, 39
mite imasu (iru), is looking, is watching, 158
mittsu, three, 45
mizu, water, 42
mo, too, 39
mō, already, 79, 96
mō, more (another), 95
moku-yōbi, Thursday, 33, 35
moraimashita, received; *moraimasu*, *morau*, receive, 108, 109
moshi moshi, hello, 88; I say, 154
mō sugu, very soon, 190
mottekite kudasai, Please bring; *mottekimasu*, *mottekuru*, bring, 137
muika, 6 day of the month, 35
musuko, (my) son; *musuko-san*, (your) son, 127, 169
musume, (my) daughter; *musume-san*, (your) daughter, 127, 169
muttsu, six, 48
muzukashii, difficult, hard, 100

naisen-bangō, extension number, 91
naka, inside, 68
namae, name, 26
nana, seven, 28
nanatsu, seven, 48
nan-ban, what number, 27, 29
nan-bon, how many (bottles), 76
nan-gatsu, which month, 32
nani/nan, what, 27, 29; *nani/nan de*, how, by what means, 62, 63
nani mo, nothing; *nani mo . . . -masen*, There is nothing, 69
nan-ji, what time, 32
nan-jikan, how many hours, 146
nanji made ni, by what time, 137

nan-mai, how many (sheets), 76
nan-nen, what year, 63
nan-nichi, which day (of the month), how many days, 32, 36, 146
nan-nin, how many people, 76
nanoka, 7 day of the month, 35
nan-pun, how many minutes, 146
nan-sai, how old, 127
nan-yōbi, which day (of the week), 32, 36
natsu, summer, 37
natsu-yasumi, summer vacation, 37
ne, Isn't it/Aren't there, 70, 73
nekutai, necktie, 110
-nen, year, 63
nengajō, New Year's card, 91
netsu, fever, 180
ni, in, at, 66
ni, on, 61, 145
ni, to, 53, 114, 115
ni, to, from, 79, 88, 108, 109
ni, two, 28
-nichi, day, 33
nichi-yōbi, Sunday, 35
ni chōme ni no ichi, 2-chome 2–1, 137
nigiyaka, lively, 99, 104
Nihon, Japan, 23
Nihon Ginkō, Bank of Japan, 23
Nihon-go, Japanese language, 49
Nihon-jin, a Japanese, 23
2(ni)-jikan, 2 hours, 133
nijū, twenty, 28
20(nijū)ppun gurai, (for) about 20 minutes, 101
nijūyokka, 24 day of the month, 35
2(ni)-kiro, 2 kilograms, 49
niku, meat, 76
niku-ya, meat shop, butcher, 76
nimotsu, parcel, 180
-nin, person/people (counter), 74
ni tsuite, concerning, about, 174
niwa, garden, 66
ni yoroshiku, Best regards to, 21, 190
no, (possessive particle), 19, 21
no ato de, after, 132
nodo, throat, 178
no mae ni, before, in front of, 68, 133
nomimasu, *nomu*, drink, take (medicine), 81, 83
nomimono, beverage, drink, 174, 183
-noriba, boarding place, 74
norimashita, got on; *norimasu*, *noru*, get on, ride, take, 145
nyūsu, news, 83

o, from, out of, 146
o, (object marker, particle), 39, 79
o-, (honorific), 69

oba, (my) aunt; *oba-san*, (your) aunt, 169
obā-san, (your) grandmother, 169
o-cha, tea, 83
o-genki de, Take care of yourself, 190
ohairi kudasai, Do come in, 61
oi, (my) nephew, 169
oigo-san, (your) nephew, 169
oishii, good, tasty, delicious, 95
o-itoko-san, (your) cousin, 169
oji, (my) uncle; *oji-san*, (your) uncle, 169
ojī-san, (your) grandfather, 169
ojō-san, (your) daughter, 127, 169
okake kudasai, Do sit down, 61
o-kane, money, 126
okāsan, (your) mother, 91, 169
o-kashi, cake, 95
ōkii, big, large, 49
okosan, (your) child, 127
okurimasu, okuru, send, 178
okusan, (your) wife, 66, 169
okyaku-san, client, customer, guest, 161
omachi kudasai, Please wait, 92
omaneki arigatō gozaimasu, Thank you for your invitation, 166
omoshiroi, entertaining, interesting, 100
onaka, stomach, abdomen, 178
onegaishimasu, Please (do) . . . , 88
onē-san, (your) older sister, 169
ongaku, music, 83
o-niisan, (your) older brother, 168, 169
onna, woman, female; *onna no hito*, woman, 32
onna no ko, girl, female child, 68
onsen, hot spring, spa, 179
orite, get off (and); *orimasu, oriru*, get off, 130, 145
o-sake, Japanese rice wine, 83
oshiemasu, oshieru, tell, show, teach, 90, 91
oshimasu, osu, push, 130
osoi, late, slow, 166
o-taku, (his) residence, 88
o-tearai, lavatory, toilet, 69
o-tera, temple, 130
otoko, man, male; *otoko no hito*, man, 58
otoko no ko, boy, 66
otōsan, (your) father, 91, 169
otōto, (my) younger brother; *otōto-san* (your) younger brother, 169
ototoi, the day before yesterday, 63
otsuri, change, 142
owarimasu, owaru, finish, end, 190

pan, bread, 76
pan-ya, bread store, bakery, 76
pātī, party, 36
pen, pen, 61, 151

pureigaido, theater booking agency, 79

raigetsu, next month, 63
rainen, next year, 56
raishū, next week, 63
rajio, radio, 42
rei, zero, 28
rekishi, history, 110
rekōdo, record, 83
reshīto, receipt, 42
resutoran, restaurant, 80
ringo, apple, 42
roku, six, 28
6(roku)-gatsu, June (sixth month), 33
6(roku)-ji, 6 o'clock, 32
ryokō, trip, travel, 106; *ryokō o shimasu (suru)*, take a trip, travel, 129
ryokō-gaisha, travel agency, 168
ryōri, food, cooking, cuisine, 106
ryōshin, (my) parents, 169

sā, well, let me see, 152, 175
-sai, . . . years old (counter), 127
saikin, nowadays, recently, 190
sakana, fish, 76
sakana-ya, fish shop/seller, 45, 76
saka-ya, liquor store, 76
sake, Japanese rice wine, 83
-sama, Mr., Mrs., Ms., Miss, 143
sampo, a walk; *sampo o shimasu (suru)*, take a walk, 116
samukatta, was cold; *samui*, cold, 104
san, three, 28
-san, Mr., Mrs., Ms., Miss, 19
sandoitchi, sandwich, 83
39(sanjūku)-do, 39 degrees, 180
san-nin, 3 people, 54
sanzen-en, 3,000 yen, 39
sarada, salad, 83
seiji, politics, 189
sen, one thousand, 41
sengetsu, last month, 57
1980(senkyūhyakuhachijū)-nen, 63
sensei, teacher, professor, 91, 189
senshū, last week, 54, 56
sētā, sweater, 171
setsumei, explanation, 104
shabushabu, shabu-shabu, 183
shakai, society, community life, social conditions, 189
shashin, photograph, 68
shashin o torimasu (toru), take a photograph, 150
shashin o totte mo ii desu ka, May I take a photograph, 150
shi, four, 28
shichi, seven, 28

shigoto, work, 36
shigoto o shimasu (suru), work, 81
shiki, ceremony, 126
shimasu, suru, do, 78
shimbun, newspaper, 29
shimemasu, shimeru, close, shut, 121
shingō, traffic light, 139
Shinkansen, Shinkansen, New Trunk Line, 63
shinsetsu(na), kind, helpful, 100
shisha, branch office, 53
shita, under, beneath, 69
shite imasu (iru), be doing, 158, 168
shitsu, room, 158
shitsurei, rudeness, 61; *shitsurei shimasu*, May I, Excuse me, I'm sorry, Good-bye, 61, 88
shitte imasu (shiru), know, 170
shizuka(na), quiet, calm, 97
shokudō, dining room, cafeteria, lunch room, restaurant, 69, 86
shokuji, meal; *shokuji o shimasu (suru)*, have a meal, eat, 100
shōshō, a moment, 92
shujin, (my) husband, 169
-shūkan, weeks (counter), 134
shūmatsu, weekend, 78
sō, so, 88
sōbetsukai, farewell party, 119
sobo, (my) grandmother, 169
sochira, there, that way, that person, 46
sō desu ka, I see, 88, 124
sō desu nē, Let me see, 180
sofu, (my) grandfather, 169
soko, there, that place, 46, 76
sono, that, 44, 46
sore, that (one), 39, 46
sorekara, and, and then, after that, 45, 130
soshite, and, then, and then, 53
subarashii, wonderful, 152
suimasu, suu, smoke, inhale, 155
sui-yōbi, Wednesday, 35
sukī, ski, skiing, 114
suki(na), like, likeable, favorite, 109
sukiyaki, sukiyaki, 183
sukoshi, a little, 134
sumimasen, Excuse me, I'm sorry, 32, 155
sunde imasu, live, is living; *sumimasu, sumu*, live, 168
sūpā, supermarket, 73
sūpu, soup, 83
supūn, spoon, 117
suraido, slide, 158
suwanai de kudasai, Do not smoke, 155

tabako, tobacco, cigarette, 155
tabemashita, ate; *tabemasu, taberu*, eat, 80

-tachi, (plural suffix, people), 100
Taimu, Time (magazine), 159
taipu, typing, 89, 138
taishikan, embassy, 22
takai, expensive, high, 100
takusan, many, lots of, 74
takushī, taxi, 61
takushī-noriba, taxi stand, 74
tamago, egg, 100
tana, shelf, rack, 67, 68
tanjōbi, birthday, 33
tanoshii, enjoyable, 106
tanoshimi ni shite imasu (iru), be looking forward to, 190
tansu, chest of drawers, 174
tatemono, building, 74
tēburu, table, 66
tegami, letter, 83
tekisuto, text, 190
temae, just before, this side of, 142
ten, (decimal) point, 41
ten'in, store clerk, 39
tenisu, tennis, 83; *tenisu o shimasu (suru)*, play tennis, 81
tenki, weather, 101
tēpu, tape, 49
tēpurekōdā, tape recorder, 42
terebi, television, TV set, 42
to, and, 66
to, with, 53
tō, ten, 45
todana, closet, cabinet, cupboard, 68
todokemashō ka, Shall we deliver; *todokemasu, todokeru*, deliver, 137
tōi, far, 97
tōka, 10 day of the month, 35
tokei, clock, watch, 27
tokidoki, sometimes, 86
tokoro, place, 189
tomato, tomato, 179
tomete kudasai, Please stop, 142; *tomemasu, tomeru*, park, stop, 138, 155; *tomenaide kudasai*, Do not park, 156
tomodachi, friend, 57
tonari, next to, 73
torimasu, toru, take, 150
tori-niku, chicken meat, 100
toshokan, library, 178
totemo, very, 95
tsugi, next, 138
tsugō, condition, 117; *tsugō ga warui desu*, conditions are unfavorable, 114, 116
tsuitachi, 1 day of the month, 35
tsukatte mo ii desu, You may use it; *tsukaimasu, tsukau*, use, 150
tsukete mo ii desu ka, May I turn (it) on, 150; *tsukemasu, tsukeru*, switch/turn on, 121

tsukimashita, arrived; *tsukimasu*, *tsuku*, arrive, 146

tsukue, desk, table, 174

tsukurimashita, formed; *tsukurimasu*, *tsukuru*, form, make, build, 189

tsumaranai, boring, uninteresting, 98

tsutomete imasu, be employed, work for; *tsutomemasu*, *tsutomeru*, serve, work for, 168

uchi, (my/our) home, house, 26, 88

ue, top, 66

ueitoresu, waitress, 139

uketsuke, reception, 70

umi, sea, ocean, 117

untenshu, driver, chauffeur, 142

-uriba, selling place, 76

urusai, noisy, 121

utte imasu, sell, is selling; *urimasu*, *uru*, sell, 170

wa, (topic marker, particle), 19

wain, wine, 166

wakarimashita, Sure, Certainly, I see, 89, 114

wakarimashita, understood; *wakarimasu*, *wakaru*, understand, 104, 174

warui, bad, 97

watashi, I, 19

watashi no, my, 26

watashi-tachi, we, 100

-ya, store, shop, clerk, seller, 44

ya, and (etc.), 66

yama, mountain, 178

yaoya, vegetable shop, green grocer, 76

yasai, vegetable, 100

yasashii, easy, 100

yasui, inexpensive, cheap, 100

yasumi, rest (period), vacation, holiday, day off, closing day, 33, 76, 126

yattsu, eight, 48

yo, I tell you, 73

-yōbi, day of the week, 33

yobimasu, *yobu*, call, 130

yōka, 8 day of the month, 35

yokka, 4 day of the month, 35

yoku, well, 61

yoku, often, 89

yoku irasshaimashita, How nice of you to come, 61

yokunai, not good, 97; *yoi*, good, 98

yomimasu, *yomu*, read, 79, 83

yon, four, 28

4(yon)-shūkan, 4 weeks, 134

yorokonde (yorokobu), (I'd) love/be happy to, gladly, with pleasure, 114, 166

Yōroppa, Europe, 176

yoroshiku, regards, 21, 190

yottsu, four, 48

yoyaku, reservation, 143

yūbinkyoku, post office, 36

yūgata, late afternoon, early evening, 147

yukkuri, slowly, 139

yūmei(na), famous, well known, 95, 100

zannen, regret; *zannen desu ga*, I'm sorry, but . . . , 114, 116

zasshi, magazine, 83

zehi, by all means, 114, 119

zenzen . . . -masen, never (do), 91

zenzen . . . -masen, (not) at all, 104

zero, zero, 26, 28

INDEX

abbreviated expression, 26, 115; verb replaced by *desu*, 32, 67, 73
address, 137
adjective, *-i* adj., 95, 97, 105; like/dislike,
174; *-na* adj., 95, 99, 105; present/past
form, 95, 105, 176

connective, *ga*, 86, 88; *sorekara*, 45; *soshite*, 53, 55
counter, *-ban*, 29; *-do*, 137, 180; *-fun*, 32;
-gatsu, 33; *-hai*, 95; *-hon*, 45, 49; *-ji*, 32;
-jikan, 133; *ka*, 35; *-kai*, 68; *-kagetsu*,
180, *-kan*, 132; *-kiro*, 49; *-mai*, 45, 49;
-nen, 63; *-nichi*, 33; *-nin*, 74; *-sai*, 127;
-shūkan, 134
counter, word order, 46

day of the month, 32, 33, 35
day of the week, 32, 33, 35
decimals, 41
desu (deshita), 20, 54
dewa/ja arimasen (deshita), 20, 33

fractions, 41

here, there, over there, 46, 70, 76
honorific, *go-*, 88; *o-*, 69, 88; *-sama*, 143;
-san, 19, 21; *sensei*, 189

indirect object marker, *ni*, 79, 109
interjection, *a*, 165; *dewa/ja*, 39, 42; *sā*,
152, 175
is/are (animate), 66, 68; (inanimate), 20,
66, 68

Model Verb Conjugation, 130
month, 35

name (instead of I/you), 21, 26
negative question, 20
nobody, nothing, nowhere, 67
numbers, 26, 45; *hitotsu, futatsu, mittsu*,
48; intermediate numbers, 33, 41; one
hundred/one trillion, 41; twenty/one
hundred, 33; zero/twenty, 28

object marker, *o*, 39, 55, 79, 109, 120, 145,
175
omission of topic, 20

particle, *dake*, 130; *de*, 53, 54; *de* (at), 79,
80, 145; *de* (by), 61; *ga* (but), 86; *ga*, 88;
kara (because), 73; *kara* (from) 32, 56;
made (as far as), 145; *made* (by), 32, 137;
mo, 39, 54; *ne*, 70, 73, 80; *ni/e*, 53; *ni*
(in), 66; *ni* (on) 61, 145; *ni* (to), 53, 54; *ni*
(to), 88, 114, 115; *ni sumu/tsutomeru*,

168, 169; *o* (from), 146; *to* (and), 66, 67;
to (with), 53; *ya*, 66, 67; *yo*, 73. *See also*,
indirect object marker, possessive particle, question marker, subject marker,
topic marker.
particle, position of, 32, 53, 54
particles (in combinations), *asoko ni*, 70;
ato de, 88; *hitori de*, 53; *issho ni*, 114;
made ni, 137; *ni mo/ni wa*, 54; *ni tsuite*,
174; *no ato de*, 132; *no chikaku ni*, 68; *no
mae ni*, 68, 133; *no naka ni*, 68; *no shita
ni*, 69; *no temae de*, 142; *no ue ni*, 66
possessive particle, *no*, 19, 21, 26; in fractions, 41
predicate, repetition of, 183

question marker, *ka*, 20, 23; rising intonation, 26, 124
question word, how, 62, 103, 104, 145;
how about, 95, 124; how long, 134, 146;
how many, 46, 76, (minutes, hours,
days), 146; how much, 39, 146; what,
27, 67, 80; what kind of, 96, 100; what
number, 27, 29; what time, 32; when,
32, 36, 55; where, 46, 49, 55, 80, 119;
which, 44, 46; which day, 32, 36; who,
21, 46, 55, 67, whose, 29; why, 73, 76

relatives, 169

subject marker, *ga*, 55, 57, 66, 67, 120,
132; preference, 174
suffix, *goro*, 86, 89; *gurai*, 101, 145; *-jin*,
23; *-tachi*, 100; *-ya*, 45, 76; *-yōbi*, 33

this, that, that over there, 39, 40, 46, 70,
76
time, 31
topic marker, *wa*, 19, 20, 55, 66, 67, 124,
132, 174, 183

verb, dictionary (plain) form, 54; *-masen
ka*, 114, 115; *-mashō, -mashō ka*, 114,
115, 120; *-masu* form, 54, 133, 138, 146,
150, 155, 170; *-nai* form, 130, 155; pre-
sent/past form, 20, 54, 56, 68, 79, 81,
110; present progressive, 159, 160, 170;
past progressive, 159, 160; Regular I,
Regular II, Irregular, 130, 131; *-tai desu*,
174, 175, 177; *-te* form, 130, 132, 133,
138, 145, 146, 150, 155; *-te imasu*, 168;
-te sumu/tsutomeru, 168, 169
verb, giving and receiving, 109; permission, 150; refusal, 156
verb, position of, 54

year, 63

KATAKANA

ア	イ	ウ	エ	オ
カ	キ	ク	ケ	コ
サ	シ	ス	セ	ソ
タ	チ	ツ	テ	ト
ナ	ニ	ヌ	ネ	ノ
ハ	ヒ	フ	ヘ	ホ
マ	ミ	ム	メ	モ
ヤ	(イ)	ユ	(エ)	ヨ
ラ	リ	ル	レ	ロ
ワ	(イ)	(ウ)	(エ)	ヲ
ン				

キャ	キュ	キョ
シャ	シュ	ショ
チャ	チュ	チョ
ニャ	ニュ	ニョ
ヒャ	ヒュ	ヒョ
ミャ	ミュ	ミョ

リャ	リュ	リョ

ガ	ギ	グ	ゲ	ゴ
ザ	ジ	ズ	ゼ	ゾ
ダ	ヂ	ヅ	デ	ド
バ	ビ	ブ	ベ	ボ
パ	ピ	プ	ペ	ポ

ギャ	ギュ	ギョ
ジャ	ジュ	ジョ

ビャ	ビュ	ビョ
ピャ	ピュ	ピョ

HIRAGANA

あ	い	う	え	お
か	き	く	け	こ
さ	し	す	せ	そ
た	ち	つ	て	と
な	に	ぬ	ね	の
は	ひ	ふ	へ	ほ
ま	み	む	め	も
や	(い)	ゆ	(え)	よ
ら	り	る	れ	ろ
わ	(い)	(う)	(え)	を
ん				

きゃ	きゅ	きょ
しゃ	しゅ	しょ
ちゃ	ちゅ	ちょ
にゃ	にゅ	にょ
ひゃ	ひゅ	ひょ
みゃ	みゅ	みょ

りゃ	りゅ	りょ

が	ぎ	ぐ	げ	ご
ざ	じ	ず	ぜ	ぞ
だ	ぢ	づ	で	ど
ば	び	ぶ	べ	ぼ
ぱ	ぴ	ぷ	ぺ	ぽ

ぎゃ	ぎゅ	ぎょ
じゃ	じゅ	じょ

びゃ	びゅ	びょ
ぴゃ	ぴゅ	ぴょ